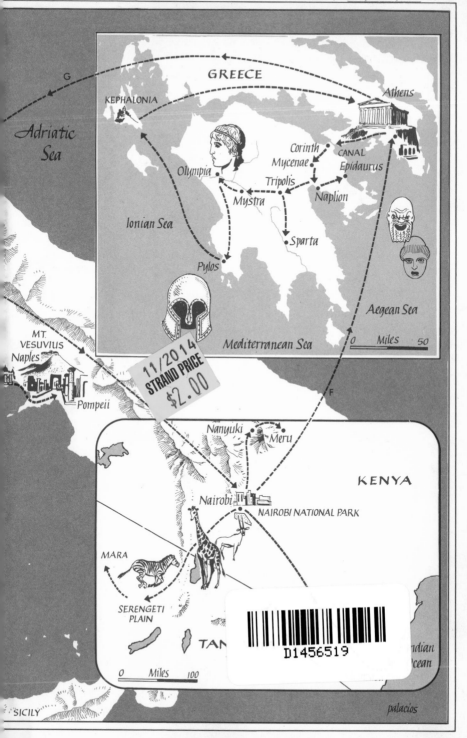

GREECE

KEPHALONIA

Adriatic
Sea

Athens

Corinth
Mycenae   CANAL
Olympia   Epidaurus
        Tripolis
    Mystra   Naplion

Ionian Sea

Sparta

Pylos

Aegean Sea

Mediterranean Sea   0   Miles   50

G

MT.
VESUVIUS
Naples

Pompeii

F

Nanyuki   Meru

KENYA

Nairobi
        NAIROBI NATIONAL PARK

MARA

SERENGETI
PLAIN

TAN   ndian
                                       cean

0   Miles   100

SICILY

palacios

THE VARIED AIRS OF SPRING

Books by Ilka Chase

THE VARIED AIRS OF SPRING

FRESH FROM THE LAUNDRY

SECOND SPRING AND TWO POTATOES

ELEPHANTS ARRIVE AT HALF-PAST FIVE

THE CARTHAGINIAN ROSE

THREE MEN ON THE LEFT HAND

THE ISLAND PLAYERS

ALWAYS IN VOGUE *(with Edna Woolman Chase)*

NEW YORK 22

FREE ADMISSION

I LOVE MISS TILLI BEAN

IN BED WE CRY

PAST IMPERFECT

ILKA CHASE

THE VARIED AIRS OF SPRING

PHOTOGRAPHS BY
NORTON BROWN

1969

DOUBLEDAY & COMPANY, INC., GARDEN CITY, NEW YORK

CONTENTS

THE VARIED AIRS OF SPRING

CHAPTER ONE

Rome   Sicily   Pompeii

"If you want to see the migration of the herds I think you should plan to be there by mid-May."

The speaker was John Owen, our friend and the director of the National Parks of Tanzania. He was dining with us in our apartment in New York and we were discussing a projected trip to East Africa, some of the islands of the Mediterranean which we had never seen, and the Middle East. Beirut, Damascus, Jerusalem, and the "rose red city of Petra half as old as time" shimmered on our horizon.

We had paid two previous visits to East Africa but now we were contemplating the kind of safari we had often dreamed of but had never undertaken; the *proper* kind, camping out under canvas in the care of a professional safari manager, and we were asking John's advice.

Having given it he finished his nightcap and left the apartment and, not long afterward, the United States where he had admirably fulfilled the admirable purpose of his visit: to raise money for the preservation of African wildlife, specifically the inhabitants of the Serengeti, one of the world's great reserves, which is in his enormous bailiwick and under his management.

We are devoted to John but mulling over his advice we had second thoughts. I said to Norton, my husband, "Every book you read, everybody you know who's been there says May's awfully early, that the rains are still on." I questioned another friend, Mary Hemingway. "What do you think? Weren't you and Ernest once there in May?"

"Yes, we were," she said promptly, "and it was grim. We got bogged down like mad, the mud was fearful."

I wrote to John. "Mary says the mud was fearful, but we regard you as the horse's mouth and will do as you advise." John wrote to me. "The roads are much better than they were when she and Hemingway were here and I also believe there is a good chance of the rains being over. Thanks for the horse's mouth but to try to prophesy African weather is to be the horse's ass yet I still think you should come."

He then, at our request, proceeded to recommend a safari manager; an old friend of his from his days in the Sudan, Colonel Hilary Hook. "He's a knowledgeable, amusing fellow with a charming wife named Jane. If you and Norton go with them you'll be in good hands."

Accordingly, I wrote to the colonel and eventually received a reply from a friend in charge of the Hook correspondence. Unhappily, at the time we wanted to come, the Hooks would still be home on leave in the United Kingdom and when they returned to Africa they would be booked solidly.

We were crestfallen but our crests rose on receiving a subsequent letter from the colonel himself. True, he could not take us on but he had a friend, a knowledgeable, amusing fellow also with a charming wife named Jane, who ran the same kind of safari they did and he counseled us to get in touch with Major Digby Tatham-Warter.

The major replied promptly on decorative stationery. Yes, he and his wife did undertake safaris and if we would let them know the sort of thing we had in mind they would do their best to comply. "Of course," he added, "mid-May seems a bit early, we may still get rain, but if you are willing to chance it we certainly are."

That seemed to be that. Possible, indeed probable rain

and the great herds on the move or clear skies and stationary, maybe even invisible, animals.

Our first trip had been in June, our second in October. Were we or were we not sporting types willing to try another season? We were. A good deal of correspondence was involved, itineraries suggested and discarded, many questions and answers exchanged, not the least of which were financial, and finally we reached agreement.

We would be in Nairobi on May 10, remaining in Africa three weeks then flying to Athens and on to Beirut and our tour of the Middle East.

Since we were leaving New York the end of April we debated going first to the Middle East and also considered North Africa but were deflected by a friend who had been there and who advised us that it would be uncomfortably hot at that time of year. Sometimes one should not believe one's experienced friends. Later we met an American woman who had spent the last two weeks of April in Marrakech. "But wasn't it hot?" I asked. "Not at all," she replied. "I wore a suit the whole time and I needed it." Among famous traitors of history one might mention the weather.

Our plan was to fly with Alitalia to Nairobi via Rome. Later, because of our projected Mediterranean island hopping, we would be weaving around the Italian skies in their handsome planes in any event. We therefore decided to get into the native spirit at the outset and go to Sicily where, we had heard, spring was poetic.

Alitalia's flight 611 to Rome is a joy. Granted, it does take place at night and in physical depletion a nighttime flight is costly. No matter how comfortable the seats or how good the service, one's metabolism is rudely shaken, but many flights to Europe are at night for the simple reason of time change. Fly by day and you arrive at a foreign air terminal anywhere from 9 P.M. to 3 A.M. and customs men, officials, porters, and taxi drivers around the world are not inclined to be up and about at any such Godforsaken hours. After all, they *live* there. So the tourist has one sleepless night. What of it? Cooperative their attitude may not be, understandable it is.

The other obvious reason for night flying is business. Theoretically your man of affairs finishes a day's work in New York, hops a plane and turns up fresh as a daisy in his Zurich office the next morning. He may turn up but I do not believe the daisy part. He must be groggy. So must the aerial diplomats who circle the globe conferring with their high opposite numbers on arrival. No wonder the world is in the state it is. Those men are exhausted, they can't reason with lucidity.

Since today the traveler automatically assumes that all planes are safe, all pilots well-trained, it is understandable that competing lines vie with one another on menus and entertainment. It is understandable that the passengers who are starting their holidays and have nothing to do but pass their few airborne hours as pleasantly as possible avail themselves of the often sumptuous meals that are served. It is one of the features I myself look forward to, but a wise and experienced friend of ours, Marcel Palmaro, who, doubling as a New York banker and chairman of the board of the principality of Monaco, virtually commutes between New York and the South of France, says the only way he survives is to fly by day and not eat at all.

As we were about to board our plane we were held up at the gate by an Italian woman, a vision in pistachio green, sprouting an orchid on her shoulder and spouting a voluble stream of her native tongue to the fellow checking the boarding passes. Her problems seemed intricate and manifold and Norton grinned. "We're out of the country already," he said.

The Italians have taken a tip from the Japanese and pass out hot fragrant little washclothes as soon as you are seated so you may divest yourself of any grime that has accumulated between your house and the plane.

First-class passengers are given toilet kits and charming little flowered sleep shades, those masks or blindfolds that fit over the eyes and have elastic loops that pass over the ears to hold them in place. They cut out light and to my way of thinking are absolutely indispensable whether at home or traveling. They have been on the market for many years yet it is remarkable how many people do not know about them in the United States. In the rest of the world they are practically unheard of yet whenever I have bestowed one on a foreign friend the reaction, after the first couple of uses, has been starry eyed. Starry because they realize they will now be able to remain sleepy eyed as long as they please and not have to rise just because the sun has waked them up.

Another Alitalia gift is writing paper. My advice is to hang on to it as many European hotels do not automatically supply it.

Disregarding the advice of the experienced Mr. Palmaro, Dr. Brown and I tucked into our delicious dinner of caviar, antipasto, cannellone, filet of beef, cheese, and fruit. We enjoyed it too. I assume I do not need to itemize wine and champagne. One expects them, does one not?

Sated by the banquet we had little difficulty in falling asleep and when I awakened around midnight, New York time, after a three-hour nap it was to a half-moon off the tip of our right wing and a crimson sky on the left. We had been flying for some time over France and were crossing the Alps, their dark flanks and snowy peaks beginning to take light, stretching below us mile after sharply undulating mile. We landed at the Leonardo da Vinci Airport in Rome at 8:20 local time six hours out of Kennedy Airport. I have flown, I should imagine, well over a million miles. It is still a miracle.

Less miraculous was the information we received on arriving at the Grand Hotel: our room was not yet available. We managed a bit of breakfast, lounged sleepily in a lounge and at last got to bed remaining there until midafternoon. That is what I mean about the diplomats and businessmen. For us any official or commercial activity would have been literally impossible.

It is not only the lack of sleep. Even flying in pressurized cabins does not fool biology which is why commercial pilots are subjected to rigid scrutiny and stringently curtailed schedules.

Once up and dressed we walked over to the Via Véneto and had tea at Doney's. The afternoon was chilly but the gay parasols were up and the street was abloom with flowers that had been set out for Easter.

Shortly before we left home I had gone to Cincinnati for a speaking engagement and I was amused when a woman came up to our table staring as though she had seen a ghost and said, "But I heard you in Cincinnati just the other day and here you *are*." She was obviously more startled than pleased and somehow the encounter had the ring of *Appointment in Samarra*, with me in the role of Death. The fable is ancient. I myself first encountered it in one of Somerset Maugham's books, but I repeat it for its curiously haunting quality.

A merchant in Baghdad sent his servant to market to buy provisions. In a short time the man returned white and trembling, saying, "Master, in the marketplace I was jostled by a woman in the crowd. Turning I saw it was Death who had jostled me. I beg you, lend me a horse that I may ride away from here. I will flee to Samarra where Death will not find me."

The master lent him a horse and digging his spurs into its flanks the man galloped as fast as he could to Samarra.

The merchant went down to the marketplace and seeing Death in the crowd asked why she had made a threatening gesture toward his servant that morning.

"That was not a threatening gesture," she replied, "it was only a start of surprise. I was astonished to see him in Baghdad for I had an appointment with him tonight in Samarra."

Strolling up the Via Véneto we passed through the old Roman walls into the Borghese Gardens, fragrant with acacias and umbrella pines. It is a lovely park with big areas of meadow grass where adults may loll about and children and dogs run free.

By chance we stumbled upon the Concorso Hippico In-
ternatzionale that had opened the day before in the Piazza
di Siena. Brilliant sunshine flooded the scene like a stage
set. Red and white hurdles were set up in the blazing green
oval studded with lavender azalea bushes. Umbrella pines
and a square tawny building formed the backdrop. The
stands were alight with the color of women's spring clothes;
yellow and lilac and pistachio green, corn, raspberry, gera-
nium, and nasturtium in every shade.

We arrived just as a company of Italian cavalry, elegant in
their bicorn hats, came trotting into the ring in time to the
music. Glamorous and gay they were, far more theatrical
than military. Parades, maneuvers, horse shows, and no killing—that's the way an army should be.

They were followed by the jumpers. The crowd was in
fine fettle, rooting for everyone and the horse and rider who
cleared the course without a fault were greeted with raptur-
ous applause and shouted *bravos, bravissimos* and *bene,
bene*'s. A sigh like wind over wheat swept the stands if a rail
was kicked off or a hurdle refused. Many of the gala pink
coats were worn by women among whom were a number of
English and Americans.

Even in such festive circumstances, however, I can take
just so much equestrianism. I am aware that many will consider my confession shameful, but after a time I find it, and
I whisper the word, boring. Furthermore, we had a dinner
engagement with Colleen Moore and time was awasting.

To some the name will mean nothing but there is a generation to whom she was the silent star who shone the brightest.
The bobbed hair, the square bangs, the big brown eyes flick-
ered joyfully and with enormous profit to their owner before enraptured audiences on silver screens in the Bijous and
Roxys around the world.

Colleen was living in Rome for a few months having
rented a penthouse apartment from a young Italian architect.
She loved the city but her knowledge of its geography was
skimpier than our own. When I had spoken with her on the

phone she had assured me that the Piazza Benedetto
Cairoli was just around the corner from the Grand. For the
dear girl's information and that of any traveler wishing to
go between those two points I can state on sound authority
—our own—that it is a good twelve to fifteen minutes away by
taxi and in the end we found number 6 only because of the
X-ray eyes of our driver.

Once unearthed we discovered Colleen was living in a cosy
pretty apartment. The other guests included a young German girl who was her secretary and a delightful Italian, a Mr.
Tallentis, and his American wife. Signor Tallentis was engaged in cattle raising and his Machiavellian mind was in
piquant contrast to his bucolic pursuit. Another friend was
the American broker, Jerry Kelton, from Merrill Lynch Pierce
Fenner & Smith. I mention the firm because Colleen herself
is involved with it. She is a woman who appreciates money so
she is a member of a not very exclusive group but she does
have a talent not common to her sex. She understands it.
Throughout her Hollywood career she made a great deal of
the delightful stuff and later she married a man who had a
similar talent and who taught her what he felt every woman
should know; how to nurture little pennies till they grow
to strong fat dollars. It is the maternal instinct at work. So
well did she learn the lesson that when we saw her she
was engaged in writing a book directed primarily to women
and the intelligent investment of their money.

She had another enterprise in the oven too, a profusely
illustrated autobiography. From her Hollywood days she had
hundreds and hundreds of photographs to choose from.
Glancing through a stack of them we came upon an amusing
and nostalgic one of Greta Garbo and John Gilbert. There
was a third figure too, a woman we had both known named
Alice Glazer. She had been the wife of a Hollywood pro-
ducer. I said to Colleen, "What are you going to do with
Alice? Nobody will have any idea who she is."

"Don't worry," said Colleen, "she gets air-brushed out." To
each generation its own liquidation.

At the height of her career Colleen was famous not only as a movie star but also as the mistress of an extraordinary doll's house. She has toured the country with it, exhibiting it for charity and she showed us the illustrated catalogue in which its beauties are retailed. I had heard about it but had never seen it. It must be quite an edifice with a tower twelve feet high, a chapel, a ballroom and many sumptuous apartments; a true fairy tale castle now on permanent display in the Museum of Science and Industry in Chicago.

Our pleasant evening was followed by a bitter morning after. I had only one shopping day in Rome before we were to leave for Sicily and to my shock I discovered it was May first, Europe's Labor Day. Every place in the city, commercial and artistic, including the Sistine Chapel, was sealed.

My bitterness was intensified because I was still tired from our flight and under the circumstances could well have spent a large part of that lost day in sleep but the dear doctor, having risen at eight and spent two hours tiptoeing around our room, not even daring to shower, could bear no more. He wakened me at ten.

Yawning and stretching we eventually took a cab and drove to the Piazza d'Espagna. We had no particular reason for so doing but we were inspired. That was where the action was. The piazza was thronged with people come to see the lovely spectacle of the broad shallow staircase banked with thousands of pots of pink and lavender azaleas that had been placed there for Easter.

We lunched afterward at George's, a small restaurant, one of the best in Rome, nestling behind the Hotel Excelsior, Via Marche 7. We walked through the dining room to the tiny terrace in the back where the only people besides ourselves were a large Italian family seated at a long table. What they had I do not know, but we had fettuccine and minestrone, fritto misto mare, sea food crisp and thistle light langoustine en brochette, and an excellent Frascati. The bill for two, $14.72.

In the early evening, after a prolonged bout of corre-

spondence with our safari hosts, Major and Mrs. Digby
Tatham-Warter, we set out for cocktails with the Irving R.
Levines. Irving has been the National Broadcasting Company's long-time European reporter and has written diverting and informative guide books about Russia and Italy.

Once again we owed our safe arrival to a ferret taxi driver
who nosed his way in and out and round about through ancient winding alleys and hidden small piazzas until he came
to Campitelli 3.

We had a moment of panic when he left us on our own as
we could not find the *portieri*, the omniscient and omnipo-
tent counterpart of the French concierge. At last, through
a ground-floor window I spotted a group of gossiping
women and knocked diffidently upon the pane. They jumped
up uttering little cries of alarm and I daresay that in the twilight courtyard I must have resembled a ghost. We were directed to the second floor where we rang the Levines' bell
and waited for quite a while. Finally we heard the tapping of
heels and Nancy opened the door. When she and Irving
showed us through the apartment we understood the time
lapse. They had fourteen enormous rooms and the flat was
a block and a half long.

We were duly impressed but it was a chilly spring evening
and an open fire would have been welcome. They themselves
were sad not to have one and Irving told us that in winter
they were very comfortable for the steam heat was efficient.
But on March the first, regardless of temperature, the gong
sounded and the furnace closed down for the season. Should
you contract pneumonia that was unfortunate, but it was
your chest and lungs and it was up to you to take care of
them. Put on a sweater or something.

There may be a point to the European-held theory that
Americans exaggerate the virtues of the radiator because the
three Levine small fry were thriving. One had not been thriving long having arrived only six weeks previously but her two
small brothers, Geoffrey and Daniel, were cherubic and ex-
hibited their tadpoles with pride. They had gathered them

from a pond that afternoon and there was considerable discussion as to what was the correct diet. In view of the fact that they were Italian tadpoles Norton suggested *polenta* while Nancy hoped they might survive on the few grasses brought from the home pond. To me they looked under-nourished already and I said, "You'd better feed them or they'll die."

"They'll die," Daniel echoed cheerfully.

We had hoped the Levines might dine with us and after the nice English girl who was looking after the children said she was willing to stay on they agreed to come along. As we went through the enormous double doors opening into the courtyard, Irving told us that when anyone in the house dies one half of the door is closed as a mark of respect.

We drove in his sleek new Jaguar to the Tre Scalini restaurant in the ancient and beautiful Piazza Navona. It was too cold to sit on the terrace so we dined inside and after-ward walked around the great Bernini fountain, its four figures symbolizing four rivers, the Danube, the Platte, the Nile, and the Ganges. The head of the Nile figure is covered by a drapery because at the time Bernini sculpted it—1630— the source of the river was still unknown. It was not until July 28, 1862, that John Hanning Speke beheld the Nile at his feet issuing from Lake Victoria Nyanza and to a baffling riddle provided the answer for which men had hankered for two thousand years.

Bernini's fountain is considered not only an artistic tri-umph but a great feat of engineering since the base is two rococo arches set at right angles affording minimum support for the massive obelisk rising above it. My own favorite bit is the lion lapping water from the basin. There is a companion piece to the fountain at the other end of the Piazza Navona but that was not erected until the nineteenth century when it was felt something was needed to balance the old master-piece.

We had thought our dinner at Tre Scallini—cannellone and boiled chicken succulent—flavorful and very good, but as we were going up to our room in the hotel elevator we heard an American woman, whom we had seen dining there, say to her friend: "My husband wasn't too happy about dinner tonight so I promised him that tomorrow we'll eat right here in the hotel. It's just like back home and dependable."

It may have been dependable but if it was like back home that lady knows a hotel I have never stopped at in all my junketing around my native land. The food at the Grand is exceptional and totally unrelated to any American hotel food I have ever eaten.

I have mentioned that I had lectured in Cincinnati shortly before we left for Rome. I had also appeared in Colorado and Chicago, in the latter two places earning a formidable reputation as a weather disrupter. In those latitudes mid-April might normally be considered spring but to Colorado I had brought a blinding blizzard and during my sojourn in Chicago, Illinois, had been swept by a record-breaking tornado.

As is usually the case when on a lecture tour the speaker having discharged his engagement can scarcely wait to get away.

In Chicago I was obliged to wait until the elements took a tranquilizer but there at least I had friends.

I do not say that the people of Pueblo, Colorado, were not hospitable and receptive to my remarks, but we were after all strangers to one another and furthermore, as I discovered on waking the morning after my talk, irreconcilably separated by snow, they under house arrest unable to venture out of doors, I trapped in a motel that was not, shall we say, the Paris Ritz. The thought of a whole day and possibly another night in my dreary room, trying to choke down the inedible food of the coffee shop was more than I could bear.

Spurred by desperation I managed to mush through the storm to the airport where I flung myself on the mercy of the personnel: one gloomy gent leaning disconsolately on the counter.

"But surely there'll be *one* plane," I begged. "I'm not asking for New York. If I can just get to Denver that will be wonderful."

His look was sour. "Lady," he said, "how you gonna get to Denver? No planes are coming in. We got no power."

I had noticed that the lights were off but I thought perhaps it was economy.

"Oh," I said, "you mean the tower. It isn't working?"

"It isn't working. And the only light in this airport is a candle on the floor in the men's room. You don't believe me, go look."

"You're more than kind. I believe you."

As I glanced through the glass wall into the impenetrable void of swirling gray and white it struck me that the little beam so strategically placed might well be the only illumination he and I would enjoy in the next twenty-four hours. Eventually I did make Denver by car—the last one as I later learned to get over the pass—and eventually the skies cleared and I arrived in New York.

The memory of these elemental aberrations fresh in his mind, Norton turned to me as we were flying by Caravelle from Rome to Catania, in Sicily. "I know about your conjuring up blizzards and tornadoes," he said, "but please promise me one thing. Don't make Mount Etna erupt while we're here. A peaceful week on a beautiful island, that's all I ask. No flames, no smoke, no lava."

"Well," I said, "I'll tell you. It's true I have you in my power but if you're terribly sweet to me and do everything I want I just *may* restrain Etna."

I lived up to my word. Not only was Etna restrained, it was invisible. The two days we spent in colorful picturesque Taormina, the traveler's joy, were mist-enshrouded, the star attraction hidden from view.

However, on our arrival, the port city of Catania was in the clear and inhabited by, among others, five thousand American troops. Why? Founded by the Greeks in 729 B.C., lying forty-two kilometers from Mount Etna, it has several times been destroyed by lava from the volcano having the awesome reputation of 130 recorded eruptions. In 1928 a stream of lava engulfed a nearby village—huge black rocks are still strewn about and in 1943 the long-suffering town underwent a rough siege at the hands of the British who shelled and bombed it before landing there to drive out the Germans.

Returning to nature's machinations, sputterings, and bubblings were recorded for a full year in 1950. But Catania is dogged and is now a prosperous city of nearly 400,000 optimistic fatalists.

We visited the Cathedral of Saint Agatha but architecturally speaking found it uninspired. It is a very large church and May being her month several Masses for the Virgin Mary were in progress. Commenting on her assumption into heaven I said to the doctor, "Supposedly, you know she rose right up, her body uncorrupted." As a man of science this caught his interest.

"How did she do it?"

"Well, uh, I don't know, but apparently in some way under her own steam."

"You mean like a rocket blast-off? Like our Saturn?"

"Those who believe the story must assume so. Though I imagine they envisage something more graceful and romantic. Kind of a floating up."

"You can't do that without thrust."

"Balloons do."

"They're full of gas."

The conversation seemed to be getting out of hand and I made a mental score: round one to science. It was a relief when the doctor turned to look at a hideous statue in the square—an elephant carved from a block of lava bearing on his back a column topped by a ball and cross. However, Catania has attractive things too: a busy fresh smelling fish market and extensive and luxuriant public gardens.

Passing through the streets we were amused to see a woman leaning from a third-floor balcony lowering a basket on a cord. The vegetable man filled it with soft green artichokes from his wagon and she hauled it up again. We thought of our friends the Lucardas, who live in Venice, and whose mail is delivered in the same way.

Our destination was Taormina. As Tauromenium it was founded by the Siculi in about the eighth century B.C. and they must have regretted it. From there on in it was nothing but razings, rapings, blood, and battle. Greeks and Phoenicians and Carthaginians, Romans, Byzantines, Normans, and Muslims raided and pillaged. The city's ups and downs were violent and prolonged causing good Dr. Brown to remark as he scanned a brief history of the territory that had he been a primitive man he would have settled in some dingy little hideaway. To choose an attractive spot was automatically to invite brigandage and destruction. In common with neighboring Naxos, however, Taormina had some consolation. She could take pleasure in small and lovely works of art: her gold coins were of exquisite beauty, elegance, and wit. I am not a numismatist by instinct—it is always easier for me to get rid of money than to squirrel it away—but I should be happy to own some of those early Greek gold pieces enhanced with bunches of grapes, stalwart bulls—Tauro, the symbol of the city—and profiles of gods, chiefly Apollo, with delicately modeled nose, curling hair and meticulously trimmed beard.

En route to present day Taormina we passed through flat and fertile fields. Geraniums cascaded over old walls, foaming white daisies spilled from the terraces and the pale lilac-colored buds of thousands of lemon trees perfumed the air.

Our destination was the hotel, the San Domenico Palace and driving into the courtyard we were greeted with the fragrance of orange blossoms. The courtyard, small and flowery, reminded us of the enchanting Parador San Francisco in Granada but the resemblance stopped there. The San Domenico Palace is huge. It, the Balkan in Sofia, and the Homestead in Virginia are to the hotel world what the word antidisestablishmentarianism is to the English language: the biggest. However, size per se has never seemed particularly praiseworthy and it was not that aspect of the hotel that we found impressive, but the situation is perfect with the classic and alluring view of orange groves, vineyards, and cypress trees sloping to the blue and sparkling sea.

Being shown to our room, we mounted a broad shallow flight of stairs debouching into a vast corridor. Later, pacing it off we found it stretched for 248 feet. Along it three horsemen could gallop abreast and at first sight we assumed the rooms would be to scale. They are not, for the San Domenico was originally a monastery and the rooms are somewhat cell-like. Luxurious cells however, even though small, with high ceilings, comfortable beds, quite handsome commodes and elegant baths very prettily tiled. The light switches are oddly set, being low in the walls, which made them awkward for us but any midgets in the clientele would find them very handy.

Along the corridor-boulevard the holy water fonts have been put to charming use for they are filled with fresh flowers, and opposite the room we occupied a tiny chapel invites the religious.

We wandered around the vast domain and had an *apéritif* in the huge ugly bar which is backed, incongruously, by a carved altar screen. The food we thought undistinguished but all right. One is comfortable and they are strong on service, for Americans a rare blessing and one to be cherished since, although we are forever vaunting our wealth and efficiency, service we seem unable to achieve. Domestic help has virtually passed from the home scene and our hotels while costly offer little. Take a nap in the afternoon, go out to dinner, come back and your room is still the untidy mess you left it. In Taormina you bathe and change, you perhaps enjoy a discreet cocktail and when you return later that night the glasses are cleared away, the bathroom cleaned up, and the bed turned down. Very pleasant.

Strolling along Corso Umberto Primo, the picturesque winding main street of Taormina, we found the merchandise to be largely baskets and small toy carts gaily painted. Today the few real Sicilian carts still in use are mostly to attract the attention of tourists, but painting one's vehicle is an ingrained custom and many pickup trucks are decorated with faces and scrolls, flowers and dots and stripes to brighten the day's grind. In Greece we recalled they do not go in so much for painting but the cab of a Greek truck is a little home away from home. Baby shoes and religious statues are perhaps indigenous to the trucking and taxi industry in any country in the world but the Greeks are also partial to stuffed toys and their windshields and windows are framed in fringe and garlanded with paper flowers. The place looks lived in.

Other popular tourist bait, beside the carts, were paladin knight puppets in shiny tin armor and helmets, brave in full sleeves and flowing capes of brilliant green and crimson silk. Sicilian puppet shows are of ancient and enduring tradition and in his book *Spring in Sicily* Peter Quennel describes a performance he witnessed in a theatre hidden at the end of a strange dark alley in a Catania slum, although there the puppets were not doll-sized like those in the shops but robust characters as large as a seven- or eight-year-old child.

"The Sicilian puppet theatre," he writes, "is genuinely popular art; no genius has ever arisen to lift it from the primitive level. It remains the occupation of large industrious families who paint the back-cloths, stitch the clothes and hammer out the armor, handle the puppets and supply the throats they speak through and the tone of voice used to distinguish each separate class of personage. Distressed heroines affect a dulcet bleat or twitter, heroic knights a magniloquent bellow . . . villains and ogres a hoarse terrific fee-fi-fo-fum . . . commonplace realism is never attempted; and the surging movement with which the actors advance, usually head foremost, while their unjointed legs trail out behind, makes them appear to be swimming or flying rather than walking on solid ground."

The most notable sight in Taormina is the Greek Theatre, more properly known as the Teatro Antico for although the Greeks built it originally they were overrun by the rampaging Romans who partially demolished and then completely rebuilt it. It was lost from those early days until the beginning of the nineteenth century when serious excavations were started.

To get to the theatre one passes through the archway in an old wall against which is propped a stall for oranges and lemons arranged in charming and decorative designs.

The theatre itself is, after that of Syracuse, the largest on the island. It is in a relatively good state of preservation and has perhaps the most beautiful view of any theatre of the ancient world. Of the modern world either for that matter since from it one may behold Mount Etna when it is in a mood to show itself, the island headlands, sandy shores and the spreading sea. When the drama dragged the audience could find solace in the spectacle provided by nature.

Today it is a tranquil lovely spot with grass growing up through the curving marble benches on which are engraved the names of the original occupants. It was also a welcome shelter from the wind, drifting mist and chill of late afternoon.

Returning to the hotel we were tempted by a sign in a shop window: THIS HOUSE IS NOTED FOR A POT OF GOOD TEA. Craving refreshment and impressed by the correct placement of the adjective we went in. For once the product lived up to the advertising claim. Not only was the tea delicious but there were heavenly little cakes concocted of delicate pastry and apricot jam. If you go to Taormina do not overlook this pleasant refuge. Myosotis is nice too and I would also recommend Ciclope, a restaurant on the Corso Umberto that specializes in seafood. It was excellent and with a good local wine our luncheon for two came to approximately $6.40.

The next morning despite a heavy fog we drove to Naxos. It is nearby and it seemed the thing to do although it has been many a long century since Naxos was a swinging center. Founded in 735 B.C. it was the earliest Greek colony in Sicily and even then it was but a steppingstone to Catania and Syracuse. Since it was named after the Greek island it is assumed that Naxians probably were among the first of the expedition to wade ashore. In the ill-fated Athenian invasion of Sicily Naxos was Athens, warm ally but in 403 B.C. it was completely destroyed by Dionysius, tyrant of Syracuse, and nothing much has happened to it since.

Today it is a quiet little port with fishing boats on which are painted mermaids drawn up on the beach. Its fish traps are decorative and it boasts a faithful reproduction of Copenhagen's famed Little Mermaid Fountain.

Of the antiquities all that remains is the ruin of a kiln and fragments of walls made from great blocks of lava. A guide almost as ancient as the relics he supervised spoke no English but made it clear that if we would be attentive while he spoke *andante* we would understand quite a bit and indeed he proved correct. So pleased was Dr. Brown at having grasped a few sentences in Italian that he overtipped the old boy with a lavish hand. Shaken when I commented on the amount, he immediately instigated an austerity regime, pointedly refusing to join me in a cup of coffee when we stopped off at a pretty, cheerful restaurant, the Stockholm, en route up the mountainside to Castello Mola. "One of us has got to start economizing somewhere," he said nobly. He does not care for midmorning coffee. I don't know why there should be Scandinavian overtones in that part of Sicily but there are.

Nasturtiums, cineraria, calendulas, sweet peas, roses, and geraniums, spilled their brilliant blossoms from boxes lining the brightly tiled terrace and they glowed and darkened as the sun won and lost its battle with the clouds. The beach spreading below us would have been tempting had the day been a little warmer but even when the sun triumphed it was a pale variety British sun rather than a hot Sicilian.

Castello Mola is the ruins of a medieval castle which is picturesque but the great attraction is the view which seems to encompass that entire portion of the world. Even through the mist and under overcast skies it was marvelous.

Two or three small shops off the main square specialize in pottery: tiles and bells and little donkeys with panniers on their backs for salt and pepper. They are colorful and fun for the country but I prefer freshly ground pepper from the mill so was able to resist temptation. Also they are comparatively bulky and brittle and tricky to pack. Today, with air travel so prevalent, a local souvenir is like local wine. Charming in situ but will it travel?

The next day the sun appeared briefly so we breakfasted on the hotel terrace overlooking the sea, surrounded by flowers and bird song and enjoying the slightly tart blood-red juice of Sicilian oranges. I had a slight passage of arms with the waiter explaining, when he brought it, that I had ordered orange not tomato juice. He set it down, looked at me pityingly and went away. On his return with the eggs I could only apologize. It is nice that it tastes so good because in Sicily where oranges grow by the millions the hotel charged forty-eight cents a glass which I consider steep.

We paid a return visit to the theatre and it was lovely in the morning light, the broken arches framing the sea. A good many people were already there and English, French, and German echoed softly across the rows of curving benches.

An Englishwoman had set up her easel and there was a whole photographic troupe, director, photographer, hairdresser, and a model in a searing orange suit. We decided that Vogue or Harper's Bazaar must be on location. Actually we had seen the same group the day before in the hotel courtyard and commented on the curious inhuman angularity now so favored by fashion magazines. Spread legs, thrusting jaws, outflung arms rigid as iron spikes. I am willing to concede it is the generation gap but to me they seem singularly unalluring. I thought perhaps it was because I am a woman but when I have pointed out the belligerent young ladies to Norton he makes a grimace of distaste and says, "My God" and "Don't ever let me catch you done up like that." But of course he has to contend with the generation gap too. Possibly their male contemporaries feel equipped to take on the spike-hard unsmiling members of the opposite sex.

Leaving the theatre we met our car and driver and started

for Syracuse. To get there we had to pass through Acireale
where there is a church with a charming rococo façade ebullient with niches and statues, cherubs and garlands.

The seventeenth-century cathedral is sprightly too. A gay
interior with an arched painted ceiling and columns embel-
lished with white and yellow scrolls. The morning we were
there the square was crowded with men standing about in
engrossed animated conversation. Nino, our chauffeur, explained it was a sort of outdoor stock exchange; they were
buying and selling crops and property.

We rolled on through the lovely countryside, the fields
bright with poppies and huge purple stains of clover, the
green wheat flowing as the wind passed over it.

Nearing Syracuse the bucolic charm diminished. The out-
skirts of the historic city are made ugly by a large oil refinery
and sulphur plant and since they are so detestable to look at
one must hope they are immensely profitable.

The modern town is on the mainland but Syracuse was
built originally on the island of Ortygia and it was in the
great harbor that the Athenian expeditionary force went
down to defeat in 413 B.C. when the Syracusans cut off all
possibility of escape with a blockade of chains and boats and
half the Athenian fleet was destroyed.

Over 7000 prisoners were taken and they were thrown into
the latomies, the city's quarries where, to quote Thucydides,
"they were crowded together in a narrow pit, where, since
there was no roof over their heads, they suffered first from the
heat of the sun and the closeness of the air and then, in contrast, came on the cold autumnal nights, and the change in
temperature brought disease among them. Lack of space
made it necessary for them to do everything in the same spot;
and besides there were the bodies all heaped together on
top of one another of those who had died from their wounds
or from the change of temperature or other such causes, so
that the smell was insupportable."

They suffered too from hunger and thirst for the daily ra-
tion was half a pint of water and a pint of corn per man.

They lived like that for ten weeks and were then sold as slaves. And Thucydides goes on to report that "their sufferings were on an enormous scale; their losses were, as they say, total: army, navy, everything was destroyed, and out of many, only few returned. So ended the events in Sicily."

Today the quarries that were the scenes of such intense suffering are sheltered gardens through which travelers may wander and perhaps, more importantly, leave at will. One may also see a curious high grotto where rope makers work as they did long ago, the continuous dampness and dripping rock being an ideal setting for their trade.

Through several centuries the Syracusan form of government appears to have been a vast sandwich, layers of democracy alternating with total tyrannies not all necessarily bad, for under some of them the city reached its greatest periods of prosperity, power, and culture.

Founded by Greek colonists in 743 B.C. it was democratic. Then came Gelon. He was a tyrant, but a nice tyrant, who won a great victory over the Carthaginians at the battle of Himera. He was followed by Hiero I, another tyrant who cosied up to culture, inviting Pindar and Aeschylus to his court. When he died democracy again prevailed and then along came Dionysius the Elder, who may not have originated the policy of keeping subjects under his thumb through threats of defeat by a fearsome enemy—in this case the Carthaginians—should anything happen to him but he was a dedicated adherent to it.

Virtues of strength and courage he undoubtedly had, as well as an enviable gift for organization, but he is said to have been ill-tempered much of the time and it is understandable. During his incumbency Syracuse became the most powerful city in Europe. Like his predecessors Dionysius too wanted to be thought cultured and he was constantly writing plays and verses which he entered in the Olympic contests where for the most part they were roundly booed. No wonder he was peevish. What maligned artist loves a critic?

The Greek Theatre at Syracuse, built probably in about

230 B.C., is one of the most famous but it lacks the magnificent location of that at Taormina and the clean curving lines of the benches lining the hillside are blurred and softened by the passage of the centuries. By millions of feet of tourists tramping over them, too, I should think. It was a big house, with a capacity of 15,000 and when sold out the take at the box office must have been heartening. Or such was my offhand assumption. Later I learned that originally every seat was free but there was also a free-for-all as citizens jostled and stampeded for the best places. People either came themselves or sent emissaries to the theatre to occupy the good seats twenty-four hours before a performance. When the play was particularly popular the local inhabitants complained that they didn't have a chance because of the foreigners who poured in usurping all the most desirable locations. There were fights and bloody noses and things finally came to such a pass that the authorities decided to demand a small fee so that the drama lovers could at least be assured of reserved seats. The same price held for every part of the theatre as otherwise, under a democratic regime, it would be charged that the rich got all the plums, that their money gave them an unfair advantage.

Later on citizens began complaining that even the small amount was too high so finally the government, to escape further headaches, said "All right. Lay off! Desist!" and arranged that anyone desiring admission merely put in a request and his entrance fee into the magic precincts was paid for by the State. Struggling to impose some limitation on the gravy train it was decreed that everyone had to apply in person and be a full-fledged citizen.

In the ancient world as in the modern corruption flourished. The government hand-out eventually backlashed to out-of-hand and the whole system was tossed overboard as the state was going bankrupt.

Behind the theatre at Syracuse is situated the Mystery. The Mystery is a deep, high cave called the Ear of Dionysius. It is a sinuous affair like the coils of an ear or shell and it

burrows into the hillside for two hundred feet, attaining a
height of seventy. There is a legend that Dionysius used to sit
above it eavesdropping on the conversations of his subjects
although it is doubtful that he would have caught more than
a rumbling mumbling echo.

It has been maintained that the cave is a natural phenom-
enon but that theory is ruled out by the thousands of chisel
marks in the limestone and Margaret Guido, a Fellow of the
Society of Antiquaries of London, in her knowledgeable
handbook *Syracuse* states that it was certainly artificially
made, but when or why no one knows.

We went on to visit the Catacombs of San Giovanni
which are large dank and dark. A small friar in a brown habit
showed us around and told us that the early Christians liked
being buried there. We gathered a bit of snobbism was involved and considerable jockeying for position, each one wishing to lie near his favorite martyr. It was interesting to see
how the other half died, but I was glad when the tour was
over and we could get back to fresh air and sunlight and to
the Fountain of Arethusa, which is more beguiling for the
legend than for the actuality.

The fountain is a D-shaped pool below street level surrounded by an iron railing. Papyrus plants grow there, gray
mullet dart and a few contented ducks paddle about. Arethusa
was a nymph in Greek mythology beloved of Alpheus, a
great hunter. She left her job in the retinue of Artemis,
goddess of the hunt and of chastity, whether of her own free
will or under pressure is not clear, and went to Ortygia where
she was turned into a spring. This meant nothing to Alpheus,
however, for he was an ardent type. He merely changed himself into a river, flowed underground, surfaced at Ortygia and
was united with his loved one. There is a river Alpheus and a
spring and fresh water so near the sea was considered by the
Greeks to be something of a miracle and their explanation
of it has more fantasy and charm than prosaic geological fact.

Should the traveler be curious about the appearance of so
volatile a maiden as Arethusa he may see her likeness on

many coins. They vary with the period and with the artists'
imagination but a beautiful one, indeed one of the most
beautiful coins in the world, is that struck in the fifth century by Kimon. It is the head of a girl, the face youthfully
soft, the mouth sensuous, the eyes large and lustrous beneath straight brows and, because this is a water nymph,
dolphins play in the waves of her hair. Her expression is
tender and a little sad. Perhaps she would have preferred to
remain a girl rather than become a spring.

I think, by the way, it is interesting that although dolphins
abounded in the Mediterreanean and Aegean Seas in antiquity today they are virtually non-existent in those parts. One
may occasionally see porpoise but dolphins have departed
for the warmer climate of the Caribbean. The assumption is
that the temperature of their former home has dropped
several degrees from what it was in ancient times.

Maintaining fluidity Norton and I moved on from Arethusa's fountain to the nearby aquarium. Ever since our trip
to Fiji, where we first saw them in their natural surroundings, tropical fish have fascinated me. In the Syracuse
aquarium they have exquisite ten-inch mother-of-pearl creatures with small flashing diamond-like spots. We learned
they were the deadly piranha who attack in shoals and
shear the flesh from your bones in seconds.

In his fascinating account of the rescue of wildlife in
Surinam, otherwise doomed to extinction by the building of
the Afobaka Dam, John Walsh tells how one of his native
helpers "was kneeling in the back of a dugout absentmind-
edly skimming the top of the water with his finger . . .
suddenly he jumped up and held out his hand; the pad on
his little finger had been sliced clean off. Another time a
Bush Negro was taking a sponge bath off the dock, sitting
with just his feet in the water. Abruptly he felt a sharp pain.
With a scream he lifted out his foot. His little toe was missing—meat, nail, bone and all."

Do not fool around with piranha. Nor with barracuda who
also will cheerfully rip you to death and sleep soundly at

night. The aquarium contained less lethal beauties with white polka dots on charcoal gray flanks and orange bands around their mouths, tiny electric blue ones and southern belles trailing white and orange ruffled wrappers as well as more sober navy blue characters and cobra fish with fluted gills and ethereal floating spines.

Among other Sicilian charms must be counted the architecture, fascinating for its variety, its age and the combination of the two. The Cathedral of Syracuse in the Piazza del Duomo, where the Museum is also situated, was begun in the fifth century B.C. probably by Gelon, as a bread and butter letter to the gods for his victory over the Carthaginians at Himera. Cicero writes of the extraordinary beauty of the doors and we know it was crowned by a great statue of Athena whose shield, flashing in the sunlight, guided mariners into harbor.

The temple was altered in the eleventh century and after assorted vicissitudes, among them ordeal by earthquake, enjoyed another heyday in the eighteenth century, when the original Doric columns were skillfully allied with a rich structure of baroque design and a sumptuous façade, the work of Andrea Palma.

Another superb façade, to my way of thinking, the more beautiful of the two, exuberant yet disciplined, is in the town of Noto, about twenty-five miles along the coast from Syracuse. Badly shattered by the earthquake of 1693, Noto was subsequently rebuilt, all of a piece. Its citizens were prosperous agricultural people and they had the taste and money to construct for themselves a real capital, even though small.

Sometimes these cities, because the artistic, intellectual, and social, as well as the political life of the community is centered there, have the richness and appeal of a small exquisitely detailed painting more winning in its way than a spacious canvas can ever be. So it was with Noto. Today it is quiet without being moribund and if, in a way, a museum, one with a good deal of lively traffic passing through it. If I were playing the word association game and somebody said to me Rome, my instant reaction would be Tawny. Rome is the lion-colored city, but Noto is almost more so. Her buildings are made of local limestone and are a delicious honey-buff in color. Three of the most notable are the cathedral, the elegant one-story palace on the opposite side of the square, and the Church of Santa Chiara.

Another delightful example of its architecture is the balconies. In the Via Corrado Nicolaci, leading off the main Corso Vittore Emmanuele, there is a balcony supported on brackets of carved stone of exceptional beauty. As in the churches the exuberant imagination is disciplined and well-proportioned so that the combination of women's heads, mermaids and galloping horses seems inevitable and right.

We did not stay long in Noto but it would be a pity to miss it altogether. Neighboring Palazzolo Acréide is a village a tourist might easily pass up unwittingly if told that today its only attraction is one more Greek Theatre but to do so would be to miss a sweet remnant of history. The community is successor to ancient Akrae, founded in 664 B.C. The well-preserved theatre is a small one, only six hundred seats but enchantingly situated on a hillside overlooking a fertile valley and a distant range of hills. From this high central plateau we could even faintly discern Mount Etna looming through the haze. It would have been a perfect place to picnic and Norton and I regretted that we had not brought along a lunch basket. Adjacent to the main theatre is another truly tiny one. We thought maybe it was the off-Broadway of the period or possibly even a children's theatre where the actors were marionettes. Later we learned that it was used as a small council chamber.

While we were wandering about an old shepherd with his flock and an ancient gray dog came along the road and Dr. Brown whipped out his movie camera. "I must begin practicing for the wild animals of Africa," he said focusing on as tame a herd as was likely ever to cross his lens.

His rehearsal period ended, he heeded the admonitions of Nino our driver that we had best be getting on to Piazza

Armerina. Although to the *cognescenti* it is one of the fascinating art centers of Italy, Dr. Brown and I had not been cognizant and stumbling upon it by pure chance considered it our own discovery. Do not mock the tourist's addiction to postcards! Because of them we had seen the extraordinary pebble mosaics of Pellas in Greece which otherwise we should have missed and because of a few cards glimpsed in the Corso Umberto at Taormina we were heading for Piazza Armerina.

Arriving there we discovered that the villa with the treasures we were so eager to behold was five kilometers farther on and that the doors closed at one o'clock. Nino dug spurs into the flanks of our doughty Chevrolet and we tumbled out at the gates at three minutes to one. I rushed up to the guardian. "*Prego, prego*, from Nueva York all the way." The man laughed, shrugged and handed us two tickets.

The great mosaics of Leptis Magna I have never seen. I have seen those of Pella, Delos, and Ravenna and the churches of Thessalonike. They are exquisite, they are impressive, I am grateful they are there. I have never seen anything with the charm, gaiety and scope of the mosaics of Piazza Armerina.

The villa itself was built between the end of the third and the beginning of the fourth centuries A.D. and is thought to have belonged to either the emperor or a prominent noble or political figure. Whoever he was he thought rich. Although the house as such has long since disappeared the floors remain and they are the glory: mosaic pavements of extraordinary variety, color, imagination, and information. The original walls have been replaced by ones of plastic which are roofed over and equipped with raised catwalks so that it is possible to tour the entire layout a few feet above floor level. In bright sunshine these plastic corridors are a bit hot and steamy but there are open windows at intervals and one puts up with the slight discomfort lost in the beauty and entertainment of the mosaics and knowing that because of the plastic they are being well-preserved.

In various apartments are scenes featuring Hercules, Poseidon, and Ulysses in the cave of Polyphemus. The three-eyed giant sits with a disemboweled ram upon his knee and Ulysses with a false-friend smile tenders him a large bowl of wine while two companions in the background are busily pouring more from a goatskin, hastening the moment when their captor shall sprawl drunk upon the floor and they can make their getaway.

In a marine scene Poseidon rises from the waves trident in hand surrounded by fish, swimming cherubs, and confronting a splendid sea dragon after whom the Loch Ness monster must have been modeled.

Best of all, however, are the scenes of daily life. Hunters returning with a wild boar slung upside down in a net borne on a pole over their shoulders, their dog, with a handsome collar, prancing beneath it eager for a bite. Previously we have seen the unhappy boar being speared to death and we come upon what must surely have been one of the earliest cook-outs. This is no fire lit in a cave but a proper barbecue with a brick hearth and an efficient chimney surmounting it topped by a small figure clad in a tunic holding a bow. There are cherubs fishing and children driving little chariots drawn by birds and ducks. One of the most entertaining and certainly the best publicized scene shows a girls' gymnasium, the feminine athletes clad in precisely today's bikinis: brief bra, briefer breeches—the Elizabeth Arden Maine Chance of the day. The young ladies are running, tossing balls and quoits, manipulating dumbbells and the victor in a game played with what looks to be a large daisy encircled by a ring crowns herself with a diadem while holding in her left hand a laurel branch balanced against her little round naked belly.

Later, in Palermo, Norton bought me a book called *Museums and Monuments in Sicily*. Among its illustrations are some of the Piazza Armerina mosaics and it is one of my cherished possessions.

Like so many Italian towns this one too has a Jolly Hotel.

They are never one's first choice but they are available and the luncheon if not outstanding was satisfying and fortified us for the drive to Agrigento.

The village of Licota on our way was in festive dress for a fair was in progress. The streets were crowded, mostly with men, and arches outlined with colored electric bulbs spanned the cobbled road. With the exception of some practical kitchen utensils the merchandise was gimcrack stuff of plastic. The plastic civilization is useful, I suppose, and practical. It is also hideous.

A little beyond the fair the crowds in the road thickened and this time there were more women than men. There were flowers everywhere and poles lashed upright to the sides of a parked truck were encircled by bright garlands. Because of the floral display we thought to have stumbled upon a wedding. Not so. We quickly perceived that all the people were garbed in somber black, the women relentlessly so; black suits, shoes, stockings, handbags, black shawls over their hair. What we had stumbled upon was an all-out Italian funeral being relished to the hilt.

With peasant faces as unrelenting as their clothes they stood in the street, heads upraised listening to a young man on the balcony of the house of the deceased eulogizing through a microphone the sister who had passed from us. He was reading from a manuscript and was in clover.

I could see him in his room at 5 A.M. that morning licking his pencil and bringing the point down sharply to form the final period at the end of the final paragraph, and I could hear him mutter with a slight licking of chops the Italian equivalent of "I guess that'll fix 'em!"

My Italian is sparse—when I attempt it it comes out a sort of garbled bastard Spanish, which I don't speak either but the sense of his oration was not hard to follow. Starting at sea level his voice sank, soared and gathered momentum as he extolled the virtues of the extinct signorina. "A virgin has left us. Let us recall the virtues of another virgin so excellent, so immaculate in her maternity." This status the local

girl had apparently not achieved. In the street below the pall-
bearers—not honorary but the fellows who did the job—
uneasily shifted the coffin on their shoulders and as the sono-
rous periods rolled on it must have seemed to them that
their virgin, growing heavier by the minute, was not too far
behind her illustrious predecessor after all and was giving
birth if not to a unique son then to full-grown quintuplets.

Since the finale was nowhere in sight we murmured to Nino
to push ahead and gradually inched our way through the
densest part of the crowd encouraged by an irreverent young
man on the fringe who waved us on with a merry wink.

We arrived at Agrigento, our destination, at a quarter to
six. We were tired and had intended driving directly to the
hotel but the light on the Temple of Concordia was so lovely
that we stopped to look and to photograph. The original
coating of hard white stucco has crumbled away and it is now
a warm rich earth color. Seen from the rear some of the columns look as though the stuffing were coming out of them.
This particular temple is well preserved owing to the fact
that although built in the Doric style of the fifth century
B.C., Christians in about A.D. 600 started worshiping there
continuing to do so until the eighteenth century.

Agrigento, for the Greek Akragas, for the Roman Agri-
gentum, was one of the glittering cities of the ancient world.
Beautifully situated on a ridge with the sea not far off, surrounded by fields and vineyards, it was a center of ease and
great luxury and according to Pindar "the loveliest of mor-
tal cities." Its wealth was rooted in fields and almonds, wine
and grain and the temples and palaces were made possible
largely because of the victory of Gelon over the Carthaginians
at Himera, the prisoners of war providing cheap and abundant
slave labor just like today. The procedure is sometimes censored but it must be said for the citizens of Akragas that if
any people were to be enslaved the Carthaginians were ideal
casting.

They were immensely successful merchants, traders, and
explorers but they were merciless enemies, brutal in victory

and no record of art or architecture survives them. Although it is said that their woven fabrics were of great beauty and highly prized.

Also I suppose one should add that most of what we know of them is hearsay handed down by the Romans who feared and hated them but their cruelty would appear to be soundly established.

They relished human sacrifice and propitiated their dreadful God, Moloch, in a peculiarly hideous and horrible manner. Small children were placed in the arms of a huge bronze statue, slipping from the arms into a blazing furnace below. Their heroes were warriors, Hannibal, Hamilcar, and Hasdrubal. The latter two were brothers and Hamilcar's son was Hanno. There was another chap named Himilco. Apparently one's name had to begin with H to join the club.

Hannibal is considered to have been a great general and has become a kind of historic pet because of the elephants and not sacking Rome, but for all that it was a sorry business when the Carthaginians got their own back, attacking Akragas and sending the gay and luxury loving inhabitants fleeing as their beautiful and beloved city went up in flames.

During their great era, however, the charm and comfort of Akragas was unsurpassed. If I may quote Peter Quennell again "as Alkinous suavely explained to his guest when he described his happy subjects, [they] ever delighted in feasts and dances and music, in frequent changes of clothing and hot baths and love and sleep." An understandable taste.

Gelon and Polyzalus were brothers belonging to the Deinomenids family of Gela and Syracuse. They married two daughters of Theron, ruler of Akragas, who married Gelon's niece so things were almost as cosy for them as they were for the Ptolemies of Egypt.

The whole family were mad about horses as indeed were most of the Agragantines. They were famous breeders and their entries in the Olympic Games were synonymous with victory. In Delphi a monument ordered by Gelon to commemorate one of these happy affairs was completed after his death by his brother Polyzalus and the famous Charioteer still to be seen there was one of its figures. Nor were chariot and horse racing the only sports at which they excelled. One of their athletes, Exainetos, won the foot race in two successive Olympiads. On his return from his second triumph in 412 B.C. a great procession from the city went out to meet him including, among other spectacular components, three hundred chariots each drawn by two white horses belonging to his fellow citizens and a magnificent coin was struck in his honor.

Nature and animals meant much to them and they erected statues to their horses and even to the little birds their children kept as pets and, according to the historian Diodorus, they constructed "an artificial pool outside the city seven stades in circumference [4249 feet] and twenty cubits deep. Into this they brought water and ingeniously contrived to produce a multitude of fish of every variety for their public feasting and with the fish swans spent their time and a vast multitude of every other kind of bird, so that the pool was an object of great delight to gaze upon."

One of the leaders of their opulent world was Gellias whose wealth, generosity and fame as a host were legendary. It is said that he once entertained five hundred cavalrymen from Gela when they arrived drenched and chilled to the bone from a winter storm "and provided them all forthwith from his own stores with outer and under garments."

His wine cellar, according to an eyewitness, consisted of "three hundred great casks hewn out of the very rock, each with a capacity of one hundred emphoras [900 gallons] and beside them was a wine vat with a capacity of one thousand amphoras from which the wine flowed into the casks."

Another expansive gentleman was one Mr. Antisthenes and the festivities of his daughter's wedding perhaps stand unique among nuptial high jinks. Again we are indebted to Diodorus who tells us that there were parties in every courtyard in the city and the bride was followed by more than eight hundred chariots not to mention gentlemen on horseback, some of them home-town friends, others guests from neighboring cities. The most breath-taking sight of all must have come after dark when altars in all the temples and courtyards were piled high with wood supplied by the generous and rich father of the bride and the simpler folk were told that when the fires were kindled on the Acropolis they should do the same and since there were many torchbearers in the procession escorting the bride to her new home the city was filled with light.

One of the more thoughtful citizens observed that they built their houses as though they were to live forever but gave themselves to luxury as if they were to die tomorrow.

And the lovely life did not endure forever. The Carthaginians came. The Akragantines made some efforts to defend their city and one of their austerity measures in their time of crisis has come down to us. It was a military order that soldiers at their posts were not to have "more than one mattress, one cover and sheepskin and two pillows." For them civilization died hard. As for Gellias he perished in a Gotterdämerung of his own devising for when it became evident that the Carthaginians having entered the city were not going to spare the temple of Athene where he had sought refuge he himself set fire to it and died in flames among the treasures.

Perhaps the sterling of the Akragantines was not in their characters but they possessed it and its sheen illumined their lives.

Our first night in Agrigento Norton and I drove to see the lighted temples and reflected that the people who built them never saw them under those precise circumstances although their silhouettes against great brilliance may well have been remembered until they remembered no more by those who beheld them at the time of the shimmering wedding or fleeing looked back at them when the Carthaginians fired the city.

After reading of such luxury it is sobering to have to report that the accommodations of present-day Agrigento have little in common with the tenets of Gellias. The Hotel Della Valle,

although clean, is second rate Jolly and the food and dining room dreary. A French couple at the table next to us
caught our attention. She was young and pretty, he elderly
and distinguished. Their rapport seemed enthusiastic for father and daughter and whether it was legal or illegal we of
course could not know but we were intrigued by the combination as Latin men usually are not so dogged nor so touch-
ingly optimistic in their courtship of girls twenty-five years
their junior as are their Anglo-Saxon brothers.

The other diners consisted of a bus tour of obviously well-
off, middle-aged American women, the ball bearings of the
travel industry, each of whom left the dining room clutch-
ing her bottle of Fiuggi, her shield against the nameless perils
inherent in Italian food and water. The tour director dined
alone. The poor man probably had all he could take of
femininity.

It was at the Della Valle that Dr. Brown announced that
he had at last discovered the real purpose of the bidet. "It is,"
said he, "the place where the husband puts his toilet articles."
He was right. Few hotels in the world provide enough shelf
space in the bathroom or a sufficient number of hooks. The
bidet comes in handy.

We woke next morning to our first really clear hot summer
day and left the hotel early to vist the Temple of Hera. The
temples of Akragas are strung out for about a mile along a
ridge. They are lined up east and west with the sea on the
left, the fields dropping away to the right and the modern
city crowning a wide rise beyond.

Their location was and is superb. Including the Temple
of Juno, one called Concord, the gigantic never finished
Temple to Zeus, one to Vulcan, another dedicated to the
cult of Hercules and others on the plain below they formed
one of the largest sacred complexes of the ancient world.
Getting there early we were fortunate for no tourist groups
had yet arrived and to my delighted surprise I found myself
a participant in a minute miracle.

On the slope below the temple I was watching a lizard

on a stone surrounded by May flowers and encrusted with golden lichen. Usually lizards run swift as fire. They flicker and dart and are gone. This one was making his way slowly and gingerly up what must have appeared to him as a boulder, one frail paw pigeon-toeing in front of the other. He stopped and looked around. I murmured to him in soft broken soothing sounds. He cocked his head, his sides working like a pair of tiny bellows. I stopped and he inched toward me. I began murmuring again. He came nearer, halted and sank down between his elbows and looked me straight in the eye for several long moments. I was speaking lizard!

Leaving my *vis-à-vis* with reluctance we went on to visit the ruins of the Temple of Olympian Zeus, the largest in Sicily. Piles of stone and some of the foundation still survive as does a gigantic broken figure twenty-five and a half feet long. It has been reconstituted and lies supine on the ground, one of the Telamons, the male caryatids, that upheld the entablature of the temple.

Excavation is in progress between the Temple of Zeus and the adjacent Sanctuary of the Chthonic Divinities, the goddesses of the underworld, Persephone and Demeter. Circular altars are set in the ground and in this area is the group of columns, the so-called Temple of Dioscuri, now used on many posters promoting travel to Sicily. The component parts are authentic but it was reassembled as it stands today, in 1836.

Another temple we were particularly interested in was that of Aesculapius. We gathered that it lay at a little distance from the others and in its photographs it looked imposing. I can only say that after driving around for half an hour, and through Nino, inquiring as to its whereabouts from a good many local characters we were unable to find it. I do not see how one can mislay a large temple but humiliating as it is to make the admission Dr. Brown and his bride accomplished it. We finally gave up and headed for Palermo.

On that morning in early May the countryside was radiant but an automobile is an intrusion and to travel in one is to

miss the essence of nature. It was only when we stopped for
photographs that we became aware of the fragrance and of
the stillness enhanced by the humming of bees and the soft
tinkle of cow bells. Part of the way we passed between
hedges of flowering cactus. They grow profusely in Sicily and
when in bloom they look like big flat green feet with pudgy
toes. Nearing the capital the landscape changed, the smiling
curved surfaces becoming serious; harsher, higher and more
rocky.

Our hotel in Palermo was the Villa Igiea. Under the same
management as the San Domenico it too is admirably situated but try for a room on the long side of the building overlooking the bay. We could see the water out of the corner
of our eye but our windows opened on a bend in the
road and motor scooters roared around it and car horns
blared unremittingly. It was *noisy*.

The hotel is set in a luxuriant garden and a broad terrace,
cunningly designed with alcoves and different levels that
insure a certain amount of privacy, surrounds a large swimming pool. There are lounge chairs and parasols and it is
inviting but one is also frustrated because the sea is right
there spread at one's feet yet swimming is not advised. A large
shipyard off to the right pollutes the water. A group of columns lends a picturesque note and Norton thought they
were phony but while they have obviously been rigged at that
spot to lend atmosphere I see no reason to assume that
the columns themselves are not old. Sicily is full of them, why
shouldn't the Igiea have its share?

Our luncheon in the large dining room was reasonably
good and we were lucky to get it as a large wedding breakfast was in progress. As we were leaving for an afternoon of
sightseeing a group of people came out and joined us under
the portecochere. A good many of them wore black but a
few were daring; navy blue and brown even olive green,
so we concluded they must be wedding guests. We were right
and shortly the bride and groom came running out, hopped
into a waiting car and were whisked away. To our way of

thinking there was a notable lack of gaiety amongst the company. I am sure the Akragas wedding was very different from *that* but we thought perhaps they were lugubrious because there is no divorce in Italy and the friends and relations were contemplating the inevitable disillusion when youthful passion fades, clean shirts have not came back from the laundry and the twins have developed whooping cough.

As Election Day was coming up loudspeakers blared in the streets and posters exhorted the citizens to VOTA SOCIALISTA . . . VOTA COMMUNISTA PER LA PACE . . . VOTA LIBERALE . . . VOTA STELLA E CORONA, that was the prettiest one, and VOTA P.I.S.U.P. The visitor got the impression that possibly the Sicilians were being exhorted to vote for pea soup but various questions to various people, none of whom seemed to know offhand what the initials stood for and all of whom asked somebody else, at last elicited the information that they meant Partito Italiano Socialista Unita Proletaria.

Since all communication and all transportation in Italy is already state controlled the role of the Communist Party is more or less limited to acting as spur and gadfly to the existing order. Also, although its power is soft-pedaled, the Vatican plays a dominating role in the government.

When his superiors learned that a priest had been interviewed on the subject of birth control he was called on the carpet even before the tape was released to television. He was worried, poor soul, as to what the consequences might be but having cautiously hedged with many "it seems to me's," and "people say's," and "as I see it's" the consequences were not too grim.

The bulk of the Italian population would appear to be divided into three categories: those who adhere to Vatican policy, those who are indifferent to it, and those who are violently against it. "In our family we eat priests" is the slogan of the disillusioned and disgusted.

Our first evening we dined in the hotel but the dining room that had been rather pleasant at luncheon was vast and gloomy and the dinner poor. I don't know why we did not think of the bar. The next night we did and it turned out to be small and festive.

Palermo is a small but vigorous city and in one aspect unique: its Museo Nazionale Archeologico houses the finest Greek art outside of Greece. The metopes, those rectangular panels between vertical bands, taken from the temple at Selinunte are carved in deep relief in limestone and are works of extraordinary liveliness and beauty.

There is a marvelous Europa in a long gown with a deep collar—what we used to call a bertha—sidesaddle upon a stalwart and engaging bull as well as a splendid quadriga, the four horses abreast facing front, called the quadriga of Apollo, Artemis, and Latona, but only a part of one head, that of Apollo remains.

There is a cheerful primitive of Perseus and Athena slaying the Gorgon who, although about to be beheaded, is grinning broadly and holding in his arms a small Pegasus, the winged horse who was born from his blood. Another spirited scene is Athena, now headless, killing the giant Enelados and, the most moving of all, the marriage of Zeus and Hera—Hera, with her wide-apart eyes, smoothly molded face and carved lips, looking remarkably like Jacqueline Kennedy.

Herakles killing an Amazon and three dogs being urged on by Artemis to devour Attis, an unfortunate youth who was turned into a deer because the lady was not expecting him at the particular time he showed up, are marvelously vivid and a group of terra-cotta heads have a serene and beguiling charm. These sculptures are as fine as some of the pieces in the Acropolis Museum in Greece or those at Olympia.

Besides the Museum, Palermo is rich in churches, the most magnificent perhaps being Monreale about five miles southwest of the city. Many cathedrals are a long time in the building but Monreale was erected more or less of a piece in the latter part of the twelfth century. The man responsible for it

was the sovereign William the Good and his church is huge,
impressive and entertaining.

Dominating the apse is the image of the Pantocrator,
Christ the All Powerful, but his expression while scarcely
cheerful is more benign than that of his famous counterpart
in the Byzantine monastery at Daphnē in Greece.

The diversion is to be found on the upper walls of the
interior above and behind the long and imposing dual
colonnade of the nave. They are encrusted with storytelling
mosaics, religious instead of comic strips. They have a blithe
quality which is endearing; Biblical scenes done with verve
and a certain downright approach. There were two I particularly liked. In the Creation of Eve—Adam lies asleep,
his elbow resting on a rock in front of a cave, his head on his
hand as God, seated opposite him watches Eve emerge from
his side and, on the other, beyond the stained-glass window
that separates the two panels, Adam is sitting up while
God, robed, stands between them introducing the naked
lady and gentleman to each other. There are other fine scenes
too: Lot's wife and flaming Sodom and martyrs galore.

The mosaics are largely Restoration. According to Peter
Quennell "In November 1811 one of the cathedral choires-
ters put a candle down beside the cupboard and started a
blaze which he tried but failed to beat out. Whereupon [he]
. . . decided to close the cupboard and went home hoping
for the best."

He didn't hope hard enough and the building was very
nearly demolished. An enchanting survival is the adjoining
twelfth-century cloisters. Two hundred sixteen pairs of columns surround the courtyard, their capitals ornately carved
with iocanthus leaves and intense vigorous small figures.
Next to the cathedral is a broad terrace, a sort of park-
playground overlooking the Oreto Valley and the not too distant sea. It is noisy and gay with swings and roundabouts
and on a small train for children a placard on a second-class
carriage proudly proclaims itself, TEXAS FAR WEST.

We refreshed ourselves with coffee and delicious little

cakes topped with whipped cream and wild strawberries, noted as we sat at the cafe that Palermo traffic was as bad as New York and that Italian children had to be nimble to survive, and made our way to the Cappella Palatina.

As opposed to very large Monreale the Cappella Palatina is a compact brilliant gem glittering with golden mosaics and figures in crimson and blue and green, and a golden honeycomb roof reminiscent of the Alhambra, natural enough when one considers the long rule of the Saracens in Sicily.

Built originally by the Arabs the palace, of which the chapel formed a part, was rebuilt by Roger II, the first King of Sicily, a gentleman who had nothing against either the east or the west and saw no point in not enjoying the best of both worlds, a philosophy followed by his son, William the Bad, so-called because the clergy and members of his court disapproved of his lax eastern ways with luxury and women taking priority over stern virtue.

William installed a clock in the chapel and had carved an exuberant inscription in which he refers to himself as "His Royal Majesty, the Magnificent Ruler, the Exalted One" and other terms of endearment. Apparently absolute rulers find it difficult not to swoon with pleasure when they see themselves in the looking glass for to this day Haile Selassie tenderly treats himself to King of Kings, Elect of God and Conquering Lion of Judah. A raised choir at one end of the chapel faces a raised dais at the other on which was placed the king's throne. Here too the mosaics have been greatly restored but the effect is rich and brilliant.

As I have said Monreale is large and sumptuous and the Cappella Palatina is small and sumptuous but we saw another church that while it does not glitter with mosaics has a charm of its own. A romantic and pretty place, it is the church or rather the cloister of San Giovanni degli Eremiti. Late Norman in style it was built by Roger II in 1132. The cloister is surrounded by a delicate double colonnade reminiscent, on a smaller scale, of the enchanting fourteenth-century Franciscan cloister of Dubrovnik. In the heart of noisy

Palermo it is a quiet oasis, its grass parterre unkempt, pink rose vines twining with feminine grace around the slender gray stone columns.

Something of a comedown from these structures, although one mounts the not inconsiderable height of Monte Pellegrino to reach it, is the shrine of Santa Rosalia. She was a niece of William the Good, son of William the Bad and taking advantage of the diligent research of others, specifically Mr. Patrick Brydone, a gentleman traveling in Palermo in the second half of the eighteenth century, and Mr. Christopher Kinimonth, author of an admirable guide book to Sicily in the twentieth century, I can tell you that she was a very holy girl who, deserting the world at the age of fifteen, retired to the mountains in about 1159. For five hundred years the world waged without her and then a terrible plague broke out. Death swept the city until a holy man claimed to have had a vision of Rosalia's bones buried in a cave near the top of Monte Pellegrino and, said he, if they were taken up with due reverence and carried in procession thrice around the walls of the city the plague would be over.

True or false I cannot say but the story goes that the bones *were* found, the procession took place and the plague ceased. It is perhaps needless to add that Rosalia became the most popular saint in that part of the world and on her feast day, July 15, there are fireworks and jubilations of every kind. Her shrine is a large grotto in the mountainside and the trickling water seeping through the walls, although it seems natural enough to me, is considered miraculous. The grotto gleams with thousands of lighted votive candles which make a pretty effect and cause one to think of the Chinese proverb about not cursing the dark and a plaque let into the wall informs you that Goethe visited the shrine and was overwhelmed by it. Some people overwhelm more easily than others.

We had planned to lunch at a nearby seaside resort so leaving Santa Rosalia to her admirers we drove to La Torre, a very nice restaurant in Mondello. Our driver thought it was nice too. We tried to explain to him that we wanted him to go

someplace and have his luncheon while we had ours whereupon looking pleased he sat himself firmly down at our table.
I am not averse to democracy but in view of the discrepancy
in language and background Norton and I did not feel there
would be much rapport between the three of us. We asked
the headwaiter to suggest to him that he go elsewhere. "I
already have," he said, "but he said no, he likes it here better." He was no fool, the luncheon was extremely good.

La Torre is set directly on the Tyrrhenian Sea, which is a
deep and brilliant blue. Homer wrote of the wine-dark sea
and in Taormina he might have written of the wine-dark
beaches too for they are of powdered lava but at Mondello
they are the color one expects them to be—sand, and perhaps because more familiar, we found them more attractive.

At a nearby table a large family was celebrating a small
daughter's first communion. The moppet was done up like
a little abbess in a long white habit with a crucifix dangling
from a chain around her neck. Norton thought the costume
hampering. He had been disturbed earlier in the day too
when visiting one of the churches we had come upon a cor-
pulent priest saying Mass assisted by four altar boys in their
street clothes. "That's not fair," he said, "those kids have
been yanked away from their play." He enjoyed more the sight
of the young communicant's little brother who, rosy from
tomato sauce, enmeshed engarlanded and ensnarled in
spaghetti was, he considered, getting real mileage out of it.

Although on rising from the luncheon table we felt it un-
likely that we would ever eat again we dined that same evening at Le Caprice, via Cavour 42 in Palermo. My diary notes
read "Simple atmosphere, nice food. Dinner for two with
wine and including service, 5000 lires. $8.00.

In driving to Mondello one passes La Favorita which we
had hoped to visit but there we were disappointed. It was
closed. La Favorita is a villa built by Maria Carolina who was
a sister of Marie Antoinette and the wife of Ferdinand I, King
of the Two Sicilies. Persuaded by his wife he declared war
on the French in 1799 but it was not a good idea for they

arrived in Naples, of which Ferdinand was at that time King, and drove the royal couple out. They fled in Lord Nelson's ship, the *Vanguard*, to Palermo where they built La Favorita as a diversion and a summer residence.

Nelson lived nearby with Sir John Hamilton and the love of his life, Sir John's overblown rose of a wife, Emma. They spent a good deal of time at the villa for the queen, a glacial and often cruel woman had taken a great fancy to the buxom, squirrel-headed English beauty.

The house is a pretty *chinoiserie*, that affectation of stylized Chinese art and architecture so popular in Europe in the nineteenth century. It contains we were told, some charmingly painted rooms. Unfortunately, we could not see them but anyone visiting Palermo should inquire if the villa is now open.

Usually visible and visitable is a treat of a quite different order, and although I am aware and indeed understand that there are those whom it may leave cold I still think it should be mentioned. This is the work of Giacomo Serpotta, an engaging genius who worked in stucco, modeling his figures free standing or in very high relief. He lived from 1656 until 1723 and while his sculpture may be found in some private houses of the period the examples the average traveler is most likely to see are a few in the museum brought there from dismantled churches or those of the Oratorio di S. Lorenzo and the Oratorio di S. Cita. In the former, two charming female figures flank the altar; an elegant smiling tender lady nursing a baby while two others reach up their arms to her and, across the way, a goddess in rich draperies holding a horn of plenty with two infants of her own in attendance. Further work adorns the walls; scenes like stage sets framed in deep niches, some Biblical, some purely decorative with swags and draperies and fat cherubs and marvelously rhythmic saints and virgins.

The churches are not easy to find but a map and a guide book will help and if one has the time they are peaceful sanctuaries housing the lively and lyrical work of a man who devoted thirty-two of his seventy-six years to an uncommonly graceful output presumably spending the rest of his time in pleasant living, although the job itself must have given him amusement and deep satisfaction.

Sicily is noted for her ceramics and in Palermo we came upon a shop where the sculpture though vastly different from his own work might have entertained Serpotta.

The shop is called Ceramiche La Musa and the address is Vio Noto 14. They make bowls, tureens, candlesticks, flower pots . . . assorted houseware but the most amusing objects to our way of thinking were busts of paladin knights with helmets and fierce mustachios and sun bursts on their breast-plates, brightly colored, comical and gay. We bought one and it took a long time to arrive but in these matters one must not give up hope. In all the shopping we have done around the world no shopkeeper has ever taken our money and not delivered.

Since we normally do so much flying we had decided to return to the Italian mainland by boat and boarding the *Sicilia* for the night's voyage we were pleased to see we had a roomy cabin but saddened, not to mention enraged, when it became evident that the portholes while having the normal complement of hinges and screws and brass frames had never been opened and that tradition was not going to be broken that night.

Dr. Brown having spent sixteen months at sea during World War II considers he knows something about portholes but the glass and hardware simply gritted its teeth and defied him. We called the stewardess who laughed, shrugged, and went away. We both uttered short obscene epithets and went on deck. There our tempers improved for matters were more diverting. To begin with there was the way they loaded the cars aboard. The system is ingenious. Two slings of plaited rope are lowered onto the pier, the car owner rolls his wheels over them, gets out and a massive crane hoists his investment onto the deck. We wondered how frequently they checked the ropes. There was, we noticed, no nonsense about draining out the gasoline and as each car swung into the air we had a moment of hopeful apprehension. Maybe this one wouldn't make it! What a glorious smash-up *that* would be. We were disappointed, every car was neatly and safely stashed.

The dock was noisy and crowded with people pushing and shoving and hauling their luggage up the gangplank and we felt rather sorry for the vendor of brightly painted toy *Sicilian* carts. Everyone ignored him and his trade was not good. Finally the gangplank was hauled up but as it swung in midair a young couple with panic cries came running frantically onto the pier. The captain showed himself sympathetic and sporting. The vital link was lowered, the young couple rushed forward but just as she was about to set foot on it the girl stopped short, nearly sending her fellow hurtling over her shoulder, fished wildly in her purse, came up with a few coins, thrust them at the man, grabbed a toy cart and dashed up to the deck. Loud cheers from the passengers hanging over the railing.

It was a beautiful night, the sea was calm and the crossing could have been delightful but we got little sleep for due to the wretched and relentlessly stuck portholes our cabin was airless. At five o'clock, after fitful dozing, we woke definitely to find the ship anchored at the dock.

The Bay of Naples is supposed to be one of the most picturesque of Europe and if you are out at sea looking into it I am sure it is, but if you are *in* it, tied up alongside a wharf, the prospect is dull. Warehouses. We contemplated them for some time as our car had not been ordered until seven-thirty.

When it arrived, bearing a compact informative young man from the American Express, we drove off just able to discern Mount Vesuvius through the harbor haze. We passed an ancient fortress known quite rightly, as New Castle, since it was erected by the Duke of Anjou as recently as 1279.

Greeks, Etruscans, Romans, Normans, and of course Sicilians, came to Naples. In 1139 Roger of Sicily added it to his kingdom and while he was Roger the two on the island he was Roger the one on the mainland and the city was his capital.

In the sixteenth century Philip of Spain used briefly to sign himself King of England and Naples, and since he was married to Mary, Queen of England, and inherited Naples and Sicily when his father, Charles V, abdicated in 1556, he probably wasn't going overboard but somehow he scarcely seems to fit one's idea of a volatile Neapolitan. Joseph Bonaparte and Joachim Murat were also her sovereigns, so it is only comparatively recently that Naples has entered the democratic ranks.

The early morning hours we spent there seemed democratic not to mention prosy for although we breakfasted at the Albergo Vesuvio which has a rolling provocative sound the dining room was full of American businessmen, they and ourselves stowing away the democratic American breakfast of bacon and eggs, coffee and orange juice. I had tea but I don't know that that is undemocratic.

Afterwards, in order to get to our car we had to cross the street, surely not too baffling an ordeal for a New Yorker but I think we should still have been there, a pair of emaciated, haggard derelicts had a sturdy determined little Italian woman not taken us in tow, holding up her hand to stem the onrushing flood of buses, cars, screeching tires, and a deafening cacophony of horns as she piloted us across the road.

Leaving the city on our way to Pompeii we passed the Royal Palace, now a museum, greeny mustard in color with a glass-roofed many-pillared arcade and drove along the waterfront—the district that suffered so terribly from the German bombs of World War II. Most of the neighborhood was razed, including some magnificent old buildings. There are now many new apartments, government controlled, erected with the help of the Marshall Plan and we were told that they rent for 35,000 lires a month, about $57. Long lines of laundry strung across the streets flutter from the upper windows. Each family has its own day for hanging out the wash and I should think by now they must all be pretty familiar with the more intimate articles of their neighbors' clothing.

"Papa, what do you think? That fliberty-gibbet Maria Rosini has *another* new petticoat!"

"Maddalena, come quick, you won't believe it, they've bought poor old Sebastiano another set of underwear at last! Now he won't have to stay in bed one day a week."

Since our driver assured us we would find superlative jewelery at moderate prices in a factory he wanted us to stop at we agreed, with misgivings, to do so. Superlative jewelery and moderate prices are a contradiction in terms in most places and so they proved to be at Torre del Greco although what we saw was not without interest. The craftsmen worked in coral and made cameos. Until I saw them doing it I had no idea of how they chip away at the coatings of a mollusk shell to form the bas-reliefs which later are so smoothly polished. The men doing it were obviously skillful but a cameo is neither a work of art nor a jewel to which I warm and I am afraid, to the great disappointment of our guide who doubtless collected a commission when travelers in his care made a purchase, we left empty-handed and drove to Pompeii.

The original town was probably established around 800 B.C. by an Italic tribe, coming later under the influence of the Greek colonies along the coast. However little was recorded before 79 B.C. One of the outstanding events of the first century of the Christian era appears to have been a fight in the theatre. A riot broke out between the locals and a visiting team from nearby Nuceria. There were so many broken bones and so much bloodshed and indeed deaths that for ten years all theatrical presentations were forbidden. History does not say what the play was or if the play was in fact the cause of the fracas but it seems to have been a violent forerunner of the riots in Dublin when *The Playboy of the Western World* was first produced in 1907 at the Abbey Theatre.

Fresh turmoil, and this time more fearsome, broke out in A.D. 63 when an earthquake caused serious damage. The inhabitants were still digging out when they were devastated by the great eruption of the year 79, the one that buried the city and proved to be such a rich source of inspiration to Bulwer-Lytton.

In its heyday Pompeii was a prosperous town, nearer the sea than at present and it did a brisk trade in wine, oil, and such specialties as perfumes, cloth, and fish sauce. The fish sauce people were perhaps the antecedents of the Progresso family and their tinned goodies.

There were about 22,000 inhabitants of whom it is estimated some 2000 perished in the earthquake. Pompeii was covered by cinders, small stones, and ashes but the material was on the whole light in weight whereas at Herculaneum the substance became water-soaked and formed a hard layer over the entire city at some places sixty-five feet deep and averaging eighteen to twenty feet.

The force of the eruption was tremendous and the lava must have spread with terrifying speed yet even so the great majority of the people escaped and it is hard to understand how others became trapped but they must have been suffocated by the fumes. In the museum one sees the poignant forms that once were living beings encased in lava. The bodies long ago disintegrated into dust and the lava casts are now plaster filled instead: a girl flung forward propped on her elbow, a small crouching boy covering his nose and mouth with his hands and a dog twisted on his back drawing up his legs in his final agony. I do not know whether or not it is true but they told us he is the same dog whose portrait in mosaic still decorates the house where he was found. In his picture he is a frisky fellow with a curly tail on a chain looking fake-ferocious and under his paws is the legend Cave Canem. I know some people who don't have any dogs at all, who in fact dislike them but a sign in their driveway bids trespassers BEWARE OF THE DOG. That is how the legend has come down to us, a sort of second courin to Caveat Emptor

—let the buyer beware—but actually the original intent of Cave Canem was quite different.

At that period in Pompeii miniature whippets weighing perhaps five or six pounds were the fashion and much loved. The real warning was not for a person to safeguard himself against the dog but to take care not to step on the family pet or to run over him in his chariot.

It is understandable that once the work of excavating began really to take form the site should have drawn visitors by the hundred thousands for there, imbedded not in amber but in ash, is The Way It Was. The straight narrow streets crossing each other at right angles, the deep ruts made by chariot wheels, the raised sidewalks and the houses opening onto their interior courtyards where the family lived. Sometimes the lower façade fronting on the street was rented out to shopkeepers and not necessarily run by the family who owned the house. Today grass and poppies grow up through the stones and the big paving blocks in the streets but one gets a clear idea of what the city must have been and can sense in the open agora, where there has been considerable restoration of the columns, the vital part it must have played in the daily life of the inhabitants.

Pompeii used to be famous for its erotic paintings and mosaics. They have endured through the millennia, cheerful proof that the Rabelaisian aspect of human nature is a hardy perennial. To our own Rabelaisian disappointment we were told that very nearly every example has been removed from the walls of Pompeii and placed in the museum in Naples where one must have special permission and, I suspect, dispense a little cash to see them. It was not edifying to learn that the principal reason for their removal had been the graffiti scratched over the pictures themselves and on the walls beside them by American soldiers during the war. The originals were hallowed by skill and antiquity. The American contributions were lewd without artistry. One or two, however, still remain.

One of the best preserved houses is the Casa di Vetti.
It was owned by two gay blade brothers and the goings-on
therein used to be a principal source of the scandalized and
greatly relished gossip of the town. Behind a small grille set
in one of the walls is a fresco and if not too many people
are about and if one passes a little judicious baksheesh to
the guide he will open it. The scene illustrates a wager as
to which of two objects weighs the more. One of them is a
sack of gold. The competing item is laid upon a scale and
I can only say it is extremely funny and wildly flattering to
the male ego.

Our own guide was a trying old party named Grimaldi—
one of Princess Grace's lesser in-laws I imagine—with a rasp-
ing voice which he never modulated but he caused us a moment of diversion when, as we were en route to Sorrento
for luncheon and he was referring to some of the bodies that
had been exhumed in Pompeii, he said, "Visita bodies in
da catacombs outsidea Napoli. Needa special permit see
them. Seea da bones, seea da artichokes." We were startled
until we realized he was referring to a field of artichokes we
were driving by at the moment.

La Favorita in Sorrento is a large airy restaurant where one
climbs up a couple of terraces to a substantial meal and a
fair local wine. In 1873, Enrico Caruso was born in the nearby
village of San Giorgio and when the incomparable voice could
be heard no longer he came home to Sorrento to die in 1921.

We returned to Naples to catch the Naples-Rome-Milano
rapido. "Great train," people had said. It was not great but
it was all right and the beauty of the countryside was rewarding; everything tender spring green, lush and fertile.

We were returning to Rome to reorganize our luggage and
leave for Nairobi the next day. Already weary and antici-
pating a long flight, we dined in our room on exotic foreign
fare—tomato soup and hamburgers—and were in bed with
the lights out at 9 P.M.

This may not sound like life a go-go in a gay foreign
capital but it was wise for leading the life of the birds.

We woke early to the cornflower sky of Rome on a radiant May morning. When inspired by primavera in full fig our driver made the normal forty-five minute drive to the Fiumicino Airport on the wings of a lark.

We were flying with Alitalia from Rome to Nairobi via Athens and the luncheon between the two European capitals was *magnifico*: caviar, paté, osso bucco, spinach, rice and wine galore. One must concentrate on the meal for the elapsed flying time to Athens is only an hour and thirty-five minutes.

After Italy Greece is arid but even Italy is not illumined by the lambent light of Greece. The light was a benediction but the wind, although the day was hot, snatched the breath from your throat. I had gone to some pains with my hair, Norton having announced that he wanted to snap me on the steps as I emerged from the plane. He went down ahead of me, motioned me to come out which I did and Whee! Fright wig! Every hair on my head straight on end.

Since we would have a forty-minute layover Norton wanted to take his camera with him but one of the plane attendants said politely, "I think better not, sir. They are jittery."

The coup of the colonels when they took over the Greek government had occurred on April 21, not quite three weeks previously and the gentlemen were still a little nervous.

An Olympic plane arrived just as we did and taxied to a stop in front of an honor guard drawn up at attention. Military men disembarked including the Minister of Defense arriving home from a NATO meeting in Paris.

Nearby stood a group composed of two nuns, a man in uniform, a few civilians, and a woman in deep mourning. Another man, a friend or relative from the military plane, walked over to them and took the woman in his arms. She broke into choking sobs, and I felt the tears slipping down my own face. Why? I did not know her, we would never meet, she could not know I existed but I cried because she was bereft and because war and violence are hideous and men die and women are left to loneliness. We watched them lower a casket from the Olympic plane and turned to re-board our own.

The flight to Nairobi, said the captain, would take about five hours and fifteen minutes. Shortly afterward we were flying over Crete, our last glimpse of Europe, and then it too slipped away. We crossed the Mediterranean and after the brilliant enamel coloring and the glittering light of Italy and Greece the dun stretches of Egypt and the Sudan seemed endless, a sort of sad remorseless penance for so much worldly pleasure, but they were swallowed up by the darkness and we knew that shortly we would be in Nairobi. Norton and I like the city, not so much for itself but because it is the gateway to a world of wonder.

CHAPTER TWO

East Africa

Our correspondence with Major and Mrs. Tatham-Warter, fairly voluminous before we left home, had slowed to a trickle while we were in Europe. They knew when and on what plane we would be arriving but no precise meeting had been set and on the flight from Rome Norton and I wondered whether or not they would be at the airport to meet us or if there would be a message at the hotel saying they would be by in the morning.

It was 10:45 P.M. local time when we touched down at Nairobi and the couple who were to be our hosts, guides, informants, and very soon friends, were there to greet us.

Our first impression was that they were very nice and very British. Jane—we were quickly on a first name basis—has a charming face and Digby is spare and upright, Sandhurst, D.S.O., and military in appearance.

With John Owen's predictions about the weather ever in mind, as we were driving to the New Stanley Hotel we asked the Tatham-Warters how it had been and what they thought was in store.

They replied, "Frankly the rains have been terrific, the heaviest since 1961. Personally we have been grateful because of our farm, but just before your plane came in we had the most frightful cloudburst. Look at the pavements."

It was true that the pavements were flooded but the water

gleamed in moonlight. As we approached the field the rain had ceased. We encouraged ourselves with the hope that we had arrived with the olive leaf between our teeth.

Over nightcaps at the hotel we discussed the rough outline of our safari. Norton and I thought we might first want to pay a flying return visit to Uganda—Queen Elizabeth and Murchison Falls National Parks had been fascinating interludes in our first trip to Africa—but that would be decided in the morning.

Although we went to bed as soon as the Tatham-Warters left us, due to excitement I was lagophthalmos, a word I came upon by chance while looking up another word in the dictionary. It means hare-eyed, a morbid condition in which the eyes remain wide open. That was me. Shortly after six I did fall into a kind of stupor only to be awakened before eight by the sharp peal of the telephone. It was a call from Mombasa, Kenya's vital seaport, and a lilting Irish voice was wishing me the top of the morning.

For this blithe importunement I had to thank one of my dearest and oldest friends, Mrs. Reginald Rose. Some months before Mrs. Rose had been smitten with a serious misery, scaring her friends blue, but she had fully recovered and this happy condition she attributed in part to the charming young Irish nurse who had taken care of her in the hospital. The nurse had since left New York to be with her fiancé, an Italian surgeon in Kenya and when Bertha learned we were going there she was delighted.

"I don't know just where Mombasa is, dear, but probably it's quite close to Nairobi" (it is not) "and I'll let Mary O'Mahoney know you're coming. She's a charmer. You'll love her and she'd adore to meet you. Her father was an Abbey player and she's crazy about the theatre and books and that sort of thing. It will be a real treat for her to talk with you."

Dear Bertha. I am as susceptible to blandishment as the next one but treating somebody to my wisdom and experience, dispensing the latest bulletins on the art and literary worlds at 7:45 in the morning after a sleepless night is not my idea of undiluted joy. I am afraid I gave the young charmer short shrift.

"My God," I said to Norton, "what an hour to telephone."

"You forget," he said, "she's a nurse."

It was obvious that my hunt for sleep was frustrated so while waiting for breakfast we stepped out onto our balcony to scan the skies. So much would depend on the weather. There were clouds but they cleared as the morning progressed and the sun broke through as did a light spring shower. Ah well, a light shower, what was that? As long as it wasn't a torrential downpour.

The trouble, Digby had said, was that even if it didn't actually rain some places might be impassable because of mud. Poor John Owen, it was scarcely his fault nor his affair but because he had suggested this particular season we muttered mutinously against him. What we should have done we felt was to have gone first to the Middle East as we had at one time contemplated doing and then come on to Africa. In the light of hindsight that, obviously, would have been the better plan but Mr. Nasser had not confided in us and, as we were shortly to learn, the one-week Arab-Israeli war would put a crimp in our future itinerary although luckily not in the safari.

I have read a good many books about safaris. The quality of the writing varies, but to me they are all fascinating because they deal with a unique and marvelous way of life. However, those I have read give little practical information on the brute facts which anyone planning a trip to Africa must know.

At the end of this chapter will be found a few statistics on cost and a suggested list of clothes to take which I hope will prove helpful. By the time this book is in print figures may have gone up or down and anyone interested in making such a journey will naturally write for price and information, bearing in mind that besides the tenting safari there are two other kinds: by private car or by bus tour, staying overnight or for more protracted periods in lodges or camps. I cannot speak from personal experience of the buses, but Norton and I traveled by car with our own driver, stopping in lodges on our first trip to Africa in 1962. It was a memorable experience and I have written about it in *Elephants Arrive at Half-Past Five*.

Regardless of one's method of getting about, however, I would suggest planning well ahead. Not only are the host-guides themselves likely to be heavily booked but in the high season getting into lodges, if that is what you prefer and many people do, requires a well-greased shoe horn, reservations are so tight.

I can give no information on hunting safaris since I have never been on one and never shall be but I do know that they cost more than the game-viewing kind because of licenses and the need for trackers and skinners. For either kind one must first get to Africa so the fare too is a consideration. Speaking for ourselves on this, our third visit, we wanted Authenticity!

Not only animals, but camp fires and stars, the hush of the bush, or the cacophony. We were to discover that in the latter half of the twentieth century the natural and the simple is the costly. Henry Thoreau would be absolutely astounded by what it costs to sit beside a hippo pool or to watch the fleet antelope soar off as man approaches. Rousseau would turn ashen over the take-home pay of the noble savage. Yet, if you wish to enter into a vanishing world, to experience something strange and lovely and unique, it is worth saving up for.

As I have said, we met with the Tatham-Warters the night of our arrival. The next morning the final financial details were ironed out and from the point of view of both time and money we reluctantly decided that Uganda was not feasible.

Norton and I then went off to see Mr. Karmali, an Indian friend of ours who keeps a shop with fine cameras and photographic equipment. We also went farther down the street to a shoe store to buy rubber boots. "Considering the weather," Digby had said, "I think you would be wise to have gum boots." That man was a prophet.

A little later he and Jane came by and drove us out to the Muthaiga Club for luncheon. The club building itself is comfortable if not remarkable but their *pièce de résistance* is a handsome new swimming pool. The old guard was bitterly resentful of such a new-fangled contraption and fought a tough delaying action but the club was losing so much money the board of governors bowed to modernity. The pool was installed and business now booms with the young splashing like porpoises and when we were there they were looking forward to throngs when the weather got really hot.

Norton and I noticed that two Africans were lunching at the club as guests and we thought that there were other innovations besides the swimming pool.

The afternoon was spent sorting and packing our safari gear and alternately cursing, weeping, and praying, for rain-laden clouds hung low in the sky and as we contemplated all the money we would be spending to sit bogged down in mud our spirits sank even lower.

"If the animals have any sense," said Norton, "they won't budge. They'll stay huddled under trees and all we'll see will be backsides of formless hunks of creatures."

As evening drew in we ordered the ice and soda and turned on the radio to cheer ourselves up. The only program we could get was a very British voice giving French lessons. The morning emission had been another British voice discussing abortion.

We dined in the cosy atmosphere of the New Stanley grille room and Norton had Mombasa oysters which he fancies and I do not and we both, for sentimental reasons and because it is delicious, ordered Nile perch.

Our sentiment stemmed from the time we had stayed at Lake Rudolf in northern Kenya and I had brought in a perch weighing sixty-eight pounds. They go far higher than that but I was impressed by my catch. We drank a toast to my five-year-old triumph and another, sadly, to Guy Pall. He had been the manager of the very primitive camp at which we stayed. He was able and amusing and somehow made us think of a tough little bantam cock. A year or so after we had been there we learned he had been killed by the Shifta.

The next morning, although the cloudy season was still with us, our spirits rose as we drove off to the orphanage and great optimistic patches of blue began to appear in the sky.

The orphanage is attached to the Nairobi National Park, the reserve only a ten- or twelve-minute drive from the heart of town.

It houses animals who are small or ill or who for some reason are waiting to be transferred from one game reserve to another. It used to be very informal but with the passing of time and increasing interest in the inhabitants it becomes ever more zoo-like. The animals are kept in enclosures that are larger and better than cages and they have trees and earth. They are still confined.

In honesty, however, I must say that the mongoose darting in and out of their little mountain of stones seemed merry and a big chimpanzee thoroughly enjoyed the cigarette our driver gave him. I imagine it is against the rules but the old boy would take a puff, lay it down, roll over, scratch his back, languidly reach out an arm, pick it up and take another puff.

After we had admired other beasties, especially the elegant and graceful little lynxes, we drove into the park proper. There were hundreds of gazelles and we passed very near two proud giraffe and very near a warthog too who, down on his knees, was busily rooting for grubs. Truffles, too, perhaps.

When we came upon two cheetah cubs happily rubbing themselves against a signpost James, our driver, perked up. "The mother must be somewhere near," he said. We went on down the road and sure enough there she was, oddly enough not much bigger than her children. She was moving quietly and watching her we became aware that she was stalking a group of impala lying on a slope about a hundred yards away. James drove on beyond them and turned off the road up onto the hillside so that the herd lay between us and the cheetah. For a few minutes we lost track of her for she had disappeared into the long grass. The impala lay quietly, unaware of their danger since she was downwind of them. Presently we caught sight of a small round furry head. She was moving cautiously, always keeping low bushes between herself and her quarry. Still the herd was quiet, most of them lying down, two or three grazing. The wind shifted and suddenly, in an instant they were stung to action. The impala, the cheetah in pursuit, broke into a gallop. Impala are swift but the cheetah for short spurts is the fastest animal on earth. The chase lasted eight or ten seconds, if that, then she leaped, bringing one to earth, its neck broken. We were so close we could hear her gasping for breath and see her sides heaving. We saw, too, the film come down over the lovely liquid eye of the impala. The cheetah never relinquished her grip on its neck although the animal kicked convulsively. I began to cry. "It's all right, it's all right," Norton murmured sympathetically, busy with his camera. "Those are just agonal convulsions, like a chicken when its head's been cut off." I hoped he wasn't saying it only to comfort me.

For a long time the only sounds breaking the stillness were the humming of bees, distant bird notes and the cheetah's heavy breathing. Then she loosed her hold, sat up and in some way we could not understand communicated with the cubs. Moments later they came romping up and fell to on the carcass.

James assured us they would be there for some time and as we had a 12:45 luncheon appointment with our friend Ken Smith we decided to leave. We had met Ken on our second trip to Africa in 1964. We had gone to Samburu, one of the most appealing of all the reserves, and he was the warden of adjoining Buffalo Springs. He was a delightful Scotsman, sturdy, forthright, and experienced in his job. He had now been promoted and switched to Nairobi but when we congratulated him on his advancement he said gloomily, "Oh yes, it's nice of course but now I'm tied to a desk. Don't get nearly enough outdoor work."

Luncheon in mind, Norton gave James the signal to go ahead. He turned the Toyota around and rolled gently down the slope. We were about three feet from the road when there was an abrupt jolt and the front wheels sank to the hub caps in mud. We had struck into a ditch edging the track.

James shifted gears. He tried to advance, he tried to back up. He took it slowly, he spun the wheels. We were irremediably and irretrievably stuck. He got out, Norton got out. They plopped on their bellies and peered underneath. It was some time before they discovered, by dint of scraping the mud away with their bare hands, that the axle was hooked over a large rock. It was maddening to be that tiny distance away from the hard-packed earth track and unable to make it.

Norton was convinced that had James kept a sharp eye on where he was going the trouble need not have happened and I think he was right but I will say for our little driver that having got us into the mess he did his best to get us out. He embarked on a flat stone strategy going to pick them up one at a time and placing them under the wheels in the hope of getting a purchase for traction. Since each trip took him several yards from the Toyota he urged us to keep an eye on the cheetah. "I fear," he said, "I fear," and somehow it sounded more fearful than "I am afraid."

If he was afraid it was brave of him to do what he did but Norton and I, while no Tarzans, are not very afraid of cheetahs knowing they are often kept as pets. Furthermore this particular family, involved as they were with the freshly killed impala, were not likely to show much interest in us.

Again and again small dark James sloshed through the mud with his heavy burdens and again and again he hopefully brought out the jack but it was too short to be effective in our ditch.

We may not have been very concerned with the cheetah family but we were bogged in a short loop of road. I could see across the great expanse of bush in front of us and up the slope behind where the cheetahs, veiled by the tall grass, were happily feasting. Anything approaching from those directions would be visible at long range but animals walk the dirt roads of the park as well as the bush and were one to appear around the bend from either left or right we would have short notice.

However, the landscape was serene. Never before had we seen Africa so green and by now there was a huge expanse of blue sky and bright sunshine. Aside from a nagging worry about our lunch date with Ken, I felt happy and relaxed when suddenly, coming up the slope opposite us heading at a businesslike trot for the narrow dirt track on which we were stuck and about twenty yards off to the right came a large black-maned lion. Being bent over the stones with his back to him, James did not see him.

"James," I said, and I hope I said it calmly, "get in the car quick. Here comes a lion." James got.

The lord of the bush couldn't have been more indifferent to us piddling humans. He had scented the impala kill and it smelled far more appetizing than we did.

From where we were trapped in the mud we couldn't see over the brow of the hill so we did not witness the dispute which must surely have taken place but within minutes we did see the magnificent thief make off with the cheetah's kill dangling from his jaws. We were incensed by such high-handedness but it had been about half an hour since the cubs had been summoned so we felt they must have enjoyed a good meal.

James and Norton got out of the car and started to work again, heaving, sweating, grunting and casting quick looks around while I kept an eye peeled like Sister Anne.

Presently in the direction from which the lion had come we

saw a great flock of vultures gathering over something on the ground. Even through binoculars we could not distinguish what it was but his lordship, although he disdained to dirty paw or jaw with muggers' work, was susceptible to the perfumes of the chase and before the vultures could settle, having presumably finished the impala remains, he came trotting back past us and was off across the plain to investigate whatever it was the vultures had spotted.

Finally with a terrific grinding of gears and spewing of mud the Toyota moved forward. Six inches. And stopped dead. It was now 3:30 and about three hours since we had been mired and no car or human soul had passed our way. Fortunately, we none of us felt hungry—too engrossed, I suppose—but I did wonder how we should fare if we began to get thirsty. Also, if we were still there when it got dark what would be our course of action?

Seeking reassurance, I said to James, "I expect around sunset the wardens make a kind of checkup, don't they? To see there's no one left in the park?"

"No," he said, "they don't. They don't know we're here."

"But we came through the gate, we bought the tickets. They *must* know."

He shrugged. "The gate man goes home. The wardens *don't* know. Besides they're not expecting people to be here now, it's early in the season." Early birds were on their own.

A stringent rule of the East African game reserves is that visitors must never get out of their cars but in our case it looked as if the rule was about to be cracked. We were four or five miles from the gate and if help didn't arrive pretty soon we'd have no alternative but to walk. The wardens will tell you, and I am sure correctly, that ninety-nine times out of a hundred nothing will happen to you if you are on foot. The hundredth time gives the place a bad name. Ours may have been the calm of ignorance but Norton and I felt that the three of us together armed with the too-short jack and the inevitable African panga and with strong voices to hoot and holler would be more than a match for any predator.

After all, animals instinctively avoid the human race, the youngest, smallest beast being haunted from birth by "The earliest trumpet note of fear, that call unheard yet clarion clear, 'Flee for your lives, it's man.'"

And of course there *was* the chance we could work ourselves free. The flat rocks and the heaving and pushing seemed on the verge of success when around the bend came a Land-Rover driven by a warden. He stopped when he saw us. We waved and shouted to him. "Thank heavens you've come to rescue us. We *were* beginning to get just a tiny bit worried." He looked surprised. "I didn't know you were here. Hadn't a clue."

This was deflating. "Oh? You weren't looking for us?"

"Good Lord no. I came because I heard a giraffe has been killed. That's unusual. I want to see what's up."

"You will give us a hand though?" He shook his head unbelievingly. "I never thought I'd live to see the day when I'd have to pull a Toyota out of a ditch." That warden was unsophisticated. In the course of the next three weeks we were to demonstrate time and again that the revered, supposedly all-powerful Toyota can succumb to mud as easily as an old-fashioned belle could swoon into the arms of her swain.

Yet even as he mocked us our rescuer was unwinding his tow cable. He attached it to the front of our car, hopped into his own, started the engine and within seconds our troubles were over. On the way to the gate we were escorted by bands of friendly baboons whom we would have liked to photograph but the cameras were too mud-bespattered. Back at the hotel Norton spent what was left of the afternoon cleaning and polishing.

There was a message from Ken Smith who had duly shown up for luncheon and who, having waited more than half an hour, had gone on about his business. We gathered from the operator that he had called several times and indeed we hadn't been in our room fifteen minutes when the phone rang. On hearing my voice he said, "Good, I'm glad you made it. I take it you were bogged down."

I apologized for having kept him waiting and poured out our story and the warden's tale of the giraffe, with what I considered a fine dramatic flourish. "And there we *were*, Ken, *stuck* all that *time. Anything* might have happened to us."

He said, "A giraffe killed, eh? I'm sorry to hear that." His heart is with the animals. He had, however, been concerned for us. "I've been calling every fifteen or twenty minutes. As a matter of fact I'm at the gatehouse of the park right now, had to come on business. If I hadn't reached you this time I was going to drive on in and look for you."

We appreciated his thoughtfulness, for the park, forty-four miles square, has over eighty-five miles of road and retrieving is not so simple a task. When a heavy shower broke in the evening we were grateful it had not occurred during our sojourn in the bush.

We made another engagement with Ken Smith for the following morning and this one happily we were able to keep. It was a pleasure to hear him say that he might possibly meet us again at Leopard Rock, even though, as events developed, it did not come to pass.

We were going to Leopard Rock because Joy Adamson was camped nearby. George was also in the neighborhood, but in a camp of his own. Ken was keen about the book George was writing, A Lifetime with Lions.

"He writes well," he said. "His reports when he was senior game warden were always good."

When we remarked that our real goal was Kenmare Lodge, about twelve miles from Leopard Rock, Ken said, "Ah, yes. Well, Charles Moore, he's the warden, will know which is the better place. They have a security problem there."

"Security?"

"Yes. Shifta about. I shouldn't worry."

Maybe he shouldn't, but I felt a small thrill of apprehension. To Ken of course the Shifta, the marauding bands of Somali who drift across the border into northern Kenya were an old story. I remembered how, at Buffalo Springs, he was never without his rifle just in case. Still, over coffee in the New Stanley lounge, they seemed pretty remote.

After Ken left us we joined the Tatham-Warters and again lunched at the Muthaiga Club, this time en route to their farm. As we were leaving, a friend of theirs came up to us and there were introductions all around. The lady was the mother of the Earl of Montrose, one of the signers of Rhodesia's recent Declaration of Independence. She proudly gave us a copy.

Later, when we had time, we looked it over. It is a curious document, candidly and admittedly paraphrasing the American Declaration of Independence but the language is not so noble. Nor the intent. The reasoning strikes a disinterested eye as spurious since no mention is made of the real cause of the disagreement between England and Rhodesia; namely the overwhelming majority of black Africans, more than 4,000,000 living with the tiny minority of ruling whites, fewer than 225,000 and denied the rights of citizenship.

I quote from the opening paragraphs. "Whereas in the course of human affairs history has shown that it may become necessary for a people to resolve the political affiliations which have connected them with another people and to assume amongst other nations the separate and equal status to which they are entitled;

"And whereas in such event a respect for the opinions of mankind requires them to declare to other nations the causes which impel them to assume full responsibility for their own affairs" and further on . . . "through two world wars having been prepared to shed their blood and give of their substance in what they believed to be the mutual interests of freedom loving people, now see all that they have cherished about to be shattered on the rocks of expediency." No mention of the blacks who might appreciate a little freedom too. The documents ends with God Save the Queen.

Leaving Muthaiga after luncheon we struck out for the farm, about one hundred twenty miles from Nairobi. The land was fertile and, after so much rain, marvelously green. We passed through sisal and coffee plantations and what used to be called the Kykuyu reserve but since Kenyan independence the term has been dropped. We passed women in bright dresses, their babies in slings on their backs and many men, the older ones, still wearing British Army surplus overcoats, the long skirts flapping around their thin shanks.

There are some buses, there are very few private cars. Africa still travels on foot and following the long red roads of his homeland that stretch to the horizon an African must walk thousands of miles in a lifetime. They are car conscious, however, and African traffic cops are as quick to pin the culprit who has transgressed the law, passing through a red light or violating a parking restriction, as are their colleagues in Europe and the United States. Unfortunately the whites resent this and there are sometimes disagreeable little passages at arms when they refuse to acknowledge that they are in the wrong. Such episodes do nothing to better race relationships.

We stopped off briefly at Blue Posts, a hotel-restaurant to renew acquaintance with it and also to see the falls, at this season in full flood, great torrents of dark brown water spilling over the dam, an impressive yet sad sight for millions of tons of irreplaceable topsoil were being washed away in the process.

The place is a favorite with Indians who drive out from Nairobi for tea, the women strolling across the lawns in their colorful saris. Indian women seem to age quickly but in youth many of them are lovely and they have smiles of extraordinary brilliance.

We drove on and nearing the Tatham-Warter farm turned into the old Naru Moru Road. Norton and I felt a warm glow of familiarity for that was where *Born Free* had been filmed in 1964 and we had spent a few days there with Joy and George Adamson as guests of the company.

The farm was pure delight but if to an American mind it conjures up a vision of a snug white house nestling under old elms and a big red barn nearby the vision, while charming, is faulty.

To begin with the farm—it is also called ranch and from our point of view more accurately—comprises five thousand acres, four hundred head of cattle, uncounted numbers of antelope, a great many horses, dogs and cats, not to mention innumerable other house pets including three daughters. The youngest, Belinda, was a beguiling child who went to boarding school during the week but came home for weekends. The oldest girl was off at another school and the middle one, Caroline, was taking a secretarial course in Mombasa.

The long low ranch house with its red-tiled roof is beautifully located, set in lawns emerald green at that season, overlooking colorful flower beds, two small ponds, sweeping fields, round dark green trees that are called wild coffee but are unrelated to the tame variety and in the distance snowy Mount Kenya, rising sharply from the range of which it forms a part.

The house is spacious, cosy, and comfortably furnished and our room and bath were attractive and abloom with charming little bouquets arranged by the hostess. Tea was shared with three black labradors, an odd red dog, a gravid white cat and a mottled semi-wild one, a creature of great magnetism with a ruff flaring out on either side of its piquant face. We also made the acquaintance of an English friend and house guest, Major Bobby Ormsby-White, and of two crested crane who added distinct panache to the lawn.

Jane told us that the African who had caught and brought them to her had tied the legs of one so tightly together for several days that it was crippled. When they undid the cord it couldn't walk at all. They fed it special nutritious things which fortunately it enjoyed so it ate well, grew strong and recovered from its cruel and literal bondage. Whether it was the ordeal that had affected its crest I do not know but it was set on its head at a rakish angle, like a little boy's cow-lick.

Dinner was not served until the elegant hour of nine since after tea Digby and Jane and the girls, when they are home, usually go riding. Courteously acceding to our non-athletic ways that afternoon they waived the riding and Jane showed movies and good ones, much superior to the usual home product, that she had taken herself of safaris they had been on and of the making of the picture, *African Cowboy*, that had been shot on their property.

Digby also regaled us with the tale of a rhino who had been a member of the cast and who caused the producers as much trouble as a human star. Not through outbursts of temperament or injudicious forays into the bottle—theirs was a cosmetic problem. It was as though the leading man had shaved off his character beard before retakes or as though the leading lady had changed the color of her hair or gained ten pounds before a sequence was completed.

Their star attraction had already appeared in several scenes when through brusque and unexpected contact with a barrier of some sort he broke off his horn. Imprecations rent the air. How to camouflage the disaster? How to keep from the public the sheepish fact that the courageous characters in the film no longer had to battle the lethal protuberance? Art saved the day! A sculptor friend of the Tatham-Warters modeled a new horn of plastic, painted it the proper color, applied it with cement to the spot on the rhino's snout where the original had been and where, like the poetic pro-boscis of Cyrano, it rode triumphantly through the film till the shooting ended.

As Jane and Digby had mentioned four hundred head of cattle and we had not seen any driving through the property, on our arrival we asked where they were. The story was ironic. During the long drought they had been obliged to send them away to good pasture. Now they had jungles of waist-high lush nourishing grass but had to continue to spend large sums for the distant rented food because there had been an outbreak of foot-and-mouth disease in that area and they were not allowed to bring their cattle home.

Bedtime in the African countryside is usually not very late as there is a lighting problem. The ranches have electricity but usually it is home-manufactured; it is expensive and is turned off at bedtime. Jane supplied us with enough candles, lamps and electric torches to read until daybreak if we were so minded but we chose nature's way. "Early to bed, early to rise" and you meet very few prominent people. Yes, I know, but you witness some spectacular dawns.

The next morning was particularly glorious. I woke early and seeing Norton's bed empty slipped into a dressing gown and set out to find him. He was on the terrace off the big living room busily photographing Mount Kenya. When I looked at him in surprise he said, "I know, I know, it's right into the sun but damn it all I want to get *some* mountain when I can see it."

My heart went out to him. In 1959 on our first trip around the world we had spent three weeks in Japan and although we were near it, although we discerned it, you could not honestly say we had *seen* Mount Fujiyama. And now, just recently, we had not *really* seen either Mount Etna or Mount Vesuvius. Mount Kenya might appear on the film in black silhouette but it would be clean cut, visible, and indisputably *there*.

Going back into the house I saw one of the African servants in a long robe, the Khanzu, polishing the floor, a piece of lambswool wrapped around his feet as he shuffled about the room. I asked if I might have morning chai. He bowed, hand over heart, I went back to bed and presently a less picturesquely clad colleague arrived with a tea tray.

Breakfast on the veranda with porridge, brown sugar and the thickest most delectable cream I have ever tasted was a sociable meal with the two crested crane cadging bits of toast. They are toothless but their beaks are nippy, and we fed a pair of Muscovy ducks, engaging creatures who wag their tails exactly like a dog when tossed a few goodies and kind words. We made the acquaintance of Belinda's caramel colored hamster and of two friends of the Tatham-Warters who landed on their airstrip; a girl, an artist, and Peter Jenkins, a bright young chap who was the assistant game warden of Tsavo Park toward which we were heading.

The talk turned to animals, elephants featured. Digby told of John Savage, a game warden in Uganda, who had been obliged to shoot an old male because his trunk was caught in a poacher's snare and he was dying in slow agony. Later, when the rangers went out to get him they found only the carcass, the tusks had been pulled out and had disappeared. The ground all around was tumbled and trampled and following the tracks the wardens found that other members of the herd had pulled the ivory from their dead comrade and hidden it in the forest. Digby himself was convinced that old males sense that they are vulnerable because of their tusks and hide in the forests emerging only in the early morning and after dark to drink and forage for food and then only when surrounded by the rest of the herd.

Norton and I accepted this but young Mr. Jenkins shot his friend an amused glance and helped himself to salt. "It's a moving theory, old boy, but I doubt it. I don't think elephants know about the ivory trade although, mark you, I do think they're the smartest animals after the primates."

We said we had heard that Indian elephants are not so well adapted to work as those of Africa. "That really isn't so," Peter said. "They can work the same as the African. It's the Indian mahouts that are unpredictable. They're always corking off under a tree and claiming the elephants are on strike. Also, as a matter of fact, using them for work is uneconomical since they can only work four or five hours a day and must spend the rest of the time feeding." Elephants are endlessly fascinating creatures. They evoke wonder, curiosity and affection as well as a strange insatiable blood lust.

Months later when we were back in the United States, Norton and I were invited to a dinner party where my right-hand neighbor told me of a friend of his who had hunted one male elephant for many years. Always the animal had evaded him but now the hunter knew he was getting old, this coming year was to be his great opportunity. This time surely he would meet his quarry and he would slay him. "God, I hope he does," added my partner jovially. "After all these years of faithful tracking and all the money he's spent he *deserves* to get him, he's *earned* the trophy." I could only think of *Les Misérables*. Jean Valjean and Javert, the implacable, remorseless police officer who so cruelly hounded him.

After breakfast we walked the visitors back to the airstrip and watched them take off in a small plane that had been donated to the National Parks by the East African and World Wildlife Funds.

Later Jane and Digby suggested a visit to their friends the Peter Whiteheads who had a farm nearby. We had met Peter when he was working with the animals and with George Adamson on *Born Free*, and he and his wife Laura keep an impressive menagerie of their own including an affectionate waterbuck with coarse yet pliant and oily hair who took a great fancy to my straw handbag and followed munching wherever I went. There was a young zebra with brown stripes —they turn black only as they get older—and front-view butter wouldn't melt in his mouth but you had to watch his rear, he was a kicker. A steinbok was curled up in a corner of a big pen looking like a well-baked cream puff. When standing and fully grown they are no more than eighteen inches high with tiny little upright horns.

There was a baby Thomson's gazelle with matchstick legs and an inquisitive cuddlesome hyrax; those who saw *Born Free* will perhaps remember the seductive furry rodent given to hitting the bottle, he was a hyrax. On another scale they had a giant forest hog named Piggy. His tusks though small are wicked, but he was a gentle beast who loved having his round flat rubber nose scratched.

The star of their collection was their cheetah, a superb animal and the tamest of pets. The Whiteheads five-year-old daughter spent a good deal of time hanging around his neck, her hands in his mouth. His cage was large but for all that it was a cage and it made us sad to see the swift lithe creature cooped up. Peter Whitehead walked him every day on a leash so he would get to know the property and some day they hope to let him run free but at that time they were fearful for the other pets should he suddenly succumb to a hunger pang. There were masses of rabbits of all sizes chiefly for cheetah fodder and an entrancing bird who seemed a cross between a dove and a parrot. His plumage was pale soft green, he wore yellow trousers and had coral colored feet. *He* was not fodder.

Leaving these lucky people we went on to visit an attractive young man, Roddy Minns. Over some thirty-six years his mother has developed one of the most beautiful gardens in that part of the world. At the time we were there she was in England but her son took us around so that we might see the magnificent trees and the extraordinary display of flowers. Lilies, dahlias, roses, mimosa, zinnias, impatients growing in great bushes, all blooming together. The scent and color were intoxicating. Apparently there had been an engagement in the young man's life but it was over and he was living alone in the beautiful garden like a prince in a fairy tale, his only companions servants and dogs.

Back at the Tatham-Warters we lunched on excellent beef and delicious homemade bread and after a nap and tea—in case we might be feeling faint from so insubstantial a meal— Jane and Norton drove off in the car and Digby took me out in the trap, a jolly affair painted red with high wheels and drawn by a shiny black horse. We were accompanied by three dogs and Belinda on her adored white pony, Spotlight. It was her duty to ride ahead of us and point out deep holes made by ant bears that were concealed by the tall grass. From Digby's description I gathered that an ant bear was, in American, an anteater and their holes were deep. Some of them Belinda didn't see and a couple of times we sank into one with a jarring jolt that I should have thought would have broken a wheel, not to mention a rib, but we were lucky and survived intact.

At that hour of the day the landscape was serene and beautiful; the vast sky, the spreading plains, the flat-topped thorn trees and the lines of tall straight slender gums, their trunks and high plumage glowing in the late afternoon sunlight, the whole tableau rimmed by the distant blue mountains on the horizon. Digby wanted to ford the little river that runs through the property but the water was too high.

Though the cattle had had to be farmed out big herds of sheep still grazed on home territory, their shepherds in attendance. The shepherds were not those of Fragonard or of the old French folk song, *Il Pleut, Il Pleut, Bergère*. They were scrawny black men in tattered clothing and they carried with them tin shelters shaped like low quonset huts into which they crawled at night. A little farther on we came to a tin cooking hut. A sweet-faced woman, a baby on her back, tended the fire and a couple of battered pots. A few chickens scratched about, and a pair of scruffy but lively dogs frisked around the woman's feet. Existence seemed marginal but Digby regarded them with detachment. The shepherd families we gathered were the province of his foreman.

We were turning toward home when we discovered that one of the dogs was missing. Belinda rode off to find him. We waited by a fence for her to catch up with us—Digby said he had strung sixty-five miles of wire fencing around the ranch— and after a bit we heard Spotlight's galloping hoofs. We heard them for quite a time before he and Belinda came into view. It is a marvelous sound and I thought of the sounds at one time so commonplace and now lost, some of them forever. Galloping hoofs, wheels over cobblestones, the clash of steel by night and torches blown by the wind. The butter churn, the night watchman's cry, the rattle of chains as drawbridges were raised and lowered, the rustle of taffeta petticoats, the long lonely whistle of the night trains thundering across the American prairies. Thank God, with determination, one may still hear the crackling of an open fire. I find the ads for flameless heat quite chilling. There they sit upon their pristine wall to wall carpeting, the happy affluent suburban American family. In the background is a functional sterile heating unit and the manufacturers and advertising agencies are trying to push down our throats the frigid concept that such sterility is more desirable than the fragrance, the companionship, the cosy crackle and the dreams that glow in a fire of logs or coal.

At the Tatham-Warters, when the group is small, dinner is served beside the big fireplace, dogs lie about deep in slumber and the atmosphere is relaxed and homelike. Norton and I enjoyed it but we were beginning to get restless. We wanted to be on safari—that, after all, was why we had come.

A good many English families in Kenya are beginning to go into the safari business and as the competition becomes keener it is natural that each of them will try to devise something a little special with which to tempt clients.

In their comfortable house and magnificent acreage and with their diverting pets, Jane and Digby Tatham-Warter have a very good thing. Furthermore on their own property they can offer fishing and bird shooting. It is also possible to arrange antelope, zebra and warthog hunting for any mongoloid element in the group. Since the traveler's common complaint is the boredom of hotels, the difficulty of meeting people who live in the lands they are visiting and of never being asked into their houses, it is a special pleasure to stay in such attractive surroundings and to meet hospitable neighbors.

There is, however, an angle to be considered. The price per day at the ranch is the same as it is in the bush under canvas. Many people have attractive houses of their own, pretty gardens and amiable friends. They are not the novelty, that is not where the wonder lies. Camping out, surrounded by wild game roaming free is the unique magic of Africa, the cogent magnet that draws the visitor and that those who live there may not always appreciate.

In our own case, while Norton and I considered the matter completely settled, there had been some uncertainty on the part of the Tatham-Warters as to whether we were definitely coming and the exact date of our arrival. Also, having agreed to their terms, we thought to pay them when we got there but until they saw us they had not seen the color of our money. For that reason the safari preparations had not been completed and they needed a bit of time to organize, but in any event, as they now state in their brochure, their plan is to bring clients to the house for several days.

At the end of our stay, when we left the Mara, they also took us to spend the night with friends of theirs at Subukia. The friends were cordial and their well-run farm attractive but by and large I think the safari-minded would probably prefer to spend the extra night in camp returning directly to Nairobi rather than make a long detour to see strangers whom in all likelihood they will never meet again.

If you do the visiting you will participate in an agreeable way of life but if you want to spend all your available time in camp it should be specifically stated in your agreement.

However, the Tatham-Warters and their friends, the Hilary Hooks—the two families are now working closely together—are set up to receive guests in their own homes and I do not know if an exclusively tenting safari is feasible for them. That is something a client would have to inquire about.

Living under canvas was, for us, ideal but sometimes it is advisable to stay overnight at a lodge. It would be a pity, for example, to miss Treetops or Secret Valley, especially as you do not pay extra. If you have planned ahead your room and board will already have been included in the over-all price of the safari. Everything is included with the exception of hunting licenses, tips, and hard liquor. These costs, quite rightly, are assumed by the client.

When in the bush I feel that one may reasonably expect beer and soft drinks in sufficient quantity to be provided by the management. Specify the beer though or you will be all awash in lemon squash. It is a British passion. If you like wine with meals it should be decided whether you or your host-guide will pay for it or if you will share the expense. The latter would seem the simpler and more friendly way since many people enjoy a bottle of wine and in Africa, although we thought that on our own safari Jane managed quite exceptional meals, the food can usually stand a little filip.

There are one or two nice South African wines but given the political attitude in that part of the continent other African countries understandably will not import them and the long hot voyage from Marseilles to Mombasa does nothing to enhance the great French vintages so by and large we settled for a serviceable Chianti, available in most of the stores along our way. The only trouble with Chianti on safari is that the shape of the bottle makes it difficult to pack but in view of the reward we did not find the lugging too arduous.

As I have said, we got together with the Tatham-Warters through something of a fluke. It turned out that we'd been lucky for on safari compatibility of temperament is of even more importance than usual. The relationship is close, and it is sensitive. The clients pay but the people with whom they travel are hosts, guides, and instructors rolled together. Ideally they are also friends and they are indispensable.

The day following our visits to the hospitable neighbors, Norton and Digby and I left the farm at 7:30 in the morning for Meru, seventy-three miles away. We were in the Toyota, accompanied by two African boys. Jane did not go. Jane is a knowledgeable and experienced woman and she did not go. She had, she said, to stay home to oversee the packing of the supplies we would be taking with us when we finally did set up camp in the Tsavo Game Reserve. That was true, she did have to. She was still a wise woman.

We had our troubles but we also saw a country of heartlifting beauty. Digby said that much of that part of Kenya was considered by agricultural experts to be some of the best farmland in the world. There can be no doubt that it is some of the loveliest. The fields gleamed green and gold under the sun and on the flame trees the trumpet blossoms blazed among the dark shining leaves. Fertile farms rolled over the flanks of the mountains and as we approached the Northern Frontier District the land dropped away to an endless spreading plain. Along in there we had our first flat tire but on the dry road it was quickly changed. I mention it only because it is customary to note the opening dates of events likely to make history through repetition and longevity. There is, for example, a record of the night *My Fair Lady* opened since that night's performance was destined to be repeated so many many times. Nearing Meru we passed brightly dressed crowds streaming along the highway. There were thousands of school children, the older girls in striped uniforms, the younger in green pinafores with orange guimpes and all the boys in clean white shirts and short dark blue pants. Even a group of prisoners working on a hillside garden in spanking white shirts and shorts looked festive. Triumphal arches flung across the road fluttered with gay pennants and banana branches set in the earth symbolized a welcome to Kenya's Vice-President, M. H. Eshimiwa who was visiting the neighborhood.

Only in Africa can the landscape seem so empty one minute and so wildly populated with milling colorful throngs the next. The secret I suppose is that to the western eye the villages, the rondavels with their thatched roofs nestling in the grass and bushes, go almost unnoticed but they are there and so are the inhabitants.

One of the big crowds of school children was being shepherded and exhorted by an African master angrily pounding the ground with his cane and shouting with a strong English accent, "All you school chaps, back to school, back to school at once I say." School chaps do not budge except to jump up and down in place yelling and waving. We learned that although Mr. Eshimiwa had passed he was coming back. After all, vice-presidents do not appear every day and the children were determined to squeeze the last delicious morsel from the excitement.

When we saw a large crowd swarming up a hillside to blend with a still larger crowd gathered around a three-sided shelter on the crest of the hill Digby turned the Toyota off the road and we started after them.

"Think we ought to do this?" Norton asked.

"Why not?" said Digby. "He's my vice-president too. If he's going to talk I've every right to hear him." He of course would have understood him but since Mr. Eshimiwa would doubtless be speaking in Swahili and as the crowd was beginning to press in closely around the car Digby thought better of it and with considerable difficulty—bodies were packed solid—finally managed to turn around and roll back down the hill. To my regret we never did learn what savory treat the politician was promising the electorate.

When, a little earlier, we had stopped at a restaurant, the Pig and Whistle, for coffee and toast the Indian manager had told us that the first twenty-seven miles of road we would be traveling toward Meru were in good condition. Regarding the remaining twenty-three . . . we gathered, Wow! and understood what he had in mind when we reached Maua and a dip in the road completely submerged under a rapidly running river.

Here began the rift in the harmonious lute as Digby and Norton argued the best way to surmount the insurmountable barrier. Mechanics was the only issue on which they split but they did it frequently and vocally.

Digby, as ardent a gadgeteer as Norton, was curiously indifferent to machinery. Norton respects the human ingenuity that contrives it and he understands the parts and their functions.

Digby admitted candidly that he preferred horses. He raises them on the farm, plays polo and the members of his family are expert equestrians. He drives a Toyota because it is a vital part of his business but considers himself under no obligation to love it.

In our particular dilemma my husband was all for the persuasive approach, for following that excellent handbook, *Official Touring Guide to East Africa,* to which anyone contemplating a trip to that part of the world should subscribe.

It is a mine of sound information and we are deeply indebted to Ken Smith who gave us our copy.

When faced with a watery impasse the guide counsels one to "engage low gear and enter the drift slowly; keep the engine turning at a constant speed and . . . keep the car moving if possible; to stop is fatal."

Digby had another plan. He is a man who believes in taking the bit in his teeth and the bull by the horns. He revved up the motor, dashed forward at a high old clip, skidded and sank into a deep hole. Twenty-five minutes, hundreds of heaves and grunts, countless rivers of sweat mingling with the river on the road and we were on our way again, eventually reaching the gate of the Meru reserve and the big compound where five so-called white rhinos brought from Zululand for experimental purposes were quartered. I am happy to say the experiments were not laboratory but merely to see if citizens of the South could survive the Kenya climate and surroundings. The five we saw were doing extremely well. Their hides were like hard dry leather badly in need of saddle soap but they enjoyed being petted. We found this out when Digby announced he was going to enter the compound although we urged him to caution. "Can't rhinos be quite unfriendly?"

"I think so. Let's see." And in he went.

He was to the rhinos what Androcles was to the lion. They loved him, so Norton and I followed suit. We were surprised to find there were no tick birds who are their usual companions but we were much amused by one who sank to his haunches with a sigh of relief like a weary fat woman submerging into a hot bath at the end of a long, hard day. He then flattened out, to the extent that a rhino can flatten, and went fast asleep in the welcome shade of a bush.

Once within the reserve gates I had assumed we would quickly arrive at the warden's house, but we lost track of time bumping over a dirt track that stretched forever; the grass grew high between the ruts and the end was not in view.

First we had to reach Leopard Rock, then we had to push on to a lodge built originally by a Lady Kenmare, where we were to spend the night. All of us, including the two Africans, were reaching a state of dogged determination and gritted teeth, yet when Norton, shaking his head in bewilderment, muttered, "Lady Kenmare must have been a bear for punishment," Digby and I exploded with laughter. And indeed it was hard to understand what could have possessed a woman of wealth and position to give up every comfort and go jogging to the ends of the earth to establish a primitive camp on a river bank.

On the other hand, what could have possessed us? We were perhaps lacking in the Kenmare attributes but we did live with comfort and the amenities and no one had taken a lever to force us from our nest into this remote wilderness yet here we were and with the exception of our present situation it still seemed a good idea.

The literal distance to the lodge from the entrance to the reserve is twenty-seven miles; to Leopard Rock, seventeen. It seemed five times as long. Digby had tried to dissuade us from the Meru trip because he rightly feared the state of the roads but when he saw we were set on it he gamely cooperated and we had only ourselves to blame for our troubles, but we wanted to go for two reasons. Meru is a comparatively small and new reserve but it has a great variety of animals including the handsome reticulated giraffe and Joy Adamson was living there involved in some way with cheetahs, the way she and George had been involved with Elsa the lioness. We wanted to see her and also we hoped for a glimpse of George farther away in his own camp.

Joy and I had had a good deal of correspondence in recent months so that when Leopard Rock loomed at last I regarded its surroundings with interest. It was the place where letters had come from and the destination to which mine had been sent winging. It is a large rock, very large, and was at one time the abode of leopards although I believe recently they have given up their lease and moved elsewhere. The first signs of human life were the shed for the warden's small plane and the shop where park machinery was maintained and repaired. Digby immediately handed over our punctured tire.

As we were walking about getting the kinks out of our legs and backs Charles Moore the warden came up to greet us. He was an attractive young man, with upspringing dark curly hair, very spruce in a green bush jacket and green shorts and he led us over to his house, a spacious open bungalow with a thatched roof and a fine view of hills, palms, and a little river rushing below the bank, but the most welcome sight was the ice-cold beer he proffered which we replaced with our own warm bottles from the Toyota. Not far from the veranda on which we were sitting we noticed, on a slight rise of land, a kind of sentinel box, a low stone parapet and a thatched canopy. We asked what it was for. "A sentinel," said our host. Besides being a warden he was commander-in-chief of a tiny army recruited to keep an eye out for any marauding Shifta.

While we contentedly sipped our beer he told us of his plans. He would be leaving for England in two or three weeks where he was to be married and would be returning shortly afterward with his bride. As we had seen a baby carriage in the front hall we couldn't help smiling but he said hastily, turning rather red, "That belongs to the previous warden. Their kid was getting too old for it so they left it when they moved away and I took over."

It seemed in good condition and we said we hoped that in their own good time he and his wife would have use for it. He smiled but his immediate concern was the reception he was planning for three hundred people in July. He wanted all his friends and neighbors to meet the bride but his mother's farm which had been offered was too small. "Can't even park one hundred cars so we're taking over the Outspan."

Norton and I were impressed. We had stayed at the Outspan, a comfortable and enormous old hotel where we had spent a night when we returned from Treetops, the enchanting lodge in the Aberdare Mountains. This is where from a comfortable balcony one may watch all sorts of game including, with luck, splendid elephants, as they come around sundown to drink at the waterhole and root for the coarse salt tossed out for them.

We fell to discussing Kenya economy and Charles Moore observed that the part of the country we were in was dependent on tourists who came to see the game but he felt the status was fragile.

"At the slightest whiff of potential trouble they shy off. Even if the blow-up is in central Africa they won't come here. They simply don't realize how gigantic this continent is but the reserves have to be established on a more solid basis than tourist whim."

Like many people he seemed to feel the nationalization of resources to be a dubious enterprise, an attitude particularly understandable in East Africa. Since the nationalization of the banks of Tanzania, for example that country's currency has little value beyond her own borders.

Referring again to the game he felt that since the cropping of herds, especially elephants who overgraze their territory, is essential for their own survival, the killing should be on an organized basis and they have already proven that practical results may be achieved. Poachers and hunters used to annihilate a thousand elephants a year and the consequence was a glut on the ivory market. Now, with better organization, only three hundred are killed and the economy has profited.

Asked if Africans would eat elephant meat to offset their lack of protein he replied that as far as he knew only one tribe did so as a regular habit but he felt that scientifically treated elephant meat could be made palatable and might gain a wide market.

He himself was giving up his warden's job, a decision that saddened us for able interested young men do not abound, but he felt there was not much future in it and on his return as a married man he was taking up a new position as manager of an enormous experimental station that a group of investors had been granted by the Kenya government. If I understood correctly they planned to combine breeding with the control and marketing of wild game and also to raise domestic cattle.

It was so pleasant where we were that we would have been glad to stay there overnight going on to Kenmare Lodge in the morning but Charles Moore said it was not feasible. Arrangements which included part of his small armed force had been made for us at the Lodge and it would be better if we went along as planned. Furthermore, Joy knew we were coming and was expecting us that evening. He himself would escort us. We set out, Norton, Digby, and the two Africans in the Toyota, Charles and I in his husky Land-Rover.

The road was grim. Since the first of April they had had thirty inches of rain, normally a year's allowance, but we were managing not too badly when, after a patch of particularly deep and sticky mud, we looked behind us. As we feared the Toyota was nowhere to be seen. We backed up a few hundred yards and there sure enough were our dear companions, mired and immobile in the ooze. Charles Moore clambered out of his car, Norton, Digby, and the Africans clambered out of theirs and the digging started. They worked for an hour and a half with varying degrees of energy and enthusiasm. Dr. Brown's enthusiasm was at low ebb.

Charles had brought along a rifle as protection against the Shifta. "Frankly," he told me, "they haven't been here for two years. It's simply that we never take a chance." When he got out to dig, however, he left it in the Land-Rover. I eyed it with suspicion, for gunlore is not my forte, and then I gingerly began to touch it. When it neither bit nor fired I hefted it up and placed it across my knees. Since it is doubtful that I could rake the side of a barn with a machine gun I don't know what I thought I was doing but the men were working some fifty yards away. Were the Shifta suddenly to pop up from the bush, and due to the heaviest rains in six years the bush was exceptionally high, old Betsy would have been of little use to them. I suspect there was a good deal of Wilhelmina Mitty in my behavior but I felt like a pioneer woman with hostile Indians behind every rock and tree and I kept a sharp lookout just in case.

The Toyota finally rolled out of the wallow, chaps repaired to their assorted vehicles and we started off again. I handed the rifle to Charles Moore who looked at it and at me uneasily. "You haven't removed the safety catch, have you?" he asked.

"Why no," I said, "I didn't know there was one." Occasionally in my life men have glanced at me with amused affection. This was not one of the times.

We had covered perhaps a quarter of a mile when . . . Don't say it! Not that! Not again! I am afraid so. Behind us we heard it, kerplunk, kersplash, crunch. There was the Toyota in a deep hole, in deep water, up to the bottom of the chassis in thick black mud. Once gain, my hearties, all hands heave to!

This time we removed the luggage to lighten the load and, at his insistence, Digby, Norton, and I took off in Charles Moore's Land-Rover, leaving him and the boys to work the cruiser loose.

It was after dark when some yards off the track to the right we discerned a blur that Digby identified as Joy Adamson's camp, but we were so tired we decided to continue on to Kenmare Lodge only about a mile away and communicate with her later.

As we drove into camp five young Africans in freshly starched khaki tunics and shorts saluted and came forward to greet us. Our private army!

The double banda overlooking the river that had been prepared for us was roomy and reasonably comfortable but we were badly in need of light. I said to Digby, "Can we ask the boys to bring lamps or candles?"

"There are none," he said.

"What do you mean? What do the Africans do when it gets dark?"

"Go to bed. But don't worry, I've got a fine light that I can rig up. The only trouble is the battery is in the Toyota. I'll go fetch it and you and Norton can get settled in."

In the pitch dark this was not easy. Actually the camp has electricity but due to its being so early in the season and to the heavy rains they were not expecting visitors and the equipment was not functioning. The absentees were sharp. They knew about the rains and the resultant state of the roads. It was only the exuberant adventuresome Browns and the knowledgeable and experienced Mr. John Owen who did not know.

Digby set off to pick up his boys and inform Joy that we were in camp. While we were waiting and groping about in the dark our army did manage to rustle up a lantern and one candle. They made the beds and Norton arranged our mosquito netting and poured a couple of stiff drinks of which, all told, we felt the need.

Sooner than we would have thought possible Digby was back and rigged up his light, a long horizontal neon bar set at right angles across the top of a slim metal pole. It was powered by the car battery and was extremely serviceable. By the time Charles Moore arrived with Joy Adamson we were beginning to feel very much at home.

Joy was in sandals and khaki shorts with a halter top. Her skin glowed like deep polished bronze and her blue eyes were shining. She greeted us warmly but quickly. With her life is a perpetual rush, and we found her the same as ever, her conversational Niagara flowing unchecked although this time the subject was not Elsa but Pippa the cheetah and her cubs. Others were supposed to help in the experiment— we were vague as to just what it was—but all they did was to exploit "ze animals." She broke off long enough to assure us she was glad to see us but protested that we should not have come at this season. "Ilka, ze roads, impassable, impassable." She was in on the secret too!

She spoke of George who was camped seven miles away. George, as we had heard from Ken Smith had had a near miss. In his Land-Rover he was crossing a bridge slung over a rushing torrent. There was a terrifying sound of rending timber, the bridge collapsed and was swept away. By an incredible stroke of luck his car, spanning the stream, came to rest on the two short ends that were still holding. It was heeling over alarmingly and the door was jammed. He finally managed to get out the window and inch his way with infinite care to the bank.

He and Joy were not seeing a great deal of each other at that time but he had been to call on her and still shaking from the experience he returned to her camp to tell her of his narrow squeak. In relaying the story to us she said, "I have only seen George cry twice in my life; once when Elsa died and when he told me about the bridge."

She referred again to our having come at this season and I said, "But, Joy, it can't be such a surprise. After all, I wrote you we would be here."

She began to laugh. "I know, I know, but the mail, here you understand, it is not like the States."

As even the most patriotic American must acknowledge, delivery of mail in the States is scarcely our star achievement but the attitude is perhaps not quite so informal as it is in the Leopard Rock district. Around there things are done on a more or less casual and private basis. If a postmaster is away, which frequently happens since many of them have large families whom they like to visit, the mail piles up. Sometimes the stoppage gets so great that it is really discouraging to have to cope with it. When this occurs they tear up a lot and throw it down the toilets resulting in clogged drains and inexplicable gaps in correspondence between devoted friends. Sometimes Joy complained because they cut the stamps off the letters she received. "You simply must not *do* that," she would exclaim. "It is not done in *any* country."

They would look at her kindly. "But of course we cut them off. Letters come to you from all over the world. They are the most interesting stamps that come here."

Charles Moore had intended to fight his way back to Leopard Rock through the mud but we persuaded him that

1. Sicilian puppets; fierce, chivalrous and elegant.

2. Antique Theatre, Taormina. The outlook was better than Broadway.

5. Noto. A façade chaste and lovely.

3. Little town of Acireale. Exuberant façade.

4. A stumper for the audio department of any TV studio. The Mystery! The Ear of Dionysius at Syracuse.

8. As it was in the beginning, is now and ever shall be. Girl in gym class. Mosaic at Piazza Armerina, Sicily.

6. Theatre at Palazzolo, Sicily. Dream spot for a springtime picnic. Hot in summer, I should imagine.

7. "Watch the Tabascol" Early barbecue. Piazza Armerina, Sicily.

10. Columns of the so called Temple of Diosceuri at Agrigento. Ancient, decrepit, still noble in their strength.

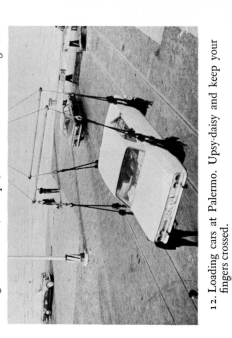

12. Loading cars at Palermo. Upsy-daisy and keep your fingers crossed.

9. Temple of Concordia, Agrigento, Sicily.

11. The rococo, lively and graceful art of Giacomo Serpotta in the Oratorio di San Lorenzo, Palermo, Sicily.

14. Overture to the great adventure. Alitalia's Rome-Nairobi flight.

16. "Hey, mate, how about it? How about a drag?" Our friend in the Nairobi National Park.

13. Ruins of Pompeii. On the right a guide. As for the others, we don't know them either.

15. View of Nairobi from our window at the New Stanley Hotel.

18. "Come and get It" Mother cheetah on impala kill. Nairobi National Park.

20. Jane Tatham-Warter and her youngest daughter, Belinda.

17. Standing on the corner watching all the girls go by.

19. Olechugu Farm. The Tatham-Warters house near Nanyuki.

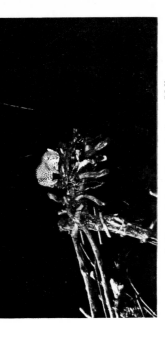

21A. Young lady at dinner in Secret Valley.

23. Our shower tent on safari.

21. In the Meru. The lyrate doum palms lace the sky.

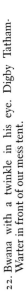

22. Bwana with a twinkle in his eye. Digby Tatham-Warter in front of our mess tent.

25. Those two old softies, the adult rhinos, Rufus and Rendi. Bipeds left to right: Caroline and Jane Tatham-Warter, David Sheldrick, Ilka and Norton.

24. David Sheldrick's baby rhino, Stub. "I know I'm ugly but I'm affectionate."

26. Lollapa, the baby buffalo at David Sheldrick's.

27. Eleanor and Kadenga in girlish play. Ilka joining in.

29. Kilimanjaro and Ngurdoto Crater, an Eden newly minted.

28. Picnic party en route to the Ngurdoto Crater.

30. Reedbuck on an early morning call at the door of our rondavel at Momella Lodge.

31. The birthday party at Ngorongoro Crater. Jane, Ilka, Digby, the birthday boy, Caroline and Norton.

32: Winsome trio in the Ngorongoro Crater.

33: Wildebeest. Four of the thousands upon thousands.

34: An inhabitant of the Ngorongoro Crater. Independent cuss going about his business.

35: Our camp in the Serengeti.

36. Kabwi in his kitchen in the Serengeti.

37. Honeymooning couple in a kopje. Note tag in lioness' right ear.

38. Three handsome gentlemen at ease.

39. Three handsome gentlemen importuned. "Those damned tourists again."

41. An obliging pair, photogenically arranged en route to the Mara.

40. Biding their time. Flock of vultures on a kopje in the Serengeti.

42. Desolation wrought by the Kykuku.

in the darkness it would be folly. Even his doughty four-wheel drive *could* bog down and *then* where would he be? In the black night, in a car, with wild animals abounding. This last, unhappily, was wishful thinking.

Our long sticks-in-the-mud would have been less tedious had there been game about to watch, but with the marvelous stands of grass resulting from the heavy rains the glamour characters were disporting themselves on the other side of the river and it would be several weeks, Charles said, before they would put in an appearance in our neighborhood.

Still, our argument held good for the dark and the mud. "Think of your fiancée," we said, "you don't want the poor girl widowed before she's wed." That did it. He agreed to stay and dine and spend the night.

We had quite a wait before dinner was ready but I considered it miraculous that Kabwi, the Tatham-Warters' stocky little cook whom we became very fond of, was able to rustle up anything at all under the circumstances—unpacking food from the Toyota, starting a fire from scratch and cooking by the light of one candle.

Norton and I had a bottle of our own but Digby had a splendid traveling bar and by the time dinner was on the table, which was set by a small swimming pool under the stars, we were in high fettle. Not only had Joy and Norton and I known each other since 1962, we had *all* known each other since 1962. Longer! We were spiritual brothers! It was a cheery evening.

By the time we parted for the night the camp was organized to the extent of providing abundant if brown hot water for baths and during our sojourn at Kenmare I accustomed myself to sharing the bathroom with a small darting bat. I am rather frightened of bats so bathing or not I wore a shower cap, having been brought up on the old wives' tale that bat bliss is tangling themselves in women's hair and I firmly believe it.

About half-past four I woke up and stepped out on the

veranda. The sky was ablaze with stars tangled in the thorn trees and to reach out one's hand was to touch the Milky Way.

Daylight and chai arrived together and we dressed, hoping George Adamson would stop off to see us on his way to Nairobi. He was supposed to pass the lodge about seven o'clock and Charles had posted one of our army along his way to tell him we were there. To our regret he did not show up. He knew about the roads.

In the daytime our romantic little swimming pool of the night before appeared less appetizing. The water was black and it was inhabited by three small crocodiles but the Rojerwero River above which we were perched ran clear and on the opposite shore, on a broken limb of a doum palm lacing the sky, a fish eagle posed for his portrait. He was a handsome bird with a white head and bib. His body was a rich sleek brown and black wings were draped like a cape over his shoulders.

We were planning to stop at Joy's camp and set off in our Toyota which was looking very spick-and-span, having been washed during the night. I felt perhaps it was a wasted gesture but tactfully held my tongue.

As we were about to turn off the road one of Joy's boys stopped us saying we must cut the motor and walk very quietly. "The cubs are here." We were delighted by the news and Norton reached for his movie camera.

We were starting quietly forward when Joy came to meet us. It developed that although she had sighted the cubs they were across the river and hiding in the tall grass. We could see nothing. She then proceeded to chew out the African boy saying he had made too much noise and had frightened them away. She turned to us. "He is only showing off," she exclaimed angrily. We said nothing and followed her to her camp, a banda—in this instance a small one-room cottage— and three or four tents.

The walls of the room were papered with stills from the

movie, *Born Free*, with pictures of stalls and shop windows around the world showing the book translated into every language, with shots of Joy with copies of the book in her hands and with dozens of photographs of Elsa.

Remains of her breakfast were on the table and we were pleased to see she had been eating the bacon and pineapple we had brought her and given to her the night before. On our way to Meru we had stopped in Nanyuki to lay in a good supply of fruit and fresh vegetables for we were worried about the fact that she was subsisting for the most part on nuts and canned beans. The only meat in her refrigerator was cheetah food.

She showed us countless snapshots, some of them excellent, of Pippa and the cubs but we did not quite understand what she hoped to achieve and why she had spent the better part of three years living in so remote and uncomfortable a place. During the recent flooding she told us she had been obliged to sit on a chair placed on the table to escape the rising water.

My heart sank at the sight of her sleeping tent for there was a rent in the top and when it rained she lay on her sagging cot, an umbrella rigged over her head. We learned with relief that she was building a house at Lake Naivasha and expected to move into it in July. In the meantime, having raised the cubs until they were a few months old and then released them she was spending five and six hours a day looking for them.

We didn't understand that either. What did she do with them when she got them? Photograph them probably which would provide a good record of their development but as far as feeding them was concerned it appeared to our eyes unnecessary. Pippa, their mother, was with them and was teaching them to hunt.

During the filming of *Born Free*, Joy had been very fond of Virginia McKenna and her husband, Bill Travers, who portrayed her and George, but the entente once so cordial seemed to have chilled. We did not understand the reason but it was involved and rather sad and we left her with heavy hearts.

On such a beautiful bright morning the camp was well enough but when night fell and she was there alone with only a couple of African servants and fitful lantern light it must have been deeply depressing.

Even in the sunshine our gloom deepened when we again got bogged down and the tractor Charles Moore had sent to help us proved of little avail. Our spirits perked up a bit when army reinforcements from Leopard Rock, seven Africans with rifles riding a lorry, pulled alongside us. There was much jacking up and down and filling in of ruts with stones, large ones hauled by the men, small ones by me, and then a tow rope was attached. The lorry strained forward with a mighty heave, there was a loud cheer and the tow line snapped. This happened three times but at last after two hours we were dragged free. We bade the army farewell since they were off to reconnoiter for Shifta and returned to Charles Moore's house for a quick cup of coffee and to bid him goodbye and good luck.

When we got back to Maua the river was still in spate but less fearsome than the day before. This time Digby very carefully reconnoitered and as the roadbed under the water was hard he decided to risk it. We got out but left the luggage in—twice the poor boys had taken out every single piece to lighten the load. Digby made a cautious dash for it and emerged triumphant on the other side. Our hero! We didn't need the tractor which just then pulled up behind us. I said I was sorry the driver had had that long rough ride for nothing but Digby pooh-hooed the idea. "Nonsense. Gives him an opportunity to visit all his girl friends and chums on the way back to Leopard Rock. He'll have a grand time."

We lunched on sandwiches Kabwi had prudently prepared before leaving Kenmare Lodge and around three o'clock arrived once more at the Pig and Whistle where we had tea and Digby changed his trousers, wet and mud-caked from our bog downs.

Heading for home and confronted with two alternatives he decided on the upper, or dry weather road, as he wanted us to see the magnificent farming country. Since the current weather could scarcely be classified as dry Norton and I were apprehensive but the beauty of the scenery, we gathered, would mollify any qualms we might have. The road was fearfully muddy and we skidded wildly, in one place making a complete 180 degree turn. Still, we did progress if at the pace of a giddy tortoise and it became evident that there had recently been a downpour of formidable proportions for we saw a whole farm that had been washed into the road, a foot of topsoil stretching for nearly a mile. It was a disastrous loss for the owner and one more impassable barrier for us. Digby was convinced, however, that he could get through it and up on to the hard grass bordering the road on the other side. Once again we all piled out, once again he made a dash for it and once again the abrupt sickening descent into implacable mud. The patience of Dr. Brown, not to mention his wife, was wearing a little thin.

True, the trip had been our idea and there had been occasions when a bog-down could not have been avoided, but this time we had had an alternative. The lower road we had been told was in fair condition.

A group of Africans were working in the field with a caterpillar tractor and Digby climbed a fence and walked over to them to ask if they wouldn't come to haul us out. They said no. He was indignant but Norton and I couldn't really see why they should have come. We were none of their business and they had their hands full with the devastated field.

He went down the road away to the owner's house and returned with the news that another caterpillar would soon be coming to our rescue. While we were waiting a car full of friends of his came from the other direction. They said they had just come from the lower road and it was appalling, worse if possible, than this one. I never saw a man more relieved than the major. He was off the hook! Our annoyance having somewhat abated, Norton and I joined in the general air of release and laughter and when the tractor did arrive it was a marvel of swift efficiency. We were hauled out and sent on our way with a fatherly slap on the behind. After an interminable drive through the black night we came at last to the ranch and the comfort of Jane and Bobby Ormsby-White welcoming us at the door, hot baths, drinks, and dinner by the fire. We were blooded troops ready for the next adventure.

Secret Valley was our destination and we had been impelled to it by the vague remark of a woman we scarcely knew who had said something about leopards.

"There's this wonderful place and you see them there. It's kind of a lodge beyond Nanyuki."

When we had questioned the Tatham-Warters about it they said the trip was perfectly feasible and they would arrange for us to spend a night there.

It was agreed that Digby would drive Jane and Norton and me part of the way, turn us over to Mr. Shamsu Din, the Indian who owned Secret Valley and return to the ranch to oversee the packing of the camping equipment. Early in the morning we went out on the lawn to find him surrounded by tents, beds, ice chests, water purifiers. The amount of stuff required for a party of four plus six camp servants is staggering.

Around noon we took off for luncheon at the Mount Kenya Safari Club. Because of previous visits it seemed to us quite cosy, even though it is a deluxe and highly manicured establishment set in beautiful surroundings. One is provided with every comfort and to fault it in any way seems niggling but to go to Africa to stay for any length of time at the Safari Club is like going to the capitals of Europe and staying always at the equivalent of a Ritz hotel. One has comfort and luxury and the true flavor of one's surroundings penetrates not at all.

We did, however, appreciate comfortable and luxurious Bloody Marys and a martini, although way off there in Africa the price seemed high—ten shillings or $1.40. Since the devaluation of the pound, $1.20. We lunched more plebeianly

on Irish stew—and very good it was—and admired the prom-
enading white peacocks and some spectacular blue and
yellow and blue and red macaws. One very funny chap de-
scended from a high limb, walking cautiously down the tree
trunk claw over claw until he arrived on the ground where he
admired himself with obvious satisfaction in a large piece of
mirror propped against the trunk for his benefit.

The club has a garden surrounded by a wall of beautiful
narrow old bricks and Jane told us that at night the lily-like
blossoms of the moonflower tree give off a quite intoxicating
fragrance.

I reveled in a shampoo. I mention it because there can
come times on safari when due to the dust of Africa one
would just as soon cut one's head off as go around with
what's on top of one's scalp. Afterward Digby drove us over
to the Sportsman's Arms. There he dropped us and departed
to supervise the rest of the packing.

On a tenting safari, nights under canvas are usually the
most memorable but sometimes there is a tempting reason
for staying in a specific lodge. While the owners can not guarantee them, usually they specialize in particular animals and
your chances of seeing them are good: elephants at Treetops,
leopards at Secret Valley.

The Sportsman's Arms is no Safari Club, but they serve
good tea. That is one thing about being with the British and
the Indians; there is always something to do; drink tea. There
are those who may not care for it, but it is preferable to being
in Detroit, let us say, drinking martinis. I once spent some
time in Detroit and they drank so steadily I marveled they
ever got a car off the assembly line.

Shortly after 4:30, Mr. Shamsu Din, proprietor of the
Sportsman's Arms as well as of Secret Valley, gathered us up,
Jane, Norton, an Indian gentleman and me, and we started
off. The rest of the party, two Indian women and another
man followed in a second Land-Rover driven by an assistant.

We very soon turned off the main road and headed into
rough country, climbing steadily, winding through a pine

forest and past a sawmill until we reached 8400 feet. It was nippy.

We ground over fearful roads, worse than any we had yet encountered but our host was an Indian and of more philosophic temperament than the impetuous Anglo-Saxon major. He took the morasses very very slowly but the wheels kept turning and we kept moving forward. When we complimented him on his technique he smiled. "It is nothing, you must simply learn to gentle the car along, like a woman."

The muddy crisis behind us, we continued on until we came to a place in the bamboo forest which, although it looked no different from any other place in the road, was our goal. We got out and walked for two or three minutes through closely crowding trees until we came to a short bridge across a deep ditch that led to the second floor of a two-story treehouse.

The large central room is deliciously cosy. A little bar adjoins it, there is a long dining table on one side, easy chairs, benches and in a brazier a welcoming charcoal fire glowed and crackled.

Stepping out onto the balcony we discovered that our surroundings were similar to those of Treetops. Treetops is a marvelous spot but the atmosphere of Secret Valley is perhaps even more romantic. It too has a waterhole—actually an artificially built pond, but completely wild in appearance; there are a few cleared areas, called arenas and the rest is forest.

Fifteen or twenty feet from the balcony are the feeding stations; four platforms about twelve feet high constructed of tree trunks and branches and shortly after our arrival two agile Africans swarmed up them to secure the carcasses that are bait for the leopards.

Originally the platforms had been placed across the pond at the very edge of the forest so the leopards would feel they were feasting without leaving home. Gradually, every month or so, they were moved forward ten feet until they reached their present positions. From there the leopards can clearly see the guests should they be interested and the guests have excellent close-up views of the superb and supple diners.

The lodge can accommodate twenty-five and during the season is solidly booked, but on our evening we were only seven and it was homelike. One may make reservations through any travel agent or write to the Sportsman's Arms Hotel, P.O. Box 3, Nanyuki, Kenya. The price of a hundred shillings ($12.00) includes transportation from and back to the hotel, a room in the lodge, tea, dinner and breakfast the following morning.

We went to stow our luggage. Warm clothes and one small bag for toilet articles are all that is required and we found that our rooms, while tiny, were well-equipped with comfortable cots, heavy blankets and hot water bottles.

Returning to the central room we had a round of drinks, were served delicious curry puffs and went out onto the balcony to await the leopards. Night had fallen and Mr. Shamsu Din turned on three floodlights. They do not disturb the animals and in their glow we saw the arrival of a herd of Cape buffalo. There were seven at first, but the clan continued to gather until there must have been twenty-five or thirty. Beyond the circle of light we could hear them milling about in the darkness, snuffling and rooting up the salt spread for them on the ground. The only other sounds to break the stillness were crisp little insect noises and occasionally the harsh croak of a tree hyrax.

It was now about 8:30 and although tense with anticipation of leopards, unworthy thoughts of dinner began filtering through my consciousness. Inwardly I was debating whether to ask our host if he didn't think it just possible that we might *perhaps* . . . when Jane touched my arm.

"There," she whispered, "one's coming. I saw the glittering of his eyes."

No leaf stirred to betray his presence but in a moment we too had spotted him; a small animal moving with silent fluid grace through the grass and low shrubs. He crossed the open space to the foot of one of the platforms, leaped nimbly up and settled contentedly to his dinner. I had assumed masculinity, but Mr. Shamsu Din corrected me.

"That's the female," he murmured, "her brother should be coming too." He knew them well, they were two of a litter, he told us later.

Leopards, we discovered, are neat eaters, very well-mannered. They tear the meat and crunch the bones but the approach is concentrated and businesslike and they balance themselves without fear on the slimmest and most limber branches. The ones we saw were exquisite creatures, tawny gold with clearly defined brown velvet spots, long gently lashing tails and deceptively soft paws. How anyone seeing such beauty can bear to destroy it I do not know.

The lodge is equipped with stronger lights than the floods and when guests have got their cameras poised Mr. Shamsu Din turns them on briefly for stills and movies. Surprisingly enough the sudden glare does not necessarily alarm the leopards. Our beautiful girl *had* been joined by her brother and they were not disturbed at all although a later visitor proved shyer.

In the interests of accuracy, I have to record that for darling Dr. Brown's movie camera the lights were not strong enough. He shot a good deal of footage but unless you had been there and remembered it you would have difficulty trying to decipher what was going on.

After about half an hour of feeding, the sated pair slipped away and we felt that we too could now dine without rudeness. The meal was long and quite elaborate with many courses including delicious fresh trout and avocado. Three of the Indians were vegetarians and although our host was not he had thoughtfully catered to their needs. Before dinner one of the women had offered us what looked to be finely shredded tobacco. I do not smoke or chew but I did not like to appear rude so I took a little. To my delighted surprise it turned out to be a very good spicy kind of sweet.

Since a man had been posted to watch for leopards after dinner we sat by the fire absorbing leopard lore rather than brave the cold throughout what might have been a long vigil.

We had observed that the platforms were very near the lodge but assumed that the chances of a patron leaping from one of them on to the balcony were slim. Mr. Shamsu Din said that was so although they had had one episode that might be called the Lady or the Leopard.

The lady it so happened was Mrs. John Mills, the wife of the distinguished actor and the mother of talented Hayley and Juliet. They were visiting Secret Valley and, just as we were, after dinner had been sitting chatting by the fire. The anecdotal tide was running high when they became aware of a great pounding and banging and muffled cries. Looking around Mr. Shamsu Din and Mr. Mills and the others realized that Mrs. Mills was missing.

"The banging, it's coming from the lavatory," the host said.

They leaped up and ran out on the balcony and down to the end where the ladies' room was situated. Behind the closed door the harassed sounds continued.

"What is it? What's the matter?" they cried.

"Get it away! Get that leopard out of there!" The feminine voice was hysterical.

"What leopard? There's nothing here."

"There is, there is. He was there just a minute ago. I opened the door and there he *stood, looking* at me. That leopard!"

It took a great deal of reassuring from her husband and the harried proprietor before Mrs. Mills could bring herself to open the door and emerge. "To tell you the truth," said Mr. Shamsu Din, as he recounted the story, "we didn't believe her at first, but later, reconnoitering, we realized a leopard *could* have walked up the outside staircase and gone along the balcony. He took off of course when he heard us coming but now, as you see, we have a gate." They have indeed and it is leopard-proof. On the night in question the leopard was undoubtedly as startled as Mrs. Mills, but at the moment of confrontation few enemies dare bank on that.

They had had another evening of crisis of a somewhat different sort and on that night a good many people were watching the drama played out in the arena before their eyes.

With subtlety, stealth and a strong sense of theatre our Indian friend—he reminded me of a bouncy smily mahogany ball—portrayed the two antagonists. A leopard and a waterbuck stood face to face and in strange nightmare fashion the buck found himself drawn by that irresistible magnetism which they say the rabbit experiences with a snake. The leopard crouched, motionless except for the twitching tip of his tail, the hypnotized victim moved nearer and nearer to its doom. No breath escaped the spellbound audience. Unendurably the tension mounted, the moment of impact was a second away and *then* . . . somebody sneezed! The spell cracked, the leopard and waterbuck leaped apart and vanished into the forest as a shout of frustration and fury broke from the spectators. Bilked of the kill! The hapless woman who had sneezed was a pariah for the rest of the night.

While Secret Valley cannot guarantee leopards it is rare that the visitor goes away totally unrewarded. Yet he must realize that unlike the gregarious lion the leopard pursues a solitary way. On the other hand, one night nine of them congregated around the bait. That, to be sure, was a record. However the lodge people are not apprehensive about a lack of patronage because the place is becoming a leopard tradition—younger generations are attending their parents alma mater.

We were told of a mother who had brought her three cubs to the feeding stations. They sat in a row and she sat facing them, obviously briefing them on how to attain the succulent goodies on the platforms. She then set an example by leaping up to one. As her student offspring were still very young their attention span was limited and they started playing with their tails and teetering off into the bush but she kept shepherding them back and in about a week or ten days they began to understand Mummy's instruction and the first thing you knew there they were sprawling and scratching their own way up the tree trunks to sample the delicious table d'hôte. It was two of those pupils, now turned professional, whom we had seen earlier in the evening.

As it was growing late, when our after-dinner vigil remained unrewarded, we decided to go to bed. "If there's any excitement we'll call you," our host promised.

As I have said the blankets in our room were warm and perfectly adequate but when we left home friends had given us a special pair and we were eager to try them out. They were made, my husband explained, out of the same material as astronaut's suits and science is fantastic and no mistake. Virtually as thin as paper, blue on one side, silver on the other, they cost little and weigh only ounces. When you cover yourself with them within minutes you are toasty warm. I do not know their official name but for campers or folk with unexpected guests they are invaluable. They may be obtained at Abercrombie & Fitch in New York and I daresay in many stores around the country. Their only drawback, and that may have been because they were new, is that they snap, crackle and crunch like Rice Krispies. The sound is not unpleasant but it can keep you awake. Possibly, when the newness has gone out of them, they are silent as swan's-down.

Nor was it only the blankets that we found mildly disturbing. Right behind our heads on the other side of the partition we could hear the crackle of the charcoal fire kept going by the night watchmen. The interior walls of the lodge are of split bamboo and there is no chimney. Unfettered the sparks fly upwards from the brazier to strike against the ceiling, also of bamboo. Would it not burn or at least smolder? When I asked Mr. Shamsu Din about it in the morning he smiled and assured me it would not. "It is green bamboo," he said, "it never catches." He must know. Nevertheless I hope he will someday have it fireproofed.

We slept at last to be awakened at half-past four by a gentle knock on our door and to hear the watchman say quietly, "Leopard is coming."

It was one of the moments when the wonder of Africa

and a sense of the extraordinary privilege that is travel swept over me. Leopard is coming!

We clambered hastily into slacks and sweaters and went out on the veranda to join Jane. There on the platform lay an enormous leopard methodically tearing and swallowing the carcass of a wildebeest. Surrounded by darkness, illumined by the soft glow of the floodlights he was a superb sight. Unfortunately, in his eagerness to have Norton get a picture Mr. Shamsu Din snapped on his brilliant penetrating beams too quickly. Our magnificent specimen, less experienced than his younger cousins, was startled. His jeweled eyes reflecting the glare stared at us for a moment, then he turned and slid like oil down the tree trunk and vanished into the shadows. Minutes later the third member of the knowledgeable litter came into view, sprang up and finished off the meal. We went back to bed grateful to have seen at close quarters creatures of such incomparable grace and beauty.

After early morning tea we returned to the Sportsman's Arms for breakfast. Digby picked us up, we drove back to Olechugu Ranch, collected our luggage and started on our way to Tsavo National Park where, after one night on the road, we would arrive in camp and our true safari would begin. We were obliged to pass through Nairobi which we were glad enough to do since it enabled us to pick up mail and gave Jane an opportunity for some final marketing.

On the way she and Digby explained that we would stop for lunch at a place that to our horrified ears sounded like Kenmare. Norton and I groaned in unison. "My God, Digby," we said, "we're not going back *there*, are we?" There was a hoot from the Tatham-Warters, "No, no, no, not Kenmare. Kenmere. It's an inn, a very attractive one in Limuru. It's run by a friend of ours, Mrs. Hugo Dent. She really knows about cooking and the food's awfully good."

They spoke truly. The inn was pretty, cosy, very English, and the food very French.

Although she did not know it, meeting Mrs. Dent made us feel like old African hands, the reason being that she had at one time been married to a charming man named Jack Hilton, the Deputy Game Warden of the Kenya National Parks. We had met him and his then wife on our first trip to Africa. We had seen Jack once more in London when he was desperately ill. His death shortly afterward, had greatly saddened us, but somehow having known him and then meeting a woman who had been married to him gave us an *experienced* feeling. We were less like tourists.

One thing that struck me about Mrs. Dent, aside from her ability as an innkeeper, was that she too, like most of her feminine compatriots living in Kenya, had the "supers." Super is their pet word and without it they would be tongue-tied. One can have super biscuits for tea, the behavior of a friend under stress may be jolly super and gazing at the majesty of Mount Kilimanjaro one observes that it *is* rather super. In this instance it was the sweater I was wearing that evoked the favored accolade. "I say, what a *super* jersey. Is it American?"

"I bought it in New York," I said, "but actually I think it's Italian."

"Well," she assured me, "it *is* super."

From then on even Norton referred to it as my super jersey. "Where's that super jersey? You'd better bring it along or you'll get the shivers."

Arrived in Nairobi we went to the New Stanley and found a gratifying stack of mail. From friendly neighbors who were looking after our dog and cat we learned that the first day of our absence they had both returned to our house and spent the day lying in the bedroom looking up eagerly everytime anyone came in. This broke our hearts. Later we were to cling longingly to the vision of such sweet fidelity. They were so well cared for that when we got home they were barely civil. The cat had a little more conscience and did deign to stay around the house but Thor, our Weimaraner, was old dog Betray. Like a teenager he rushed in for food and then off again with the gang; Tony and Sally and Kathryn, Tencci a female dachshund and countless finches and parakeets, that swinging crowd were so much more fun than his stodgy gallivanting family.

Jane had told us that Digby's birthday was imminent and that she had brought along a bottle of champagne. While in Nairobi I bought another and we were busy plotting how we would secret it in the cases of supplies to which of course he had constant access so that it should not be discovered. I forget what strategy we used but it was a success.

For a few miles out of the city the road was paved but then we hit Sultan Hamud, a huddle of miserable tin shacks where Digby tried to get the tailgate of the Toyota adjusted so that the dust would not sift in. The Africans looked at us with pleasant smiles and the Indians crowded around us curiously but nothing was accomplished. Our destination for the night was Hunters Lodge, some fifty miles from the gate of Tsavo National Park where, for the first time, we would be under canvas but at Sultan Hamud the paving stopped and the drive was long, rough, hot, and dusty.

It was late and we were longing for showers when we pulled up at a small filling station beside the lodge driveway. The drive itself was blocked by oil drums. Digby spoke to the African attendant and from their conversation emerged one of the few words of Swahili I understand. The word was funga and it means closed. It was the old story of being ahead of the season. Tired, hot, and hungry as we were it was a bad blow. The lodge would not be open until the 6th of June and it was then the 18th of May. Digby was especially upset because while we had been in Nairobi he had mentioned to a travel agent with whom he does a good deal of business that we proposed spending the night at Hunters and the man had said nothing about its being closed.

Maybe he didn't know himself. African arrangements are sometimes casual, hotel owners may come and go as the whim moves them and notifying an agent in Nairobi is the last thing that occurs to them.

Everyone is aware of the need for insuring accommodations *in* season. Out of season one is less concerned, but it is still a good idea. Maybe one's dream destination is closed or if open may be functioning with only a skeleton staff and slim larder. Notify them of the arrival of your party so it won't be a case of "Not a crumb in the cupboard, not a sheet aired and the Duke at the gates."

Digby, who had been driving all day, was exhausted. "The next place is fifty miles away," he said shortly, "Tsavo Lodge." Jane who is an excellent driver herself took the wheel and we started off again. We none of us spoke for a while but I think we were all wondering what we would do if the next place was closed too.

However, when after an eternity of driving through the black night over dreadful roads we finally arrived at Mtito Andei, the place was heaven. It didn't matter at all that the Hunters Lodge people had run out on us. We bathed and dined. Our beds were comfortable and not only did we have mosquito netting canopies we had screens in the windows. Tsavo Inn was unique in Africa. It was even more attractive in the morning. Unlike Kenmare the swimming pool was large and usable and walls and doorways were festooned with purple bougainvillea, which while lovely is perhaps a little commonplace. But there were also great sprays and fountains of variegated pink and white blossoms and others of a rich glowing salmon shade. There were fragrant frangipani trees and trees with slender trunks freighted with luxuriant green leaves and golden flowers, not wattle, not acacia but of that family: tecoma stans.

After breakfast we entered the Tsavo reserve itself and almost immediately the animals appeared. We saw that fine fellow the Kori bustard and our admiration for Jane, already begun, shifted into high. Not only is she an outstandingly able executive when it comes to organizing ambulatory housekeeping arrangements for four, she is experienced with a camera, she is a professional ornithologist and she has the eyesight of an African. Superlative. Had more Africans been scientifically trained sooner the X-ray would probably never have been invented, there would have been no need. The range and penetration of their vision are incredible.

We would be jouncing along in the bush, looking hopefully around but seeing nothing when Jane would say to Digby, "Just a minute, darling, I think over there . . . yes, I'm sure, a lioness and two cubs." Digby would turn the Toyota, more jouncing and bouncing for some little time before we reached the place she had indicated and there—what else?—deep in the grass, a lioness and two cubs.

She pointed out and named the birds and was the first to spot two warthogs. A herd of elephants and two hartebeests we had the wit to see for ourselves. On reaching Mzima Springs we got out and walked around. This is a delightful place with high beech trees, palms, and tamarinds. Crystal water gushed from the ground to form a little rivulet and many deep pools, the home of happy crocs and hippos. Millions of gallons of water are tapped from the springs and piped down to Mombasa about one hundred and sixty miles away to form the city's water supply.

A stage has been built out over one of the pools, affording a good view of the hippos, the huge weightless shapes moving silent as shadows under water then surfacing with great snorting and blowing, the grunts and gasps diminishing as their vast maws close and they submerge again, the round pop eyes, the round little ears the last portions of them to vanish.

There is a small underwater chamber to which one may descend to watch them as well as schools of fish who live in the ponds. Artistic vervet monkeys, soft fur of greenish gray, pink penises and blue testicles swung from the trees and when we opened a box of biscuits they came swooping down to demand a share.

Norton took a Polaroid picture of the African ranger who had shown us around and of his little son informally clad in open pants. They were discreetly closed for the portrait which Norton gave the father who accepted it shyly but with obvious pleasure.

We drove on to Poachers Lookout, a thatched shelter

perched on a high hill overlooking one of the great views of the world. You think, surely there can be only one such location from which to see what appears to be most of the earth, but on the vast continent of Africa they are commonplace yet always breathtaking. Surrounding Poachers Lookout are endless plains and two mountain ranges and peering through the telescope we could see far away herds of elephant, giraffe, and one lordly rhino.

Lunchtime found us at the Kilaguni Game Lodge, a good hotel with a broad veranda from which one may watch the ungainly and unpleasant marabou stork who frequent the place but also the endearing and amusing spectacle of elephants as they slowly approach the ponds and waterholes, drink, bathe, spray themselves and each other and in their own good time wander off again. Over the bar hangs a sign: ANIMALS ARE REQUESTED TO BE QUIET WHILE GUESTS ARE DRINKING AND VICE VERSA.

For our own taste Kilaguni is a little too hotely but it is well run and comfortable although we understood that such is its popularity that in the full season they assign four people to a room.

In the course of the afternoon our road at one point ran between two large bull elephants one on either side and very near. They swung and raised their trunks and I myself was a bit apprehensive, thinking they might close in on us but Digby was reassuring. "They may look threatening," he said, "but raised trunks don't really mean anything. It's when they lower their heads and tuck the trunks under that you want to watch out. That's when they may charge and as their trunks are their most vulnerable part they are protecting themselves." I was glad to learn it.

We drove past the Yatta Plateau, a curious formation, a kind of palisades, probably formed eons ago by a lava overflow that stretches for miles and is as flat on top as though it had been sheared off with a knife.

A decorative silhouette against the sky was a bare thorn, hung with weavers nests. It looked like a Christmas tree and was alive with the owners, buffalo weavers with buff fronts and white circles on their brownish wings. They seem rather staid but when they fly a flash of brilliant lacquer orange under their tails mocks their sobriety. The weavers are appealing but my heart went out to the herd of giraffe we passed shortly afterward. Giraffes are improbable faery creatures at any age but this was the first time we had seen babies. I wanted to own one and name him Mr. F. A. O. Schwarz, for if ever a creature was out of a toy-shop window it was that spotted stiff-legged infant who watched us with grave curiosity.

At a quarter past five we arrived at Ndololo, our campsite. Jane pronounced it "absolutely super" which it was and to Norton and me it brought a little thrill of fulfillment. The super tents, should you wish to buy or rent one you will get further if you call them Aruba, had been set in a clearing in the shade of newtonia, tamarind, and wild fig trees. There were three of them, one for the Tatham-Warters, one for ourselves and a larger and well-equipped mess tent where the boys had placed the food chests, the portable iceboxes which ran on butane gas and the apparatus for distilling drinking water. Although in the Serengeti we were in a more open area and in the Mara more dramatically located, this must have been the best place from the point of view of the African boys. There was a well behind a small stockade from which to draw water while in our other camps it had to be transported a considerable distance in big drums.

Across the clearing from our own tent was a big sleeping tent for the six servants and toilet and shower tents were placed at discreet distances. As I was to learn a little later on in pragmatic fashion, we were very near the Voi River, where game came to drink, but it was hidden from view by thick growth and underbrush.

The tents were roomy and airy, double tops and screened openings on four sides insuring ample ventilation and there were flaps which could be let down in case of rain or wind. The feature I found most reassuring was the floor cloth attached to the sides so that when we retired for the night with our front flaps zipped we were cosily insect and snakeproof. Indeed throughout our three weeks in Africa we never saw so much as a garter snake.

I have mentioned the shower tents and although at first crack they take a few calisthenics and juggling with equipment we quickly became proficient. One enters, tosses dressing gown and towel over the top, stands on a duckboard and pulls a chain and from a large tin can suspended overhead emerges bountiful hot water, drawn in this instance from the nearby well and heated by Kabwi over his cooking fire. The only drawback is that you have to balance on one foot while drying the other and then there is no place to put it down. Having gone to all that effort you don't want to step on the bare earth and dirty it up again, so we suggested to Digby that maybe another small duckboard, one that would be in the corner of the tent and remain dry might be a good idea. He agreed and perhaps now they have them.

Clean and refreshed we gathered by the fire for our pre-dinner drinks. The night was not cold but the fire made of long logs the boys had dragged into camp was irresistible.

Digby was very funny about his light, the one we had been introduced to at Kenmare Lodge. It was his pride and joy but also the source of much concern. "Do you think it's too much?" he would ask. "Do you think it's vulgar?"

We used to tease him. "It's the third degree. It's Times Square on New Year's Eve." Actually it was very nice. During cocktails and dinner it suffused the camp with a soft glow and afterward we would turn it off and have coffee by fire-light under the stars. Also it had a practical virtue. Digby's hope, which sometimes proved to be fact, was that it would draw insects and that, as it was several feet over our heads, they would leave us in the clear.

The first night we were handed kerosene lamps and candles and a couple of electric torches. We were told we must zip up our front flaps and leave a lantern burning on the ground outside and we should be safe as churches. Our mentors spoke gospel. It was only Dr. Brown, a prudent chap who thinks ahead, who experienced a weasel doubt.

The basic amenity was set up across a narrow path and a good many yards away. "I don't like your wandering over there in the night," he said. "After all, there are wild animals around here." And he spoke to Digby, "How about it? No old-fashioned chamber pots handy?" There certainly were for tyros like us, only they were new-fashioned: pink plastic. They reminded me of my childhood country holidays but I dutifully placed them under our beds.

That night we turned in early and I awakened only twice to peace and a stillness intensified by small delicate insect noises.

About a quarter to six I awakened for good. Looking through the screen in our tent wall I could see the first pale gleam of dawn. I could also feel that need that will not be denied. Norton normally sleeps like the dead but he can have sneaky interludes of alert restlessness so I pulled down the tent zipper as quietly as I could hoping not to disturb him and, modern version in hand, stepped outside. Maestro, it so happened, was on the qui vive.

"Where are you going?"

"Just outside, dear."

"Must you?"

"That's a stupid question. Yes."

Grumble, mumble. "All right, but don't go far."

I would have stayed where I was but across the clearing, in the boys' tent I heard the faint ringing of their alarm clock. Realizing that they would probably be getting up and under the circumstances desiring a little privacy, I went around the corner of our tent. Norton's voice stopped me. "That's far enough."

"O.K., O.K., no need to wake the whole camp."

There I was in contemplative mood absorbing the tranquil loveliness of daybreak when looking up I beheld, about ten yards away—we later measured—a lion on his way to the river. In the breathless hush I looked at him, he looked at me

then, with the leonine equivalent of "Good God," he bounded
off. I returned, shaking only slightly, to my loved one. "Believe me, dear," I said, "the people who live here and those
toilet tents, they know what they're doing. At least you're
zipped in. You have some *privacy*." Norton's whoop of laughter I found uncompanionable. Nor was he the only one. A
couple of the boys had emerged from their tent at the moment of confrontation and they were doubled up with glee.
It was the most glorious thing that had happened in donkey's
years. They couldn't wait to rout out Jane and Digby and tell
the bwanas what had happened to the memsahib. Chez the
Tatham-Warters the old courtesy still holds. Our dear hosts
were pretty entertained too and it was then that Digby got
out his ruler and measured the distance I indicated. I had not
exaggerated the nearness, there were the pug marks. "I say,"
he said and he too shook with mirth.

When I had recovered a little I was able, if with some
effort, to see the lion's side. I could imagine him returning
to the pride. "What do you know! Here I am, going as always
down to the river for a drink. How many times have I taken
that path! It's peaceful, it's deserted, I'm appreciating the
sunrise and all of a sudden what happens? A city! Tents,
lorries, people, dames on pink plastic pots . . . I tell you,
there goes the neighborhood."

By 7:30 we had had tea and crackers—biscuits to the
British—and set off on the morning's game drive. Mackerel
clouds had veiled the clear sky of dawn but we were not too
unhappy. A mild overcast is preferable for game viewing as
in hot bright sunlight the animals tend to withdraw deep into
shade.

Our first stop was Aruba Lodge on the edge of a big dam
in the Tsavo River, where Jane wanted to buy fresh fish for
lunch. A good many ugly marabou stork were fishing too but
the lodge itself we thought attractive. Five small adobe
brick bandas with thatched roofs, each containing two double
rooms and a bath. There are also tents for those who prefer
camping out but who do not have their own equipment.

We drove around for nearly three hours having fine luck in viewing. Tsavo is famous for its elephants and when first seen they are surprising for they are not elephant gray at all but elephant red, covered with the rich red Tsavo earth. They moved leisurely along the track and across the bush tucking in great mouthfuls of grass and flapping their ears to ward off flies.

A pride of ten warthogs crossed our view, traveling with that air of businesslike concentration so peculiarly theirs. I always feel that the French word *affairé* suits warthogs perfectly. With their big heads, small curling tusks like old-fashioned mustachios and short legs they hurry along full of affairs; busy, preoccupied serious citizens. They are saved from pomposity by their slim, erect tails with the jaunty pompom on the tip and one senses they were gay blades in their heyday but now they have stanchly accepted responsibility and have matured into bourgeois family men, their wives and children trotting in their wake.

Herds of oryx patterned the plain and handsome beasts they are with their faces striped black and white and their long slim grooved horns. Near them grazed congoni and zebra. When we stopped the Toyota they raised their heads and gazed at us unblinkingly but if we started toward them they moved away, not in panic, not very quickly, but definitely away from man.

Further on were Egyptian geese, chic types, modern in feeling with plumage designed by Braque: white and brown and black with a glinting flash of orange. Near them was a small dainty yellow billed stork and a flock of the so peculiar pelican, oyster white with pale yellow bills. All in all a rewarding bag and we returned to camp ravenous about a quarter to eleven.

Digby had a business letter he wanted to send off and later in the day he asked me if I would write it for him on my portable typewriter. I cherish that little machine but sometimes a person has to face the stark fact that even after years of experience he is never going to become proficient in certain aspects of his profession. There are old actors who say, "I have been in the theatre all my life. I know my business," when the sad truth is they have never learned it. I have now been in the writing business a good many years and have typed, I suppose, hundreds of thousands of words in writing thirteen books, but I have never really learned to cope with the machine.

For Digby's sake and because it was a business letter to the resident magistrate I did my best but the results were peculiar. The lines of type waved up and down, not by the way, an easy thing to accomplish, and words sprang syllables where normally they are not. Digby was annoyed with the resident magistrate who, he felt, had been unduly officious in the matter of issuing a license for the lorry that transported the camp equipment, swathing the transaction in needless red tape, and he wished to lodge a complaint. Looking at my achievement he nodded with approval. "This *will* be a poser for the R.M.," he said happily, but he still suggested we write *On Safari* at the bottom as a kind of explanation for the oddities. I did not like to confess that at my own desk they would have been the same. He went off to Voi to mail the letter and I wandered around camp basking in the peace and charm of our surroundings. Norton was writing post-cards and Jane was reading, this time not in her bird book, a fat volume that was almost an encyclopedia. She herself had made little alphabetical thumb tabs for it, the kind dictionaries have, and she could turn in an instant to the correct page when seeking information or answering our never-ending questions. "What kind is *that*? What's *his* name? Are they the same family as the ones we saw this morning?"

For those who pass their days in cities and in the inevitable repetition which is part of even stimulating work that must be sustained for long periods, life in camp is a marvelous change and relaxation. For the safari managers these happy interludes are naturally their working periods although the real work is in the preparation. Planning what routes to take, selecting and reserving campsites, pulling together the enormous amount of indispensable equipment, engaging an efficient personnel, all this can be a formidable matter of logistics and one which, in our experience, we consider to have been admirably thought out.

One lives with them closely and camp servants make an important contribution to one's well being. The head boy, Kenyua was an able young African who drove the heavy lorry and directed the setting up of the camp. When the Tatham-Warters were on a hunting safari it was Samwell who acted as gun bearer and tracker. For us he was the telescopic lens, after Jane, who spotted the game and he often rode with us in the Toyota. He was also invaluable in bog-downs and for changing tires, as due to long thorns we had a good many punctures. There was also a clean and spruce butler, Theuri, who waited on table, very neat in his khaki uniform and there was Kabwi the cook whom I have mentioned before. His kitchen was a rigged-up shelter, a canvas roof and one canvas wall and his range was that of earliest man, an open fire. Upon it he cooked very good meals and made delicious homemade bread. There was Mwangi, the general boy who dug the latrines and wielded the panga when the grass was tall, cut wood for the fire and brought the water, and Joseph was our tent boy, a knotty, able little fellow who made the beds, swept up and did the laundry. Rarely have we had such laundry service; everything washed and pressed every day. I do not say one cannot run an enjoyable safari with fewer hands but I do say that having them is true luxury. As I recall Digby had hired one extra for the trip, the others worked for him and Jane in the house and on the farm. They liked going on safari for they got an increase in wages and also it made a change. Sometimes we would alternate and take one of the boys other than Samwell to give him a chance to see the game too and always the animals filled them with wonder and excitement just as they did us. Because you are an African and live there does not mean that elephants and rhinos and lions come strolling into your front yard.

Nor does it mean that because in the past the white man—chiefly the British—has established thousands of square miles as game reserves that an African is born understanding their value. Tanzania owes a great debt to John Owen for he managed to arrange a trip to the United States for fifteen members of the government, whose primary concern is their country's agriculture and wildlife.

They met Mr. Fairfield Osborn, the president of New York's Zoological Society that does so much for wildlife in general, they were received by Secretary of the Interior Stewart L. Udall and best of all they were taken on a trip through the National Parks of our West and Middle West. These last were true eye-openers and they returned home with renewed interest, determined to strengthen and enlarge the administration of Tanzania's great reserves.

Our own men in camp were intrigued by the animals but they were prudent too, preferring to travel in the lorry than to walk and if they were obliged to go afield for water or wood they traveled by twos.

It was while we were so thoroughly enjoying life in the wild with all the amenities that Jane and Digby fearing perhaps, but quite wrongly, that we might get bored suggested a trip to Mombasa en route to Kilifi, a resort on the water. The Kilifi creek they said was the abode of beautiful and exotic birds.

Norton and I had been in Mombasa in 1962 and while we had not regreted the visit the city exerted no pull. If we never got there again it was all right with us. Also it was over one hundred miles away and we had had enough driving to last us for some little time. Our lack of enthusiasm must have been apparent but Jane and Digby were persuasive. The bird life in the creek was, they assured us, unique and Norton had his Questar with its incredible telescopic lenses. What an opportunity for him!

We began to weaken. That the Tatham-Warters genuinely

wanted us to see the birds we did not doubt but, also at Mombasa they would have a chance to see their daughter Caroline, the seventeen-year-old who was studying shorthand and typing. In the end we agreed to go.

"At Kilifi," said Digby, "we'll stop at Mnarani. It's a simple fishing club where we can spend the night. And we'll take a picnic lunch up the creek the next day."

That night in camp was made noisy by bush babies in a nearby tree. I wouldn't have minded the noise at all if we could have seen the babies but there was too much darkness and too much foliage.

The next morning we took off at half-past nine, driving for a while through Tsavo, spotting elephant and a herd of more than two hundred oryxes, their horns like a forest of masts in a small harbor. We also spied three cheetahs and Peter's gazelle, a small species of Grants, well known to Digby and Jane.

Jane had assured us that one reason for going to Mombasa was because it was such a pretty drive. Beauty lies not only in the eye but in the heart of the beholder. To strangers and to a perhaps jaundiced eye the drive from Tsavo to the coast on the Nairobi-Mombasa highway is long and boring. Stretching as it does for three hundred and twenty miles the road must occasionally curve and bend but the traveler does not get that impression. To him it continues in a perpetual straight line with nothing to see until about fifteen miles outside the city when the vegetation does pick up a bit.

Many of the Mombasa buildings are dilapidated and the climate was as we recalled; stifling and clammy and the African women who wore only skirts and no tops we considered to be very sensibly dressed.

Digby and Jane were in high spirits. "We'll have luncheon at the club," they said, "and we do hope Caroline will be able to get in to see us." Since it was Sunday there was every likelihood that she would. We assumed they would be meeting old friends but we were astonished to find that we met some ourselves, Yolande and Francis MacConnel who had been managing Samburu Lodge when we were there in 1964. Just as we were exchanging greetings Caroline rushed in and threw her arms around her mother's neck. There were introductions, she presented a young man and the four of them went off to chat while the MacConnels and ourselves caught up on the news over drinks at another table.

It was a pleasant reunion but we all felt sad about Samburu, one of the most attractive and rewarding lodges we had ever been to. It is situated on the banks of the Uaso Nyero. Birds flock there and game in abundance comes to drink and bathe. The MacConnels ran it well and the food and accommodations were above average. They were now living just outside of Mombasa where Francis organized parties for deep-sea fishing and although Samburu was still open few people went there. It is in the Northern Frontier District and the Shifta with tiresome repetitiveness were making things uncomfortable. Those who did go flew in from Nairobi, a quick and convenient way of getting there and a welcome alternative to driving, for the Shifta mined the roads.

When the MacConnels got up to join friends in the dining room Jane and Digby motioned us to come over to their table. We sat down and after chatting briefly were flabbergasted to hear Digby say, "Look here, Caroline *has* had a bit of luck. Her headmistress is ill and the school has been closed down for a fortnight. You don't mind if she comes on safari with us, do you!" And she came.

It had not been our intention to turn our safari into a family outing, but once under way we found that Caroline was a well brought up girl, helpful and unobtrusive. Although as English as her parents she had a personalized manner of speech, a slight accent that was amusing to listen to and the affection she and her mother obviously felt for each other was a heartwarming change from the snarling generation gap.

Yet objectively speaking I would think it more prudent to confine any safari to the principles. The host-guide, and, when there is one, as in our own lucky case, the hostess, the camp personnel and the clients. That is already a fair number of people to take care of. Supernumeraries added to the cast are a gratuitous risk, a potential liability. Indeed Caroline developed a bad throat and was miserable for two or three days. Had she become really ill she would have had to be taken to Nairobi and the safari which we had been looking forward to for so long and which meant so much to us would have been badly dented.

Fortunately her own youthful constitution and her father's remedies pulled her through. A Tatham-Warter safari is equipped with an impressive and reassuring medicine chest. Digby makes no pretense of having studied medicine but he has consulted good doctors and followed their advice. On the inside of the lid is a list of likely safari maladies or, for that matter with the exception of insect and snake bites, for maladies at home in the city. Sore throat, earache, nausea, fever, chest colds, hysteria, pain, right side, pain left, broken bones—what to do until reaching the surgeon . . . that cabinet is a hypochondriac's paradise. Not only Caroline but at one moment or another we all felt, for brief periods, under the weather and Digby and Norton spent happy moments consulting together and browsing through bottles and boxes.

After our luncheon in Mombasa, Caroline and Jane had hurried off to get Caroline's clothes and when they returned we drove on to Kilifi and to the fishing club which, from the way Digby had spoken, Norton and I had imagined to be extremely simple, something on the order of Aruba in Tsavo. If we had to leave our beloved camp that was second best. We were mistaken. Mnarani, "the place of the lighthouse" was nothing at all like Aruba. It was in fact a swinging country club on a summer Sunday afternoon; barking dogs, a swimming pool full of screaming children and chattering parents and friends gathered around tea tables and the bar. Norton took one look at it and his aside to me was short and sharp. I was so bitterly disappointed that I ran to the ladies room, locked myself in and sobbed my heart out. I couldn't help it. Our unique experience, an adventure cherished beyond all others, had been violated. The beauty, the stillness, the sense of wonder reawakened by the savannahs and the forests and the wild free animals had been desecrated at a stroke. Also, I was reading Evelyn Ames' beautiful and poetic book about her own African safari, A *Glimpse of Eden*, and her singing phrases were fresh in my mind.

I pulled myself together as best I could and went out to join the others. Digby and Jane realized that something had gone awry but they were at a loss to understand why. For them it was a fine day. They had corralled their daughter and here they were in this nice place among their friends. Digby said something about its being one of the nicest clubs in that part of Africa, the best people, all the rest of it.

"But you don't understand," I blurted out. "We do this three hundred and sixty-five days a year."

Obviously we do not for the very reason that it is not the kind of life that appeals to us, but it is the kind to which we, along with a large segment of America, have access. I do not denigrate clubs as such and I am glad we belong to the ones we do. They are pleasant rendezvous and in these servantless days frequently life-savers, but as Ecclesiastes so aptly remarked, there is a time for everything and clubbing it at Mnarani on a Sunday afternoon was not what we had traveled more than 7000 miles to do.

However, we were there, stuck at least until the next day, so we tried to make the best of it. Jane lent me a bathing suit and while we were on the beach she told me that they had come there the previous December for the Christmas holidays. One day, crossing the inlet on the ferry she saw bobbing in the water what she at first thought was a coconut. Closer inspection revealed it to be the head of a drowned African who had been bound hand and foot and tossed into the water. Horrified, she pointed him out to the boatman who shrugged indifferently. "But look here," she said, "aren't you going to report it to the police?"

Another shrug. "Maybe," and he began to laugh, a small chuckle at first, burgeoning into an all-out hilarious guffaw. "And to think," he said, when he could finally control his mirth, "to think that only yesterday he paid three and six for a haircut." Such delicious irony sent him into fresh spasms of delight.

When we had had enough swimming we wandered back to the club cottage where we were housed and turned on our portable radio. For the last several days the news that filtered through to us on the 7 P.M. broadcasts had not been reassuring. The relationship between Israel and the Arab countries was becoming increasingly strained and our interest in a flare-up, if one occurred, was I am afraid more subjective than global. Our itinerary called for us to fly from Nairobi to Athens, arriving there early in the morning of June 5 and leaving that same afternoon for Beirut and a trip through the Middle East. If war broke out our plans, along with those of several thousand others, would be abruptly changed. Should it happen where would we go? What would we do?

After tea when Jane and Digby suggested driving "just a couple of miles down the road to see a lovely headland we once owned" I was seduced into going. Some people learn slowly. Dr. Brown declined. He had had all the motoring he cared for. "Besides," he said, "I want to write a letter to Papa in Athens and ask him to work out an alternative schedule in case we can't get to the Middle East."

Papa was Dimitri Papaefstratiou, the head of the Greek Travel Bureau in Athens and an old acquaintance.

The four of us, Jane, Caroline, Digby and I, set out in the Toyota and it was brought home to me that I should have left them to their nostalgia. The headland of their dreams was nearer five miles than two and due to heavy morning showers the narrow dirt road, little more than a lane, was in appalling condition. It was Meru accentuated with the added attraction of coarse waist-high grass choking the tracks which Digby was obliged to negotiate since it was impossible to turn around.

Once we had reached the cherished promontory the view over the ocean was nice but I would have been content to look and let it go at that. Nothing would do, however, but that

I must follow Digby as he leaped like a mountain goat over the curious rock formations that cascaded from the bluff on which we were parked down to the beach. Then, just as I thought it was all over and we could go back, they decided it would be fun to push on a bit and look at the house. To this day that house remains a mystery to me and although they were voluble in their commentary I never did gather whether they had built it, thought of buying it or had rented it. All that came through to me was that the previous December, only five months before, some rich friends of theirs had spent holidays in it. The paint was peeling, the cement cracking, the windows were broken and an engulfing aura of desolation and decay emanated from it. The friends, I concluded, must have been rich spiders.

We plowed our tedious way back, reaching the club as darkness fell. Caroline leaped from the car. "Thank you, Daddy," she said enthusiastically, "that was super." Too inexperienced perhaps to perceive the reason behind an interplay of mood and viewpoint she nevertheless had the antennae of loyal youth. One or two of my remarks to her father had been pointed. As far as she was concerned that awful American woman was being bitchy to her Dads and she would comfort him and if some people couldn't appreciate lovely spots where they had all had so much fun that was just too bad.

The awful American woman didn't intend bitchery but tether's end was nearing. She had her emotional problems and they were beginning to make her feel physically wretched, a state which a drink before dinner did little to heal nor did it alleviate the long dreary menu. The meal began with something called Rollmops—curled up herrings—and ended with a dish dear to the British stomach, the savory. We drew Angels on Horseback, a little heap of God knows what piled on an underdone bit of toast. The whole ploy was especially trying because in camp, our lovely camp, the meals were always thoughtfully planned by Jane and well prepared by Kabwi. Sometimes she herself would do the cooking and then the food was even better. The saving grace at the Mnarani dinner was a bottle of reasonably good Graves.

Incredibly enough next morning's breakfast was as delicious as dinner had been gruesome and we were served the best bitter orange marmalade I have ever eaten. We also met the two women who ran the club and liked them on sight.

One of them had read *Elephants Arrive at Half-Past Five* and had been touched, she said, by my account of Kitu, our bush baby who had died shortly after we got him home. She had had one for a long time and loved him with all her heart. They are winsome creatures. Dirty around a house but winsome.

When in Nairobi I had gone to call on the people who ran Tropicals, the pet shop where I had bought Kitu, they were apathetic over our loss. They were now pushing mongoose. "Angelic pets, have it all over bush babies. You *must* take one to New York." I would have been happy to but the U.S. customs will not allow them. We are as pigheaded about mongoose as the English are about dogs. Although I don't think we have as potent a mongoose lobby.

When Digby said we should be getting along we went down to the water and at the foot of the jetty found a diesel motorboat awaiting us. We cast anchor and started off only to discover a few minutes later that the tide was not high enough for so large a craft to negotiate the creek. A dinghy heaved alongside and the major said briskly, "We'll do the creek by dinghy, even better." At this point I balked. I was feeling too ill to cope with the hot sun and discomfort were it to view the most ravishing plumage ever seen or to listen to the most sublime bird song heard by the ear of man. Jane said she would stay with me. I know she stayed out of kindness, I *suspect* that in the blazing sun a dinghy with an outboard motor was not her idea of a psychedelic trip either.

The captain, Norton, Digby, and Caroline piled in and chugged off. We stayed rocking at anchor. In my condition the

gentle motion of the boat was bad enough but the smell of
the diesel engine was nauseating. Discomfort was acute and
prolonged and there was no means of escape for in the
shade of the housing it was airless and in any location on
deck where there was a breeze the sun was burning hot.
Jane and the boatman engaged in desultory conversation in
Swahili and I spent the endless time hanging over the rail
retching and wishing I were dead.

Eventually the bird lovers returned with the ironic information that there had been virtually no birds to see. It was
surprising too in view of the fact that the tide was low and
feeding conditions ideal, or so a human would have thought,
but the feathered ones had departed. The great *pièce de résistance* had bombed. In fairness to Digby one must say that
that was not his fault. That's Africa. One goes to places
where usually birds or game abound but sometimes they
do not and that is the luck of the safari. Later I asked Norton
what the creek itself had been like. "A mangrove swamp in
Florida," he said.

Jane and Digby, worried by my appearance, suggested that
perhaps we should stay on at Mnarani to give me time to
recuperate. Having seen myself in the mirror I understood
what they meant but here my husband stepped in profes-
sionally. "The cure for what ails her," he said, "is to get the
hell out of here and back to camp, which we were fools to
have left in the first place."

We made Mombasa by lunchtime. While Jane did some
marketing and Caroline went to gather up more clothes for
the safari I called Mary O'Mahoney, the Irish charmer who
had wakened me so early our first morning in Nairobi. She
came to the club in a few minutes and we sat talking about
my friend and her patient, Bertha Rose, about the theatre
and the world in general. She was a pretty girl who wore her
shining chestnut hair in a braid over one shoulder, balanced
on the other side by a red hat with a turned-up brim.

She said that in September she and her Italian surgeon
fiancé would be going to Rome where they were to be mar-

ried. She was looking forward to it as to the gates of heaven for she too hated Mombasa. Due to the enervating climate she had had a bout of real illness. "In March," she said simply, "you can't breath at all."

She told me that they had gone on a safari through Shifta country and to their dismay, on official orders, had been accompanied by an army escort fifty strong. The fiancé knew Somalia and the Somali well. He had worked there and was confident he could cope with trouble should any arise. By themselves they would be all right. With an army of fifty they were a conspicuous target but they had no choice. Actually they got quite fond of the men who were charming and full of guile. "You go first," they said courteously, "and we will follow and protect you."

There was a delicate point involved in going first since, with the roads mined by the Shifta first goers, unless extremely careful and resourceful, could hit a sticky wicket. Mary O'Mahoney laughed as she told me the story. "Africans are very like our Irish, the simple way they shift responsibility."

In an hour or so the others returned and we set out for camp. I like to think it was the last time I shall ever be in Mombasa. We had not thought much of it in 1962. This time it struck us as the nether end of hell.

Our sentiments must have been clear to our host-guides yet it is true that some people want to go there for the deep-sea fishing. Should any of their clients wish to do so I imagine the Tatham-Warters will escort them although after their experience with us it will probably have to be at gun's point.

I had a fever and ached in every bone but I have never been so glad to get any place as I was to get back to our peaceful delightful camp and into bed. Under the astronaut's blanket I finally stopped shivering and fell asleep but my loved one, practicing his profession, kept coming into the tent and waking me up to see if I was all right. What I needed was a starched white dragon at the entrance to say respectfully but firmly, "I am sorry, Doctor, we are asleep and we must not be disturbed."

David Sheldrick, the warden of Tsavo East (there is a Tsavo West also) and an old friend of the Tatham-Warters came in to camp to dine. He knew the spot well, having lived there for eighteen months when he first took over his job and was reconnoitering his vast mileage and waiting for his house to be built. I could hear him and the others talking by the fire but I was too miserable to get out of bed. The cold jellied consommé that Joseph, our tent boy, brought me was a sufficient and delicious dinner.

Afterward, when he came into our tent to get ready for bed Norton relayed a story Mr. Sheldrick had told them of an African who walking alone at twilight had glanced behind him and had seen, somewhat to his discomfiture, that he was being followed by a pair of hyenas. He shook his fist at them and shouted and they fell back a bit but when he resumed walking so did they. As he accelerated his pace so did they. In a few moments there was no longer any pretense, it was a flat out chase. Terrified, the African leaped up the first tree he could navigate and as his feet left the ground the hyenas sprang at his legs but fortunately their only reward was a remnant of his trousers. Still, the poor devil was treed for the night.

At a much later date I happened upon an article in *Animal Kingdom*, the magazine of the New York Zoological Society, contributed by Patricia O'Connor in which, writing of the epidemic of sleeping sickness that befell Uganda in 1908 and 1909, she tells of hyenas who "became so emboldened by the regular supply of corpses they began to raid native villages graduating from corpses to the sick and helpless and eventually to healthy people."

Despite the cheerful nightmare that had been so thoughtfully relayed by Dr. Brown, I managed a good night's sleep and woke up cured if still feeling a bit like Alice through the Knot Hole. After breakfast, sped on our way by a great chattering of baboons and vervet monkeys swinging through the branches of a nearby grove, we set off to pay a return visit to David Sheldrick and his pets.

This fortunate man lives surrounded by baby and young animals who become as tame as cats and dogs. The first one we met was a three months old rhino named Stub. They had found him in a sisal plantation, the umbilical cord left dangling when his mother had been frightened away by a tractor. He was ugly and touching with a head like a tortoise and he came trotting after us like a puppy not wishing to be left behind.

Rhinos, we learned, are very neat in their toilet habits. They have several midden heaps and they make their rounds impartially but they always use the same ones, kicking their hind legs afterward like dogs. Stub had two full-grown play-mates, adult rhinos named Rufus and Reudi, the latter named after a friend of the Sheldricks, Mr. Reudi Schenkel, an expert on animals who had been rudely treated by his name-sake. He had been rolled over and pushed around—but he survived and charitably forgave the assault.

In their wild state rhinos are often ferocious for their eye-sight is poor and when they see some vague thing looming their instinct is to charge. Yet they are among the quickest and easiest of animals to tame. Since the vogue for African-made films, picture companies have found to their cost that after a rhino has been penned for a while and fed well he becomes so devoted that he will not dream of charging any of his colleagues in the cast. They are obliged to go out and rustle up a stranger and shoot the scene before he too becomes accustomed to a life of ease.

Rufus and Reudi, although they came back to their com-pound for the night, roamed free during the day accompanied by an aged African, a sort of tutor, who went with them to see that they did not frighten visitors in the park and also that they did not roam outside its boundaries where they would have been fair game for hunters.

Other Sheldrick babies were a buffalo named Lollapa and Bobby, a lesser kudo. Our favorites however were two ele-

phants one of whom was Eleanor. We had made her acquaintance in 1964 when she was appearing in *Born Free*
with Virginia McKenna and Bill Travers and were enchanted
to see that she had attained splendid and secure young wom-
anhood. Her pal was another elephantine beauty, Kadenga.
Watching them at play was undiluted amusement. They
would stand trunk to trunk and then braid them together in
a two-stranded plait. They would kneel down and one would
crawl under the other's belly. They lay on their sides making
gargantuan efforts to roll completely over and in the process
failing completely but having a whirl of a time. Watching
them it was heartbreaking to think of lonely bored elephants
in zoos standing all day long in hideous cages one great foot
chained to the concrete floor. The sheer stupidity of this
kind of cruelty rouses one to blazing anger.

We knew that David Sheldrick was married and had hoped
to meet his wife, Daphne, but she was away from home for
a worrisome reason. Her young daughter had been seriously
hurt in an automobile accident and she had rushed to Nairobi
to be with her. Mrs. Sheldrick had written a book called
The Orphans of Tsavo, filled with stories of their pets. Jane
lent it to me and the story I liked best dealt with an elephant,
not Eleanor or Kadenga, who had developed a bad sore on
her neck. In order to cure it David was obliged to treat and
dress it every day, a painful procedure which she bore stoi-
cally as though she understood the necessity. In time it
healed completely but when David would pet her and stroke
her neck she would lean against him rumbling gently, recall-
ing the bad time they had gone through together.

Although we missed Mrs. Sheldrick we had the good luck
to meet Dr. Richard Laws, a young scientist who was living
at the park doing research on elephants. He has since left but
he was intelligent, well-trained, extremely good-looking and
he had ample material to work with. The Tsavos, east and
west, cover 8034 square miles and are bordered with 4000
more square miles of empty bushland. It is estimated that

the whole area is the habitat of 20,000 elephants, the largest concentration in the world.

Dr. Laws told us they usually begin mating at the age of twelve but with diminishing territory and its attendant change of habitat affecting their nutrition and social habits they now do not breed until they are fourteen and sometimes eighteen and nineteen. The span of pregnancy is twenty-two months and the period of lactation another twenty-two, meaning they can breed once in about every four years. They are devising their own system of birth control.

This particular study he told us had just begun and they had enough money from a grant to continue for three years. In the small airy laboratory were jars full of elephant ovaries and spread out in neat formation on the ground 640 lower jaws awaited study. To the envy of their human brethren, elephants grow six sets of teeth in a lifetime. Some population control is practised by the wardens, but men who pass their lives in the game reserves are as a rule reluctant to take any drastic measures. Nature herself maintains a balance. This does not mean that habitats do not change, but when they do it is with rhythm and meaning.

Elephants smash and tear up trees but this sometimes works to the advantage of the rhinos who are able to get at leaves and branches otherwise inaccessible to them. In his magnificently illustrated and fascinating book, *Africa*, Mr. Leslie Brown, formerly the chief agriculturist of Kenya, describes the recurrent cycle of the land. "The trees smashed and broken by elephants lie on the ground; their canopy of leaves no longer shades the grass; their roots which could have sucked up all the moisture of the early rains, are twisted or point forlornly at the sky. The grass now has its chance. It germinates in the torn up soil and it grows dense and thick. After a year or two what was once dense bush is covered with a mass of broken branches, stumps and long dry grass. Then fire comes and consumes all . . . The converse pattern now begins; grazing animals come in after the fire and eat the grass. Over the years they suppress the grass so that what remains will not carry a raging fire; seedling trees are thus enabled to survive, and their thorns protect them from animals with sensitive muzzles. Little by little, as once again the grass is kept down by grazing or through shading by trees, the trees regain their ascendancy. The cycle may take many years to reach a stage when a good stand of elephant fodder is once again available."

One concludes that the lesson to be learned is, let nature alone, the lady knows what she is about. She has been going to school through eons upon eons of time. Furthermore she has a very well thought-out and tidy arrangement for the grazing animals of the plains. As Mr. Brown explains it, "Zebras, wildebeest and hartebeest all tend to eat grass at a slightly different stage of growth. Their effect on the grasslands is complementary rather than competitive . . . No species of animal subjects the grass to very heavy use . . . an effect that cannot be duplicated by domestic stock."

Reverting to the elephants, Mr. Brown says that they are great well diggers especially in "sand filled water courses where behind rock bars or similar obstructions, water collects in the sand. Here the elephants use their feet to dig a series of holes; these soon fill up with water . . . when they [the elephants] have gone other creatures from the rhino to myriads of small birds, benefit from the elephants' spade work."

When we asked Dr. Laws if hunters would ever be allowed in the reserves to shoot surplus elephants at those times when the wardens or scientists felt there was no alternative but to diminish their numbers he looked surprised. "Why no," he said, "one can't trust a hunter with a job like that. It's got to be an absolutely sure thing. A hunter might wound an animal who would start a stampede and send whole herds into panic, alarming the entire population. A special company does it and they get paid so much per head. They used to have four guns now they use only two."

Their marksmanship, we gathered, was swift and sure and an entire group can be exterminated in a matter of minutes. Shot directly through the brain or heart an elephant dies in a minute to a minute and a half, infinitely better than having them die slowly of starvation or be killed with insensate cruelty by poachers.

When matters are left to nature the male as a rule dies before the female just as in the human species so it can't be only the tension of life in modern civilization that kills off the fellows.

Many European game wardens doubt the Africans interest in their country's fabulous and unique wealth. They will spend a lot of money advertising and trying to drum up tourism and then kill the goose that lays the golden egg by neglecting the game itself. It was to counteract this kind of thinking that John Owen worked so hard to get the Tanzanian wildlife people to the United States and so far his vision and determination have had an admirable effect in that country. It is to be hoped that Kenya and Uganda can do as much.

While we were with David Sheldrick in the morning the weather was sunny and pleasant and in the afternoon truly glorious. Leaving camp shortly after three we dropped Digby and Norton off at Waressa Rock, a bare stone platform with a great view where they are planning to build a hotel for tourists.

When we were there fortunately, to our way of thinking, they had not started but I understand work is now complete and that they have made a good job of it.

The men wanted to experiment further with the temperamental Questar so Caroline, Samwell and I, with Jane at the wheel, took off on our own.

Almost immediately we met up with a mother, father and baby elephant grazing very near the road. Jane stopped while I tried to photograph them but they wanted none of it and came for us trunks upraised, according to Digby the nonthreatening posture, but even the baby looked so irate that we lit out of there and for a minute or so they thundered down the road after us.

We passed a heard of ten giraffe floating over the ground

and Samwell spotted a mother lioness and two cubs. Our destination was Mudanda Rock, an extraordinary high outcropping, a kind of long ridge of stone and rock from which one has a marvelous view over the plains and a nearby waterhole.

As we watched a herd of oryx wandered up and a rhino came to drink and bathe. He was mucking about in the mud on the edge of the pool minding his own business when along came a young elephant. He shooed the oryx away, thoroughly disturbed the rhino and waded into the pool where he proceeded with a long leisurely bath. When he submerged entirely Samwell turned to Caroline and asked her in Swahili if he was dead. She said she thought not and in a few moments he surfaced, seconds later to take a nose dive, rump in air, tail wagging like a semaphore. Regaining his balance he gave a great snort and ears flapping, trunk at the ready attacked two large stones sticking up out of the water. Having cowed them he approached and rubbed his backside back and forth against them. All in all a blissful afternoon.

Just as it was time for us to leave a big herd slowly approached the pond. We wanted to stay and watch them but it was getting late and we had promised our lads we would not desert them for too long. Comparing notes we found our matinee had been a good deal more entertaining than theirs. They had seen almost no game and the wind blew the Questar about so much there was little point in shooting. Although I take my life in my hands when I say it, to my way of thinking that Questar is a fraud. For photographic purposes. Used as a telescope to watch the moon it is marvelous but if you want to use it for its primary purpose you're in trouble. It is almost impossible to set up a firm-enough foundation to keep it from swaying if there is any breeze at all and if there is a dead calm and bright sun the lens is so powerful that what results is mostly shimmering heat waves. Its owner looks at me coldly when I say as much but I don't care. I still think tenderly of the box Brownie of my youth.

Early the next morning, for the first time we watched the

boys breaking camp, a task they performed with efficiency and amazing speed. I turned to look at the light on the trunk of a tamarind tree and when I turned back our tent was down!

On these occasions Digby was at his most impressive, striding about in khaki shorts, sleeveless bush jacket, and a black turtle-neck sweater, his one concession to the bitter chill of early morning. Sometimes he would oversee the activities electric razor in hand, thus killing two birds with one stone. Tall, lean, erect, hands on hips or locked behind his back, he looked like Don Quixote. Rex Harrison could play him to perfection.

Jane too was wonderfully efficient, checking with the boys to make sure that everything was in its proper chest, nothing forgotten. Watching her that morning Caroline observed with a small hoot of laughter that someone had said her mother was beautiful. "One's own Mum beautiful, what an idea!" She is though. Hers is not an obvious beauty, it does not overwhelm you on impact, although the line of her throat is lovely, the planes of her face skillfully arranged, yet her real grace derives from her courteous, gentle, and affectionate manner. She is one of the most courteous women I have ever known and to her own family as well as to friends and acquaintances. She is no milksop, however, and her devotion to her husband, the way she frequently defers to his wishes, does not prevent her from appraising him with quiet humor.

The courteous beauty having seen everything stowed to her satisfaction and Bwana having given the signal we set off in the Toyota for the Kenya-Tanzanian border and our destination for the night, Momella Lodge, near the Ngurdoto National Park. It had been decided that we would stay at that lodge and the one at Ngorongoro because the two craters were to be one night stands and it would be impossible for the boys to cover the distance in the lorry and set up and break camp as well.

As we approached the border we came upon an open air market, one of those colorful spirited African markets that somehow always have an air of fiesta about them. It is due largely to the women who wear hues as bright as their native birds. They were shabby but gay in hot orange, incandescent red, electric pink, glittering peacock blue and vivid tangerine. There were wasp stripes of black and yellow and dazzling floral patterns. Striding with queenly carriage they bore on their heads baskets, logs, and bundles of grass.

While it was a beautiful day, the sky high and clean, the vicinity of Mount Kilimanjaro, was cloud-enshrouded. The spectacle sent the Browns' spirits plummeting as low as the mountain was high. Were we *never* to see a great peak? Our thoughts once again turned sourly to Vesuvius and Fujiyama. We were about to pull out our swords and commit hari-kari when Jane, turning in the front seat of the Toyota and glancing backward cried, "Look!" We looked. In that moment the clouds had parted and there it was, the great broad snowy crest glistening against the clear blue sky. We gave a shout of triumph and Norton swung his big lens into focus.

The sight illumined the rest of our journey across an immense plain and down a fine road that divided an undulating sea of grass.

At the gate of Ngurdoto National Park we got out and while Digby was paying the entrance fee we bought little pins, or badges at five bob apiece. Within a circle of green and gold enamel an impala leaps over a thorn tree. He is the emblem of the Tanzanian parks and the money he brings in goes toward their maintenance.

Passing through the gate we drove along a ridge through a luxuriant rain forest guided part way by a very large giraffe who moved ahead of us with measured pace occasionally tossing us a disdainful backward glance. Reaching his own destination, he left the road and we proceeded as best we could on our own.

We were headed for Buffalo Point where, the ranger at the gate had told us, we would have a memorable view. Jane's sharp eyes caught sight of a narrow path off to our left with a little sign saying RHINO CREST. It looked tempting so Digby stopped the car and we got out. The path wound upward fairly steeply but after walking for two or three minutes we emerged from jungle growth onto a small open plateau to gaze upon a sight at once pastoral and sublime.

We were on the rim of a small crater. Down on the floor to our left was a wood of soft feathery trees and shadowed glades. A carpet of tender green bathed in the glow of the late afternoon sunlight, jeweled with pools of blue water stretched to the crater walls. Animals grazed peacefully. Herds of buffalo lay quiet as velvet-covered rocks and near them three white storks stood immobile like ibis on an Egyptian tomb while elephants drank from the pools occasionally raising their trunks and spraying themselves. Above the far rim of the crater Kilimanjaro, glistening, majestic, remote, its base enveloped in rosy clouds, hung in the evening sky.

This dreamlike spectacle was enhanced by silence rippled only by distant bird calls and the soft stirring of leaves. The traveler may absorb the crater with a full heart and an over-whelming sense of nostalgia but he may not enter. No road goes there. No path leads back to lost innocence. It is Eden newly minted, the garden before Adam and before woe be-fell the world.

As the light faded the spell dissipated and we drifted away almost as silently as mist, back to the landcruiser and down to the disenchanted world and Momella Lodge.

Momella Lodge, while not an abode in Eden, was by no means unpleasant. The altitude was lofty, 5000 feet, and the thatched rondavels were clean and freshly whitewashed. If they could manage small fireplaces or open stoves one could not ask to be more snug and comfortable.

As we were waiting near the front office for someone to appear to show us to our rooms a minibus with five Germans drove up. Der Führer leaped out, clicked his heels and, all but saluting Digby, demanded their accommodations for the night. The temptation to ask for payment in advance and send them off to distant non-existent rondavels was strong but just then the management appeared so we settled instead for drinks, a reasonably good dinner, and early bed.

Spoiled by our life in camp we resented the few Germans yet we were fortunate to be there when we were. Momella has seventy-five beds and they told us that in season they were booked solid by package tours for the next two years.

The time has gone by when, among the other delights of travel, one might anticipate privacy, although in Africa on a camping safari even in season considerable sequestration is still possible for those who desire it.

The crowing cock brought up the daylight if not the sun for the morning was overcast and rainy with dark clouds shredding over the mountains and Kilimanjaro obliterated.

As we were dressing a tame ginger colored reed buck came to our door extending his patent-leather nose to nibble greedily on the crackers we offered him. Reed buck are enchanting creatures but their little pointed horns are capable of nasty digs if they are frightened or angry.

After breakfast we set out to visit Big and Small Momella Lakes, meeting on the way an ebullient, curly-haired gentleman named Vesy Fitzgerald, the scientific officer of Ngurdoto Park. We stopped our cars and he leaned out to talk with enthusiasm of his projected lodge and campsites. Under his management and John Owen's direction, Tanzania is opening a new park, Mount Meru Crater. It covers about twenty square miles of the western slope of the mountain and abounds in waterfalls and streams. The plan is to merge it with Ngurdoto and Momella. It will make an enormous, beautiful and varied reserve and will probably be known as Arusha National Park. According to Mr. Fitzgerald, elephant, buffalo, rhino, and small game are plentiful and he added "it's the best place to see Colobus monkeys." They are the black and white chaps with long shining fur. The Fitzgerald enthusiasm was contagious. Digby caught it and began planning a return trip for purposes of reconnoitering campsites. While peering into their crystal ball the directors have spotted what they consider to be a superb location for a hotel at 6000 feet, from which the view will be another of Africa's triumphs.

Momella's lakes are handsome and under gray skies, surrounded by coarse dark green growth the countryside was reminiscent of Scotland. We saw a pair of tiny dik-diks—I doubt that anybody has ever seen a solitary one—and the little deer—they are scarcely larger than hares—seemed tamer than usual but a dik-dik's tameness does not mean you can gather it up in your lap. They leap across the road and disappear into the bush while you blink.

Leaving the park we drove through a dense rain forest beautiful and eerie in the gray light but the sun broke through as we reached Arusha at lunchtime where we cashed some checks. Tanzania will accept Kenyan and other currency but since they have nationalized their banks their own money is not popular beyond their borders so the prudent traveler draws no more than he is likely to use locally.

We lunched and very well at the Arusha Hotel which by now may be comfortable and handsome but was a mess when we were there for the very reason that comfort and handsomeness was their goal. That day the whole place was ripped up and torn apart in the process of remodeling.

The manager, Mr. Tony O'Brien, was a friend of the Tatham-Warters, an Irishman with the legendary Irish charm who had taken on the hotel partly as a lark and partly because of need. A true soldier of fortune, he was currently somewhat down on his luck but witty, strikingly handsome and with a gleam in his eye. He is a married man with a family and while they may sometimes be distressed by his light-hearted antics I should imagine they can rarely be bored.

Our teatime destination was the Lake Manyara Hotel, high on a ridge with a sweeping view of Lake Manyara and the thousands upon thousands of acres of Masai Land. It had been enlarged since our last visit, a whole new wing, but the fine swimming pool was an old friend as was the telescope through which one views the plain below. For the first time we saw a tree called the Bombox, an extraordinary affair, its green peeled trunk and limbs covered with shell-like protuberances. At that season it was bare but Jane said that when in bloom it was loaded with the most magnificent purple flowers.

She and Digby had suggested that we stay there overnight but as we were headed for the Ngorongoro Crater which was no great distance away we said we would like to go on in line with my philosophy of not packing and unpacking any more than is inescapable when traveling. Would it not be all right? "Yes, fine," said Jane with her unfailing courtesy but I sensed a lack of enthusiasm. However, no valid objection being offered, we went on our way, driving finally through the well-remembered gate with its little lodge where one pays the entrance fee and along the ridge with the rain forest dropping away on one side and the crater on the other. The Toyota nosed around a curve and there, on our right, sitting behind a low bush no more than ten feet away was a large lion.

"I say!" murmured Digby. He stopped the car, lowered the window and we looked upon our treat and bade him good evening. His silent reply was, I am sure, courteous and in a few moments he got up and ambled off. Caroline was shaken. For her the safari was not unmitigated joy. She liked camping and being with her parents but despite having been born and brought up in Africa, animals on the loose frightened her. The call of the wild was one thing, that of wild game quite another and she was happier in camp when her mother accompanied her to the shower and toilet tents.

We passed the grave of Michel Grzimek, the young man who lost his life in 1959 when his small plane crashed into the crater. A vulture had become tangled in the struts while he was on a game count with his father, the distinguished director of the Frankfort Zoo and author of many books on animals.

Like the Lake Manyara Hotel the lodge too was much enlarged since the last time we had stayed there. It had many more cottages and was now run by a young American named

Levitt. The cottage to which we were assigned was larger than the one we had been in before. It had a welcome open fireplace, which we had also had, but this time the bricks were painted red with white lines—an unnecessary labor in my opinion. What's the matter with plain bricks? We were also promoted to indoor plumbing which we had not had before and which, oddly enough, detracted from the general charm. The reason, I think, was that although we had to traverse some fifty yards to get there, the view from our original basic privy had been superb and this one opened on to the blank wall of the adjacent cottage. Norton and I looked at each other and with the same thought in mind: beware the sentimental journey. In honesty he had not been as eager to return as I had.

Our mild disillusion was transitory and as Jane reminded us this was our special evening: Digby's birthday, the moment to crack the champagne. In view of so gala an occasion I washed my own hair, an enterprise I do not normally undertake since I am not skilled in setting it but it had reached the state hair frequently does in Africa. A clean noggin seemed the least I could offer a birthday boy.

Champagne we had. Presents presented a problem. The doctor, a gadget king, came up with something rather handsome: a traveling kit of tools which although diminutive in size were entirely functional. Rooting about in my office— a briefcase with working materials, travel brochures and the like—I produced a Clippit, that encased curved claw invaluable for cutting columns from newspapers and magazines. Gifts, though humble, did exist. Second step: wrappings. What we devised was a far cry from the mouth-watering papers and ribbons and ornaments with which shops at Christmas time so shrewdly and so expensively enhance the merchandise but in the bush you make do. Kleenex tied with bright wool from my needlepoint was what the major had to settle for.

All the same our evening was merry and reminded me of that scene in *The Diary of Anne Frank* when, trapped in their Amsterdam attic, hiding from the Nazis, Anne and her family and friends with makeshift presents high-heartedly celebrate the Feast of Hanukkah.

Later that night after we had gone to bed I wrote in my diary and fell asleep breathing the delicious fragrance of the wood fire as the embers slowly winked out.

When tea arrived, in what seemed minutes later, our watches said 7:30 so we assumed it was morning, but the fog was so dense the whole world was shrouded in a gray blanket. At breakfast, as we were debating whether or not to venture down into the crater, we were encouraged by an American woman who said to us, "Never mind the fog, it was like this yesterday morning too but it's beautiful down there. You folks go ahead."

To our regret we were obliged to go without Jane but she was miserable with a bad back and it seemed wiser for her to stay in bed with a hot water bottle and Caroline to nurse her.

A new road for descending into the crater has now been opened up and when we reached the floor about 2000 feet down it was as beautiful as we had remembered it. The clouds were high, not nearly so enveloping as they had been on the rim but the sky was still overcast and it was nearly two hours later before the sun burst through.

The game was chiefly wildebeest and Tommies and the lordly waterbuck, every sheik surrounded by the seven or eight damsels of his harem. We had a fine close-up view of a rhino but the animals were far flung for not only was the lake full, there was water everywhere. Yet surprisingly the ground was not marshy but firm under our wheels. That is not to say it was not treacherous. Digby drove cautiously to avoid pot-holes completely obscured by the high grass and indeed it was not long before we caught sight of a motion-less Land-Rover angled at that unmistakable tilt that denotes one wheel sunk deep in the earth.

Rather than risk the same fate we got out of our Toyota and walked over to see what was the trouble. The stranded people were a German couple and their African driver, and his short jack, the only tool he possessed, was of course useless under the circumstances. One would think that by now those living there would realize that in the bush a long jack is indispensable. Even that doesn't always do the trick but it is a step in the right direction.

Like ourselves in the Nairobi National Park the strandees had already been there some little time and had no idea as to how or when they would get out. Sizing up the situation Digby went back and fetched the Toyota and progressing gingerly, jockeyed into position. He and Samwell were able to attach a tow rope and with one good jerk pulled the Land-Rover free.

In return they told us where to look for a lioness and four cubs and later on we saw them but they were high on a rocky ledge and we decided not to push our luck. Three fine elephants were more conveniently located for easy viewing and we came upon a great troop of baboons chattering wildly as they leaped across the track and swung up into the branches or settled momentarily, scratching, on fallen tree trunks. We estimated that there were about 125 of them and Digby said he had never seen so large a troupe. We tried for pictures but were not too successful for they were nimble and shy and leaped away as we approached.

Norton and I had begun to think ourselves rather professional at naming various breeds of game. Hartebeest or congoni, which are the same, we never failed to recognize. Digby indulged our fatuity until he had had enough then he snaked in for the kill. "Hartebeest, yes, but can you tell Coke's from Jackson's?" We could not and hung our heads in shame. "Jackson's are darker, the horns are set more erect on the head. The horns of Coke come forward a little."

"Thank you, Digby."

When it came time to leave we drove back up to the lodge over the old road. Originally, when it was the only one, there were up hours and down hours strictly observed since for two vehicles to pass each other is out of the question. Now the situation has eased but they have not thrown

caution to the winds. As you reach the road a sign says:
UP ONLY. WATCH FOR DOWNCOMING CARS.

It is a good road though one must travel six or seven hundred yards of what Digby called "the dicey bit." There the grass along the outer edge is thin and one is aware of the steep drop to the crater floor. The rest of the way a ridge of earth and coarse grass and brush hide the facts of life and death and give one a sense of security. It is perhaps illusionary but it serves. People who live there and negotiate the road frequently think nothing of it and even tourists quickly become acclimated. The thing to bear in mind is, Easy does it.

It occurred to me later that possibly it was that stretch that worried Jane and we would certainly have understood if it had been the case and she had said so. Quite possibly of course it was not. When, just before we went in to see her, I said to Norton that I hoped we would find her better. He smiled. "Now that we're about to leave the crater I anticipate a miraculous cure." And in effect she was much better although the misery was genuine enough. We never learned why but Ngorongoro was her Kilifi and she wanted no part of it.

Shortly after leaving the lodge we stopped for a picnic luncheon on the ridge. It was a bit windy but warm and sunny and as we sat munching our sandwiches and looking down into the vast and fertile bowl Digby told us that before World War I the entire crater had been owned by a German. He sought to exterminate the game and hired Masai to help him drive them out but always they came back to that safe rich territory and after the allies won the war it was the German who was driven away by the British and ever since then it has been the beasts paradise. Nineteen different kinds of animals are listed and the list is not exhaustive.

We had seen only the aloof lion family on the rocks but we were looking forward to the famed prides of the Serengeti. The plain lies eighty-five miles from the Crater at an altitude of 5300 feet and as we entered it we passed under a glorious rainbow. Norton and I had been there before but crossing it this time was a phenomenal experience.

The term, migration of the herds, may be interpreted in various ways and directors and wardens of the game reserves are apt to grow a bit testy when amateurs try to pin them down as to when is prime time for the spectacle and just what is it anyway?

John Owen had mentioned but not defined it.

My own feeling is that what the traveler hoping to witness it usually has in mind is a never-ending column of animals moving, perhaps rapidly, perhaps slowly, hour after hour in one direction, preferably through a narrow defile, en route from one area to another in search of new grazing grounds and water. What we ourselves saw as we crossed the Serengeti was a migration on a scale vaster than anything we had ever dreamed of. Yet, since the animals were not herded together in a column, the purist might consider that it was a gathering preparatory to migrating rather than the migration proper. No matter what you called it it was a unique and unforgettable spectacle.

For ten miles we traveled through thousands upon thousands of wildebeest, gazelle, and zebra. We learned later that by aerial count they estimated the wildebeest population at approximately 380,000, the zebra at 200,000 and they would shortly be numbering the gazelle.

Some wildebeest stood quietly grazing, others were bucking, frolicking and kicking up their heels or they would set off at full tilt for no reason at all, their bodies seeming with awkward fluid grace to be moving in two directions at once, forequarters racing straight ahead, rear ends following at right angles. They are a dark frosted silver with silky beards reaching from chin to chest, with heavy bodies and slim fragile appearing legs that gallop at incredible speed.

As far as the eye could see they covered the plain in a thick pattern and on the far horizon what we at first took to be trees turned into an encircling frieze of wildebeest against the sky. We progressed slowly and from time to time Digby would stop the engine and a great symphony of grunting snorting and mooing sounds filled the air.

We drove through the Naabi Hill gate and on for another thirty miles to Seronera Lodge. This too had been enlarged and I suppose I should say improved since we were there. They now have an outdoor bar with slate table tops set on piles of stone. Keeps the primitive atmosphere. Where we had dined in a one room shack a big circus tent now served as mess hall. The commissary department was run by a cockney woman who complained bitterly of the cost. "The eyes in our 'eads for this 'ere tent, the eyes in our bloody 'eads."

Not far away, on an outcropping of rock the directors are planning to build a hotel. Digby had seen the plans in John Owen's office when we were in Arusha and pronounced them "jolly nice." John had not been there when we passed through and we were sadly disappointed to learn that he would not be back in the Serengeti before we left. We had been counting on meeting him and had been happily looking forward to seeing him wandering free in his natural habitat but he was off on one of his periodic money raising tours in the United States in order that the habitat might be maintained.

For those who care about wildlife, it is heartening to realize that many others care too and obviously, if they are to survive, the parks must have money and money only comes from people. But people mean lodges and hotels and buses and package tours, all that lovers of wildlife and wilderness wish to avoid. It is an ironic business and one to which I am afraid there is no solution although a safari under canvas comes close. Also, John Owen estimates that since they would not all be there at the same time the Serengeti's 5600 square miles could accommodate 50,000 visitors yearly and still maintain its wild uncluttered beauty and operate comfortingly in the black.

Our camp was a short drive beyond the group of bandas, the dining tent and little general store that comprises Seronera and the location was even more appealing than that of Tsavo; the three tents had been set under thorn trees and we had an open view of the plain.

Around teatime Terry Matthews drove up to say hello. He was a friend of the Tatham-Warters, also a safari host-guide and Norton and I had met him at Samburu in 1964. Terry is a young chap, but with a lot of experience behind him. He has worked for Kerr and Downy and he was squiring a couple from California, the Londons, around the reserves. When Mrs. London was in movies her name was Jane Greer and we had known each other slightly the way people do who are in the same profession.

Terry said they had had marvelous luck with lions—they had seen many prides and many mating couples too, and he told us where he thought we would be most likely to come upon them. I would have been happy to start off then and there but for once Digby and Norton were in automotive accord; neither wanted any further jouncing over rough terrain for that day at least.

That night we had chicken for dinner and I was charmed to learn that the Swahili word for it is *coocoo*. Later, after the others had gone to get ready for bed I sat alone by the dying fire looking at the stars and listening to the camp settling down for the night. Sounds of tooth brushing and final forays to the toilet tents. After a bit Digby came and asked me if I minded if he unplugged the light. When I said of course not he detached it from the battery and went back into his and Jane's tent and moments later their lamp went out. Norton turned ours down too and with the exception of the flickering flame of the two lanterns set on the ground in front of the tents and the glow of the fire I was in darkness. Presently the gentlest of snores drifted across the grass and from the African's tent came voices and soft laughter. That too ceased and there was no sound other than the hissing of the fire, a log crumbling and the call of a distant night bird. I looked up through the lacy branches of the acacias to

the stars and the drifting clouds and sat for a long time
utterly at peace.

On a first visit to the game reserves—on subsequent ones as
well—the traveler tends to assume he must hurry immediately
to places where certain animals have been reported or otherwise he will not see them as they will have moved away. The
experienced bush dweller on the other hand assumes that
having staked out an area a pride of lions or a herd of elephants is going to stick around for a while. Usually the assumption works but it is not infallible.

A day slipped by before we went to the places where Terry
Matthews and the Londons had had such good luck and although we saw lions we did not see masses of them. Massed
lions I flourish on.

Our day in camp was one of relaxation. Jane organized a
delicious curry luncheon and spent most of the afternoon
engrossed, apparently, in *Fresh from the Laundry,* my book
about our trip through the Communist countries of Eastern
Europe. It had been recently published and I had given her
a copy. Seeing her reading, it occurred to me that the Browns
upon the printed page, and day and night in person as well,
might become a bit thick, but if she felt that way she was
too polite to say so.

In the afternoon, at her request, we left her in the Balkans
and Digby, Norton, Samwell, and I set out to scout leopards.
Despite some clouds the light of late afternoon was luminous
and we rode along peering up into the branches of the
thorn trees where leopards are likely to lie but all we saw
for our efforts were a couple of buzzards and two giraffes.
We also got stuck. Following a rough track we came to a
bad muddy wallow but Digby the Dauntless feeling that to
skirt around it by driving over the hard grass along the sides
would be a milksop refusal of a challenge stepped on the gas,
we rushed it at high speed and *plop!* Over the hubcaps,
bogged for fair. For an hour the three men struggled and
heaved and pushed and when we finally worked free they were

so plastered with mud as to be unrecognizable. As Digby settled himself behind the wheel for another go at it, Norton said, "Take it slowly, don't spin your wheels." The major exploded. I didn't blame him. The voice of reason can be very trying.

A deluge, but only of shower baths, engulfed us that night and the next morning the sun rose in glory, with the thorn trees silhouetted against a streak of gold between the earth and a gray cloud bank flushed with pink on its underside. By the time we left camp the day was bright but a transparent wafer of moon still hung in the sky.

We stopped off at Seronera where Digby transacted some business and Norton attempted to persuade him of the advantages of oil in the engine of the Toyota. As I have said Digby is a cavalryman and his understanding of and patience with horses is notable but he harbors a personal animosity toward the requirements of machinery, and the feeding and care of automobiles does not rivet his interest. Before marrying Dr. Brown my own attitude was similar. They're machines, aren't they? Let them machinate. I have since learned differently.

To humor Norton, Digby did have them check the oil which was a good idea and while waiting for our little mechanical friend to be nourished we visited Seronera's one-room museum and in the butterfly collection saw a specimen that looked exactly like a cosmos flower. Its name was Colotis Puniceus. I don't know why the scientific names for plants, insects, and birds always have to sound like diseases.

That day we were lucky and the Serengeti lived up to its claim of supporting a great variety of game. We saw topi, silver-backed jackal, warthogs, ostriches, congoni, the spice-colored elands, large, handsome and very shy and thousands of little Tommies. The wydah bird with a tail like a ragged black pennant flew across our sight lines and greater and lesser bustards lumbered about. They appear to be cumbersome creatures but they are capable of great speed both in running and flying.

Crossing the Serengeti plain is like crossing the sea only the element is grass instead of water and the islands are out-croppings of rocks, the kopjies. Animals gravitate to the *kopjies* for they provide shelter and protection and the opportunity for limitless clambering about. Baboons play in them and lions are attracted to them. Perched on a high perpendicular stone like Saint Simeon Stylites on his pillar we even saw a leopard but as we drove near him he flowed down and disappeared. We were however rewarded by a pair of lions, a honeymooning couple, who obligingly posed for their portraits.

Passing great herds of zebra we marveled anew at the way they will graze quietly within a few yards of a lion when they know that he has recently fed and has no interest in them. As we ate our picnic lunch under a tree we watched them, some 200,000 of them, and gazed off to a horizon crenelated by wildebeest.

Since we were not too far away Digby suggested Lake Lagarja. Its special charm is its inhabitants; thousands upon thousands of flamingos strewn over its surface like blown pink blossoms. They float on the water or, on the sandy shore, step delicately on their coral pink legs. From time to time impelled by what we did not know, they would rise, soar, wheel and resettle creating a fascinating spectacle of rhythm and color.

Returning from the lake we came, to our joy, upon a pride of lions; a male with five or six females. One of the damsels he was courting but she appeared indifferent to his advances. After a bit she raised her head and gave him a gentle love bite then, as he became importunate, one not so gentle. Digby drove very near and we tried hard for movies but were foiled by a sudden downpour. The lions seemed completely indifferent to it except that now and again the male shook his great mane and a shower of silver sparkled against the pelting rain.

In this instance, with better fish to fry, the lions paid us little heed but sometimes as we neared them in the Toyota they would look at us with antagonism, rise and amble away. For a long time they have been curiously indifferent to motor vehicles. Presumably the attendant smell kills the smell of humans and also, in the reserves, they have never been hurt by a car or any one in it. But science has got to work.

Scientists dart the animals to tranquilize and immobilize them for brief periods in order to tag them for research purposes. The lions recover quickly and are none the worse for their experience but in one ear a darted lion sports a rakish plastic clip with little fluttering streamers. Visitors are asked to keep track of the colors of the tags and to which ear they were attached and to hand in their notes at the lodge. It helps the scientists in categorizing the number of animals and their movements and is, basically, probably a sound idea but there seems something a little ludicrous in a wild lion with a plastic-tipped ear. And the reason they now tend to wander away from Land-Rovers is because that's where that sharp momentary sting in the haunch comes from. Later, in New York, John Owen told me they didn't feel a thing but how does he know? They're sentient creatures and we all feel a hypodermic in the behind to a lesser or greater degree.

Mr. Owen works more closely with the Serengeti scientists than do some of the other park directors but his cooperation can make them uneasy for he will say things like, "You are the scientists. I trust you implicitly. Whatever *you* say we will do." The uneasiness comes from the silent implication "and the results, whatever they may be, are *your* responsibility."

Miles Turner, the senior warden of the Serengeti, and his wife, Kay, joined us for drinks before dinner. Mr. Turner is not all that seduced by the Intellects now infiltrating the reserves and he muttered with some asperity, "If they could speak Swahili they'd *run* the bloody parks."

In any culture the battle of science versus experience is likely to be brisk.

Another day we tried for Lake Magadi but the track was overgrown and muddy to such an extent that any progress was impossible so turning back we followed the course of the

Titushi River. Because of the grass we could not see the water but the trees along the banks were lovely in shape and color and Digby was sure that *there* we would sight leopards. Having seen splendid ones at Secret Valley we were not overly enthused but he had not been with us there and was leopard hungry.

We kept peering up into the thorn and fig trees where they might be slung and the car, with difficulty, kept inching forward. This time we weren't worried about being stuck in the mud but we had a good chance of being trapped and bound into a huge bundle by the high coarse grass. We were also worried by Digby who kept hopping out of the Toyota to reconnoiter. He strode about pipe in mouth, hands on hips, bush jacket flapping, *determined* to spot a leopard. The trouble was, in that grass had he stumbled upon one asleep the ensuing encounter could have been, in his word, dicy.

Jane was unhappy too. She kept calling out to him "Darling, really don't you think . . ." and her voice would trail off. "Darling, never mind. It doesn't *matter* if we don't . . ."

But Digby won. A leopard did emerge from the impenetrable growth and strolled casually across the track not ten yards away from him. For a few moments after he disappeared into the grass on the other side we could see the tip of his twitching tail. Then it vanished. We waited hoping he would climb a tree but he was obviously heading for the river.

The next time Jane spoke there was a distinct chill in the air. "Digby get *back* into the car." Bwana meekly complied and with difficulty we worked our way free of the entangling grass.

As we turned into Seronera we passed a hyrax family sunning themselves on an enormous rock. They are sweet creatures, hyrax, fat and furry with black eyes and black noses and bright inquisitive little faces. The smaller of the two babies, endeavoring to scratch himself, lost his balance and turned a complete somersault to his astonishment and our delight.

One of the Seronera boys came running out to say that Miss Drews of the Express Transport Company, the affiliate of the American Express in Nairobi, had been trying to reach us so Norton put in a call on the radio telephone and in twenty minutes had his connection. He was in his element. The one-way conversation took him right back to his Navy days in the war—all that business of "Over" and "Hear you loud and clear." I expected a "Roger" at any moment, but he refrained. However he got her message that New York had cabled strongly advising against our going to the Middle East and he was able to assure her that news of the impending unpleasantness was percolating into the bush and that we would change our itinerary on reaching Athens.

Returning to camp we were charmed to see that seven giraffes had taken up residence quite near us. They stared at us inquisitively, intrigued by the odd shapes that were our tents and equipment. Giraffes cooperate on safari for they rub their heads together and twist and cross their necks in obligingly photogenic fashion.

Although the plain was bathed in voluptuous light our afternoon drive netted us little beyond four topi and four zebras. They looked lonely in that vast expanse of grass but they had two tables for bridge and seemed content.

The next morning was clear, cold, and very beautiful. We passed some of the kopjies we had explored previously and then suddenly there it was, a spectacle unique in our lives. Thousands upon thousands of wildebeest in a close-packed column streamed past us at full gallop leaping over one another's back in long drawn arcs as they piled up in crossing a narrow gully. The older animals dropped behind, exhausted babies struggled to keep up. Their panic had probably been sparked by the death of one of them, a kill made by two lions moments before we arrived.

Digby moved cautiously ahead but although they kept coming they split around the car, like water around stones and veered off, the momentum gradually diminishing as the column broke and separated. We drove over to the lions who lifted blood-stained muzzles from the carcass they were devouring and then went on with their breakfast.

That morning the animals were out by the thousands—gazelle, zebra, two large herds of eland and of course the wildebeest. Vibrating with life, the vast plain swept to the sky and on the horizon animals rimmed the world. We caught sight of a wind-swift cheetah and racing gazelle but this time there was no kill. The gazelle escaped and the cheetah vanished. Later we came upon a very large lioness moving away, sated, from her own wildebeest kill. As long as she was there vultures and a small jackal kept their distance but as she turned away, indifferent, they zeroed in. From the far corners of the sky the birds came planing down and in a moment they were fighting, hissing and tearing, their great wings flapping. The jackal was a pretty creature, pitiably thin and we were elated when he was able to snatch a piece of meat but the strong ugly scavengers tore it out of his mouth.

We drove on to Naabi Hill and seeing a fine big tree thought it would be pleasant to lunch in its shade but drawing nearer we saw it had been preempted by two demoiselles, two charming young lionesses who were lying in its branches, trying to escape the flies. They were playful, but a slight nip of her companion's foot elicited a growl from the nipee so we decided that since they were there first discretion was perhaps the best policy. We moved off to another tree for our picnic but as we were at the base of a rocky outcropping, a likely habitat for lions, Jane and I prudently closed the hatch and the windows leaving the door open on the plain side should it seem advisable to make a quick retreat into the car.

Since, when he had come to have a drink with us, Miles Turner had told us about a family of wild dogs we made a slight detour on the way home and sure enough there they were in the place he had said they would be. There were several adults and many babies who made noises between puppy barks and bird chirpings. For a mile around their colony no other animals were to be seen. Antelopes and zebras fear wild dogs more than lions for the dogs hunt in packs, leaping upon their prey when it is exhausted and tearing it apart while it still lives. Caroline said, "They are cunning. They arrange so that they take over from each other when one tires."

At twilight we drove back to camp and the scene that so quickly infiltrates the heart: the clean line of the tents and the lacy branches of the acacia trees dark against a pale green, glass-clear sky with Venus blazing low on the horizon. The boys had lighted a fire of long logs but it was still chilly so we dined in the mess tent and it was one of our best evenings, warm and companionable. Digby and Jane asked us which part of the trip we enjoyed the most and we told them all that was true safari: living in the tents, seeing wild game, and meeting the people who devoted their lives to its conservation and well being. For us it was a marvelous experience and one we long to repeat.

The next morning those same tents, so comfortable, so atmospheric, were dismantled by the boys as the clock struck six. It was moving day and Bwana had us really cracking. The scene changed with the rapidity of a revolving stage and when you consider that there was gear and equipment for eleven people the dispatch was impressive. It is the pride of every safari manager to leave his campsite in immaculate condition and as we pulled away in the Land Cruiser only a circle of white ash where the fire had been showed that we had ever passed that way. It was like the closing sentence of Kipling's short story "Without Benefit of Clergy": "So no man may say where this house stood."

Shortly after crossing the Tanzania-Kenya border we came to Keekorock Lodge, one of the best. The building, constructed of stone and wood is well-designed and it has a fine big swimming pool. There is also an airstrip and Digby had had fresh meat flown in so we were to dine sumptuously that night. We lunched at Keekorock and in order to give the boys time to set up camp we whiled away a couple of hours photographing the beguiling black-faced vervet monkeys

who live there, writing postcards and swimming in the pool.
We also observed deep scratches on the trunk of a tree very
near the house where a lion had come the night before to
sharpen his claws. The Lodge manager bewailed the defacing
of so fine a specimen, and it was rather the equivalent of a
mustache scribbled on the face of a pretty girl in a subway
poster. Yet although we sympathized, to cat lovers like
Norton and me, scratched bark was preferable to mauled
furniture. In our living room in New York we have a sofa, not
too strategically placed, because of the condition of the back,
attributable to a beautiful green-eyed creature, one Puss Cat
Brown.

When Digby estimated that the tents should be about
ready we set off for our new camp in the Sianna Hills, some
seven miles from the lodge, the dauntless Toyota making
its way through grass that came halfway up the windshield.
We followed as best we could in the wake of the heavy
lorry that had preceded us by a few hours. The grass, forced
down by its wheels, had sprung back again but a faint change
of color where it had been bruised, the play of light on the
angled blades, led us finally into camp. While still a fair distance off we were able to spot the tents set on a rise of land
sloping down to a stream.

The men were busy cutting grass with their pangas. We
all pitched in and in a short time we had created a small
open arena in which we could move about with comparative
ease.

Before dark we were settled in and as we dined and sat
around the fire afterward it occurred to me that there is some
similarity between a camping safari and a theatrical company
on tour. No matter how different the surroundings the stage
setting is always the same. Within that confined area everything is familiar; the actor is cosily at home and so is the
camper.

We stayed in the Sianna Hills camp for three nights and
left it on the third day wakening three times to a light that
was surely the morning light when the world was new and

dawn still a fresh wonder to itself and to the animals that shared it.

On our last full day we had a rewarding early game drive seeing several buffalo, six giraffes and countless impala and topi. We also spotted a rhino and almost overran her baby who was so small we were upon him before we were warned off by his irate parent.

Later on we decided to stay savoring the pleasures of camp while Digby and Jane went off to look for lions. That was one of their many compatible qualities. Although animals were an old story to them they too cared about them and did everything they could to locate and bring us into contact with them.

While they were gone Norton and I wrote letters, he caught up on his picture log and I took a shower. Thanks to Kabwi and his perpetual flame the water was always hot but the evenings, when we normally bathed, were chilly and to be able to revel in hot water *and* hot sunshine was luxury.

Jane and Digby returned lionless, nor indeed did we see any when we went out in the afternoon although the Mora is almost as famous for them as the Serengeti. Once again we were frustrated by the high lush grass. Happily we did see some lovely birds including the bare-faced go-away, so-named because his call seems to be saying "go away, go away." We saw the brown and black and white hoopoe, glittering superb starlings and the glorious bishop bird, a flash of vermilion and flame. A small yellow beauty with a black breast and buff back swayed on the branches as we drove by.

"It's called a long claw," said Jane. For some reason this did not set well with Bwana. "Why?" he demanded testily. "Its claws are no longer than any other bird's."

"I don't know why, dear, but that *is* its name." Low mutters and rumbles from behind the wheel.

At Keekorock for the first time we picked up an African ranger with a rifle and drove to the Mara River to look for rhino and hippos. Leaving the Toyota we made our way through trees and undergrowth down a fairly steep bank to a small sandy beach and a pool churned by rapids. We saw some hippos or, more accurately, their ears and the tops of their heads and secretly I was relieved to have the ranger with us as rhino tracks led to the water and I peered around uneasily hoping, if one was in the neighborhood, to spot him before he spotted me. We crossed the little beach and, following our African through a thick glade, came out above another pool. Here the water was placid and the deep silence was broken only by the huffing and snorting and splashing of four enormous contented hippos.

After we had dropped the ranger I asked what he would have done if we *had* come face to face with a rhino. Digby laughed, "Be the first one up a tree, I should imagine." But I'm not so sure and even if the sense of security was illusionary it was nice to have had it.

We drove across the plain to eat our picnic lunch on a high hill in a clean airy little shelter with a sanded floor that had been built and left there by a movie company on location.

Because the grass was usually up to the windshield the car radiator was chock ablock full of seed heads and weeds and steaming since no air could circulate. Driving up the hill Digby chose to demonstrate his theory, not shared by the rest of us, that the thing to do was to race the engine and proceed at the highest possible speed. "Cools it off," he explained. True enough, we did reach the crest without mishap but the poor Toyota was panting like Paul Revere's horse.

Returning to the lodge in the afternoon we came upon an enormous herd of buffalo strung out over the plain. Digby and Norton estimated between six and seven hundred. As we drew near every swinging black hulk turned to stare at us. It was curiously disconcerting to see that many dark faces topped by long curving horns waiting to see what we would do. Actually we did nothing but stop the car and sit and watch them. Reassured they continued grazing and shoving one another about and quite suddenly, on the periphery of the herd two of them copulated. It was a performance more remarkable for speed than technique, but Digby said that compared to the mating of lions it was rather prolonged. With lions apparently it is frequency rather than elapsed time that counts.

At Keekorock Dr. Brown was unexpectedly called upon to practice his profession. The manager, a pleasant Norwegian woman named Mrs. Ringberg, asked if he would see her daughter who was ailing. Her condition was not serious but her fiancé, a bearded English scientist named Dangerfield, accompanied us back to camp to get the medicine Norton prescribed and of which fortunately he had brought along a supply.

The young couple were to be married in Oslo in September but the prospective bridegroom was sad for he loved Africa and longed to live and work in the national parks but those jobs are being Africanized at a fairly rapid rate and the chances of a white foreigner getting employment were slender.

He stayed for tea which was served amidst a good deal of hilarity on the part of the camp boys for they were still amused by the unexpected intrepidity of their colleague Kabwi, the cook, who although he rather enjoyed safari life was made nervous by the proximity of wild game. He rarely strayed far from his fire yet spurred on and accompanied by Kenyua, the head boy and lorry driver, he had plucked up enough courage to walk a considerable distance through the tall grass where might be lurking God knew what to visit his mother who lived in the neighborhood. We thought him brave but to his chums the filial pilgrimage was a huge joke.

The next morning our dream ended. When we left camp it was for the last time. We had rehearsed our brief farewell taught us by the Tatham-Warters and as we drove away we shouted, *"Kwaheri, watu wote,"* which means "Good-by everybody," to the six men who had done so much to make our safari unforgettable and comfortable. They laughed with delight and raised both arms in salute and waved the

Polaroid pictures of themselves that Norton had taken and given to each of them.

Our road led through the Masai and Kykuyu reserves although one no longer calls them that since now the whole country belongs to the tribes. What the Kykuyu are doing to *their* territory is a grim business since they burn the trees for charcoal and to clear the land for corn. The watershed is being destroyed for they never reforestate and they leave the charred mutilated trunks piercing the sky or leaning crazily against one another. The landscape is indescribably sad and bleak.

A little farther on, in magical contrast to the devastation lay the beautifully cultivated farms of what used to be called the white highlands, the source of so much bitter controversy between the British and Africans, the latter claiming that the white man appropriated all of Kenya's best earth. This was largely true but the white man was skillful and hard-working and the farms paid off in money and beauty. The Africans are only very gradually learning the ways of agriculture and beginning to appreciate its rewards.

We ate our luncheon in the car overlooking the lush rolling land and then settled down to a grueling eight-hour drive over fearful roads.

We had enjoyed the Mara even though we were not there at the good time and friends who have gone later in the season tell us that the wild game was some of the best and most plentiful they saw.

The choice of where to start or end a safari is reasonably fluid, but I would think that the Mara should certainly be given priority in one's considerations. I also think that the way to arrive or leave is by plane. When we were there charter planes were easily available and had we known what we were in for we would certainly have engaged one. By the time this book appears in print there will probably be scheduled flights from Nairobi to the Keekorock Lodge strip. It is only about an hour by air and the cost is moderate. If doing it that way, one would either be picked up by the safari-mana-

ger at the lodge or one would bid him an affectionate farewell after having been able to spend an extra day in camp.

The next morning driving to Nairobi the two punctures we
had on the way were mitigated by the glory of the cape
chestnut trees laden with pink blossoms and the spacious
miracle that is the Rift Valley. Also, baskets have for me an
irresistible attraction and about twenty-five miles from the
city women sit weaving by the roadside tempting both tourists
and the locals who drive out on Sunday, with their colorful
and practical wares.

We arrived at the New Stanley about three o'clock and
after a late luncheon Jane and Digby left to put Caroline on
the train for Mombasa to go back to school and Norton and
I packed our safari gear which Digby had been kind enough
to say he would have shipped after us. When it was too late
we felt we should have left it in storage at the hotel since
we do not wear those clothes much at home and we are ever
desirous of returning to Africa.

In the evening the Tatham-Warters came back for a farewell drink. We had lived closely together for three weeks
and despite some difficulties and inevitable differences of
temperament we had grown very fond of them. They were the
agents through whom we had enjoyed a unique experience,
not the least pleasant part of which had been their own enthusiasm for wild game and their warmth of manner that
had made us feel comfortable and secure.

Other clients might be keener on the social aspects they
offer than we were, that is a matter of taste, and there is no
question that Olechugu Farm is delightful. And when on
safari proper it is hard to imagine that one could be in better
hands than with Jane and Digby.

We were sorry to see them leave and glad of the companionship of Ken Smith when he came to dine with us. He is
cautiously optimistic about the chances of wildlife in Africa
and was at that time working to get Amboseli saved from the
marauding herds of the Masai. He was hopeful of success
since it is a small reserve, two hundred square miles, and

immensely important to the economy in that part of Kenya because of the tourists it attracts.

Jomo Kenyatta, Kenya's president, is keenly appreciative of the money the wild game brings into the country and he knows the valuable services performed by the white safari managers. But Mr. Kenyatta is about seventy-eight years old. Inevitably what those interested in the preservation of wildlife both for itself and as an important source of their own livelihoods must ask is, what will be the policy of his successor?

Perhaps not in the immediate future but eventually the wardens and park directors will be Africans. There is no reason to think that eventually they will not be good ones if they have a sufficient period of apprenticeship and are convinced of the necessity of the animals and of their rights.

The same thing perhaps holds true for the safari business although there of course they need both experience and capital in order to establish themselves.

We spoke of some of these things and then Ken left when it was time for us to drive to the airport for our Alitalia flight to Athens.

We were no sooner airborne at 1 A.M. than an imposing array of drinks including champagne was set before us. There were small open-faced sandwiches of caviar and smoked salmon and other costly and exotic fare.

One may exult in wild game and savannas and the boundless skies but life's little amenities are pleasant too.

CLOTHES FOR SAFARI WEAR

Depending on the duration of your safari you may want more or fewer of the articles of clothing suggested but I believe this will act as a practical guide. The list is intended primarily for women but works for male equivalents just as well.

A hat with a brim that sticks to your head and will stand up to sun, wind, and rain.

A couple of scarves to wrap your hair in. The dust can be unbelievable.

2 pairs of long pants or slacks.

2 pairs of shorts or culottes or a couple of neutral-colored skirts.

3 or 4 blouses.

You may want a couple of pairs of brighter slacks or shirts to change into for dinner but most of the game reserves lie between 2000 and 9000 feet—the Serengeti and the Mara are about 5400, Secret Valley 8400—and nights and early mornings can be cold. Take cosy clothes.

2 sweaters, 1 heavy, 1 lightweight.

2 pairs of good stout shoes, safari boots or their equivalent.

1 pair of moccasins or lighter shoes for evenings in camp or at the lodges.

1 pair of rubber boots if you are traveling toward the beginning or end of the rainy season. Your chances of getting bogged in mud are good but boots can also be useful in camp where you may get an occasional bout of mosquitoes or tsetse flies although this is rare.

En page 8: Les dernières informations en français

Athens News

FIRST WITH THE NEWS IN ENGLISH · 3, Hariaou Street, Athens · Tel.: 27.446 · TUESDAY, June 6, 196.. · Seventh Year, No. 4... · Price · 1.00 Drachmas · TRIPLE THE CIRCULATION OF ANY FOREIGN LANGUAGE NEWSPAPER IN GREECE

WAR IN MIDDLE EAST: ARABS RALLY TO U.A.R.

U.S. POSITION 'NEUTRAL IN THOUGHT, WORD AND DEED': TRAVEL BANNED

Cairo claims line holding, heavy plane losses inflicted on Israel

Israel says key town captured

MINISTERS END TRIUMPHANT FOUR-DAY TOUR IN CRETE

RUSSIA ACCUSES ISRAEL: SECURITY COUNCIL IN SESSION
POPE PLEADS FOR JERUSALEM
WHEREABOUTS OF U.S. SIXTH FLEET

COMMUNIST DANGER

Henry Ford says he spent a very nice holiday here

FORMER DEPUTIES: MINISTER QUIZZED

Britain 'not taking sides'

Greece watching

NEW POWER FAILURE IN U.S.

43. Athens, June 6, 1967. An abrupt change of plans.

44. Ruins of Corinth, Greece.

45. Ruins of the public privies in the market place of Corinth. Real companionable arrangement.

46. Lion Gate at Mycenae and footsore tourists relaxing from culture.

47. Bourdzi. Ex-fortress, ex-prison, current picturesque hotel in the harbor of Nauplia.

48. The foundations of the Palace of Nestor near Pylos, Greece.

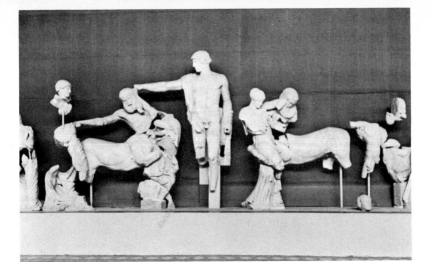

49. Figures from the pediment of the Temple of Zeus in the museum at Olympia.

50. Those old libertines, Zeus and Ganymede. Fourth century B.C. Reflected in glass case: plaid shirt of Dr. Brown, twentieth century A.D.

51. Nike as she appears today. Museum at Olympia.

52. Restoration of Nike. Faint aroma of tombstone cutters art.

53. Columns in the Altis at Olympia.

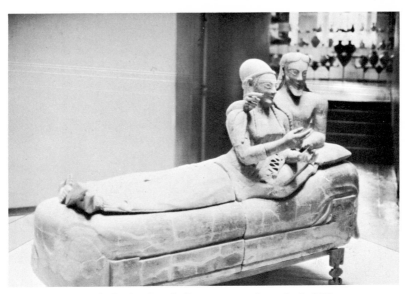

54. The Loving Couple. Etruscan sarcophagus in the Villa
Guilia, Rome. Approximately 600 B.C.

55. The Parsons house near Benisa, Spain.

56. The late abode of those late strange creatures, the Nuraghi. They lived in central Sardinia around about the Bronze Age.

57. Hotel Cala di Volpe on the Costa Smeralda, Sardinia.

58. Hotel Romazzino, Costa Smeralda, Sardinia.

59. One of the squat cottages of the Hotel Pitrizza and the splendid pool.

60. Patio of Hotel Porto Cervo. Very pleasant.

61. View from the hotel balcony of Porto Cervo itself. Picturesque and gay.

62. Garibaldi's pine tree, Isola Caprera, Sardinia.

63. Ajaccio, Corsica.

64. Rue Fesch, Ajaccio, where we had the delicious luncheon in the Restaurant Pardi.

65. Garden of the Villa dei Mulini, Napoleon's first house in Portoferraio, Elba.

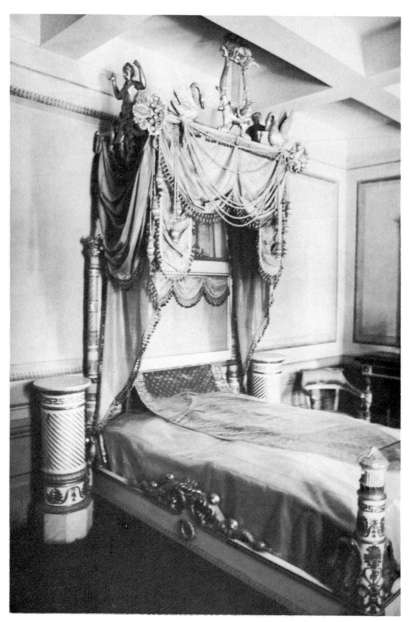

66. Napoleon's bed in the Villa dei Mulini.

1 lightweight raincoat.

1 pair of warm gloves for Treetops or Secret Valley.

1 lightweight wool dressing gown.

1 pair of bedroom slippers. Not mules. Something that covers your feet entirely and stays on. Practical protection when walking to shower and toilet tents.

Bed socks if you suffer from cold feet.

A bed jacket is useful on chilly mornings when you will have put on your long pants and socks and shoes for warmth but still have a bit of washing and tooth brushing to do in front of your tent.

On well-appointed safaris the service is admirable and laundry is done every day so you do not need many changes.

Usually your host-guide will be well-equipped with insect repellents, flashlights, clothes hangers and hot water bottles but the prudent traveler will have a few resources of his own including sun tan cream, dry shampoo (vital) and hard water soap.

A few clothes pins aren't a bad idea either. Not for laundry but Norton and I used them to pinch the tops of our rubber boots together to act as baffles to unwelcome guests. Bugs and such like. Digby and Jane laughed at us but they worked very well.

I assume it is unnecessary to mention to the safari-minded dark glasses, binoculars, and camera equipment.

A LIMITED LIST OF SAFARI MANAGERS

Major and Mrs. A. D. Tatham-Warter
Olechugu Ranch
P.O. Box 250
Nanyuki, Kenya

Our safari with them lasted twenty-one days. They now charge $250 a day for one couple. Two couples together do not pay double. They pay $300 or $75 a day per person.

Colonel Hilary Hook
P.O. Box 45
Kiganjo, Kenya

Their charge is the same as the Tatham-Warters. If handling large parties the two families work closely together.

They are both represented in New York by the travel department of Abercrombie & Fitch, the well-known sports store at Madison Ave. and 45th St.

Mr. Terry Matthews
P.O. Box 7448
Nairobi, Kenya

We met him briefly two or three times and liked him very much. He charges $150 a day for one client plus $30 per day per guest up to three guests. For four people this works out at $240 per day or $60 a guest. There is an additional 15 percent charge for safaris into Tanzania and Uganda.

Mr. Robert A. Lowis
Trans African Guides
Box 9538
Nairobi, Kenya

Evelyn Ames, her husband and friends traveled with him and she wrote about him in her book *A Glimpse of Eden.*

For thirty days his charge for two people is $4200. For three people $4650 and for four $6500. He observes that "lower prices are quoted for November and December and although these months are not suitable for safari in parts of eastern Kenya they are among the best for the Mara River and the Serengeti." Mr. Lowis is an ardent and knowledgeable ornithologist.

Ker, Downey and Selby
P.O. Box 1822
Nairobi, Kenya

This is one of the oldest firms in the business and the largest. They quote basically for hunting safaris although there is little difference in cost between a hunting and a photographic safari except that in the latter one does not have to pay for licenses, gun bearers, skinners etc.

Their charge for two clients for thirty days is $5430. If no extra transportation is required additional guests pay $30 per day per person.

Our own feeling is that while four people in a Land-Rover is ideal five may travel with reasonable comfort. This would include the safari host-guide and allow two couples to share expenses. The prices quoted are usually all inclusive with the exception of hard liquor, cigarettes, and tips.

Anyone interested in making a safari would naturally contact the above firms directly. They are all flexible and prefer to consider and plan for individual requirements.

Round Trip Fares New York to Nairobi:	first class	$1577
In winter	economy	$1045
In summer	economy	$1130.50

There is also an excursion economy fare of $784. One may book individually and does not have to stay with a group. You must remain in Africa for either 14 days or 21 days.

CHAPTER THREE

Greece   Spain   Sardinia   Corsica   Elba

We arrived in Athens at 5:30 A.M. on a pellucid morning but we came trailing the remnant vapors of Africa for as the hours slipped by Greece the golden turned to Greece the gray.

It was the fifth of June and theoretically we were to have been leaving Athens for Beirut that same afternoon but the Greek press informed us that the war of which we had heard rumors in the bush had that day broken out in full-scale fighting.

Visiting our friend Papa, Dimitri Papaefstratiou, in his office in the American Express building, we found him glum. Their own political situation had made people uneasy and tourist travel through the Middle East was now non-existent. Nor were the optimistic predictions of the Greek government—that with the war all that delicious money would automatically be diverted to Greece—being borne out. Witless tourists were going to Italy instead, although in Italy the refrain was that they had lost two million beds (night's lodgings) because of the Middle East.

Our friend and guide, Mando Aravantinou, with whom we had traveled before, came to meet us in Papa's office. She was a bit plumper than we remembered but as ebullient and outspoken as ever. Commenting on the exodus and now the non-arrival of Americans due to the April coup, she said with a small malicious twinkle, "Dear Ilka and Norton, you know your countrymen, they get nervous. Tanks roll into Constitution Square, there are rifle shots from the roof . . . Americans are not accustomed to it. It makes them uneasy and they go away, quick, quick."

That might have been true, but as far as we were concerned we had no intention of going away quick quick. Suddenly we had an inspiration. It had arrived in a left-handed manner perhaps but we saw this as our golden opportunity. We had visited Greece twice before but had never been to the western part of the Peloponnesus and we had never seen Olympia, which we had long wanted to visit.

"Let's do that," said Norton. "Olympia and the rest of it, I mean."

At this Papa brightened perceptibly. "If you are going to that part of the country," he said, "I suggest you visit Cephalonia. It is one of the Ionian Islands, still completely simple and unspoiled."

That sounded pretty nice. We agreed to Cephalonia. "And I tell you what else we might do," said the doctor.

"What?" I asked, although the glint in his eye should have given me a hint. He is a man who likes Spain.

"How about the Parsons?"

"Spain?"

"Why not? Drue and Geoff have asked us several times. They want us to see their new house."

"That they do, that they do. Why don't we cable? Invite ourselves in some devious, subtle, imaginative way."

"Such as saying, 'Can we come?' "

He chilled me. How stark! How crass! How lacking in sensitivity! In the end the cable we sent was *much* longer, a rococo valentine. WILL YOU BE SPAIN BETWEEN 16TH AND 21ST JUNE? CAN WE COME?

We had to inquire about the dates because while the Parsons have recently built in Spain their main base is the enchanting old apartment on the Quai d'Orléans in Paris where, on various trips to the French capital, Norton and I have spent so many happy days as their guests.

While Papa and Mando arranged our tour we decided to spend a day or two in Athens, reorganizing our luggage and catching up on the news. Sitting with friends over a drink, sipping coffee and lemonade under the blue umbrellas of Constitution Square, we learned that the position of our warm acquaintance, the publisher Helen Vlachos, was worrisome. When the military seized the government she had closed down her newspapers and it had been said of her that "among all the members of the Greek press there was only one man—who turned out to be a woman."

We went to call on her in her Kathimerini office in the building that she and her husband owned. Off the vestibule is a sort of well, below street level and through the glass wall we saw the great press, immobile and silent, a huge roll of newsprint still in place. A silent press is a sad sight, a potent and bitter commentary on much of our time.

In view of the United States' noisy protestations of Democracy it is curious that we seem so frequently to side with governments which, even in the most charitable terms, can scarcely be called anything but dictatorships. Over small glasses of Ouzo and iced water she discussed the situation in approximately the same terms that were later quoted in an interview in the Italian La Stampa and in the New York Times.

She was sympathetic to the king but felt he had behaved weakly. "Of course," we said, "he's very young." She admitted his position was difficult but added, "Youth is an excuse up to twenty, twenty-two perhaps. Not at twenty-six and -seven. After all he had appointed the colonels to their posts and held them there under considerable opposition. In my opinion he should have placed them under arrest at the moment of the coup. I am absolutely certain he would not have been shot but he feared civil war."

Also, I suppose, arresting a group of armed, determined, powerful men is easier said than done.

The only comic aspect of the whole sorry business had been the attitude of the rebellious colonels toward herself. Among liberal Greeks, Mrs. Vlachos has the reputation of being extremely conservative, not to say rightist in her viewpoint and sympathies. It was also the opinion held by the military and when she stopped publication of her two daily papers and magazines they were astonished. Their feelings were hurt.

"But we thought you were our friend," they said.

"I am your friend," she replied, "but I am a newspaper woman. What kind of a paper do you have when not only is the news censored but you are obliged to print government handouts?" Apparently the great majority of her three hundred employees had applauded her decision to close down and remained loyal to her although the duration of their support must inevitably have been influenced by financial considerations. She told us that she herself had been expecting some sort of coup either from the left or right for the last two years. She did not seem unduly concerned about her own position and did not worry about the arrest that some of those who knew her feared might happen, although she knew she would not be allowed to leave the country.

It will perhaps be remembered that a few months later Helen Vlachos was placed under house arrest and eventually escaped and flew to London in truly spy thriller fashion. The story was printed all over the western world but the Greek military government countered by saying there was nothing to it. She had been arrested, yes—after all in an interview she had described the government as a circus and their feelings had again been hurt. Dictators are very sensitive but they were quick to give assurance that since the Friday preceding her melodramatic departure she had been free to go any place she liked. Some people do not believe that. Some people do not subscribe to house arrest to begin with.

When we left Helen Vlachos we went to lunch at Costis, one of those spare, clean Greek restaurants where the food is often excellent. It was good here with the exception of the bread which betrayed us. In 1965 the bread of Greece had been delicious, nutritious, and flavorful. In 1967 it was as vapid as that set upon most American tables. It would be gratifying to ascribe the deterioration to the military dictatorship but I am afraid it would be fanciful.

Although disillusioned by the bread we were entertained by a brief legend printed at the bottom of the menu. *Responsible: Alice Roussopoulo.* That was placing the blame squarely where it belonged!

Costis is one of the many unpretentious restaurants of Athens where one may eat well at moderate cost. Two good ones near Constitution Square and the Hotels King George and Grande Bretagne are Zonar's and Corfu. At the latter a very nice dinner for two including wine and the tip came to 225 drachmae or $7.50.

Returning to our hotel after lunch we found a cable from the Parsons in answer to ours. "Will be Spain your dates. Come. Stay longer." We agreed to do so after our tour of the Peloponnesus and having sent a reply to that effect I puttered around our room while Norton went off to do some errands including taking my portable typewriter to be repaired. Ever since Tsavo, when I had struggled with Digby's letter to the Resident Magistrate, it had been steadily deteriorating and the moment had come for action.

When he had not returned by 5:30 I decided to go downstairs, order tea on the sidewalk terrace in front of the King George and wait for him. As I sat sipping I was picked up in the classic manner by an American gentleman.

"Haven't I seen you before?" said he to me.

"It is possible," said I to him and our little gambit was on. I do not appear that much on television but I am there occasionally and as is the case with anyone appearing in a person's own home the person, seeing the apparition elsewhere, is likely to think him an acquaintance. I remember very well one evening in a friend's house all but falling on the neck of my old, old pal, Chet Huntley, who, never having seen me before in his life, understandably parried my advance with some surprise.

As matters turned out that afternoon in Athens I was glad to have been picked up, for my gentleman was Mr. Schwartz, one of the lawyers working to free Andreas Papandreou who had been jailed on principle by the military junta. He had seen him that morning in prison. He was, he said, a charming man of forty-eight with a wife and children. Mr. Schwartz had been with the ministers on the Cretan tour that had received so much publicity in the Athens newspapers and they were, he said, full of sweetness, light and love for their fellowman and he was convinced his client's chances of a fair trial were zero. He was trying however and was plumping for exile as preferable to imprisonment and death. Months afterwards it was gratifying to read that Mr. Papandreou had graciously been granted amnesty.

As it got to be later and later and my loved one did not appear I excused myself and went around the corner to the typewriter shop. Yes, the man said, a large American named Dr. Brown had been there and left an Olivetti to be repaired but that was some time ago. No, he had no idea where he had gone after that.

I returned to the King George and continued to chat with Mr. Schwartz but I was nervous. The atmosphere of persecution and no trials or trials in camera began to disturb me. Had something happened to him? Could he have had a heart attack? Had he been kidnapped? Cases of the kind were not unknown. Who, I wondered, was the American Ambassador in Greece? Aware that my concentration lay elsewhere Mr. Schwartz drifted away and I hurried up to our room where, hopping mad, I found Dr. Brown.

"Where the hell have you been?" he demanded. "I was beginning to think something must have happened to you."

"But, darling, I was right there, right down at one of those tables by the front door."

"Well, I didn't see you. Who were you with?" Suspicious glance.

"Nobody. A Mr. . . . well, that is to say . . ."

We cleared it up. We had given each other the slip when I went to the typewriter shop and in those few minutes he had returned to the hotel.

"But what were you doing all that time?"

"Me? I was buying shirts." I was so charmed that he should have been buying shirts without force majeur having been applied by me that the interlude ended in honeysuckle and hugs and a visit to the Acropolis where, at half-past six in the evening the light was a miracle; the sky the milky blue of a star sapphire turning to cool cyclamen. There were few people about and we took many pictures.

Speaking of the Acropolis I might mention that on Tuesdays the museum does not open until eleven and on some Tuesdays, depending on the mood of I do not know who, it may not open at all, a bitter loss should one's time be limited.

Later we went to call on Mando. She had moved since we were last in Athens and her new apartment was charming. Small but with a balcony and a view of the Parthenon and of many television aerials. She said she had two neighbors, two old women who used to lean on *their* balconies and shout their opinion of the new military regime to each other across the narrow street. The opinion was not complimentary but they were quite old and one hoped their age would protect them.

At nine o'clock we strolled back to the hotel. Earlier in the day, in the same neighborhood, I had chanced upon a pet shop where they sold Korean squirrels. They are enchanting little creatures, unavailable in the United States and I longed to buy one. But I knew perfectly well that though he is an animal lover the master's reaction to any announcement that we would be continuing our journey escorted by a Korean squirrel was likely to be explosive, so I summoned up strength of character and desisted. I still find the Spanish dining hour of around eleven a little hard to cope with but somehow the Greek nine-thirty to ten or ten-thirty seems not unreasonable. The cafes along the sidewalks were crowded with homeward bound Athenians in no hurry to get there. They sat at little tables, a few sipping Ouzos but many more taking soft drinks and ices, reading the papers and chatting vehemently of current events. Fruit shops were open dispensing their succulent wares and there was a brilliant, fragrant row of flower shops with magnificent blooms at possible prices.

Despite governmental crisis and a standard of living sneered at by American politicians, most of whom have never experienced it, the pleasures of life in Europe are available to many more people than they are in the great, rich U.S.A.

In Papaefstratiou's office we had decided that our tour was to be a kind of cross-hatch of bus and private car. Since some of the places we would be going to see were served by bus and seats were available it seemed a good idea to save money when we could and then splurge a bit for those spots not on the tourist routes or when the independence of a private car would be particularly desirable.

Accordingly, one bright morning we set off at seven-thirty headed for Corinth. We had gone only a few blocks when it became evident that the loudspeaker was on the blink, so the tour guide could not enlighten her passengers when passing the birthplace of an historical legend.

We stopped at Daphne, only a short distance from the city, while an engineer was rushed from Athens to fix it up. The guide knew our Mando and asked her if she would take the English-speaking group around the church while she herself shepherded the French.

Although it was not part of the deal, Mando was agreeable. She had taken us to Daphne the last time we were in Greece for its Byzantine mosaics are world renowned and I remembered some of the things she had told us. I stood very near her drinking in every word and asking intelligent questions and I couldn't imagine why she refused to catch my eye and kept moving away from me as briskly as she could.

The loudspeaker was at last resuscitated and we proceeded to Corinth passing on the way bushes of pink oleander blazing against the blue sun-struck sea. At the canal the bus stopped and everyone got out and walked across the bridge taking pictures of that cut across the narrow isthmus so long dreamed of, begun but never completed until 1893. Statistics: 4 miles long, 70 feet wide, 26 feet deep. Nero, of all people, began digging in A.D. 67 but the project was abandoned. He got involved while on a trip to Greece where he went to compete in the festivals. He entered various competitions. For his sake the Greeks crowded them all into one year, 66. He scrupulously complied with the formalities, obeyed every rule and waited atingle for the decisions. He was like those rich and pretty young society ladies of today, who yearn to act and who become modest, ephemeral celebrities, but who remain unable to convince the public or the producers that they are professionals.

In Nero's case, however, he was humored by the Greeks. After all he was an emperor, they saw to it that he always won. Against every moral precept their duplicity paid off for when he left Greece it was in such a state of euphoria that he conferred upon them immunity from the land tax and the gift of the Roman franchise.

I always thought of Nero as a fat old duffer but in fact he became emperor at the age of seventeen and killed himself when he was thirty-one, rather than be captured and executed by his own troops when the Roman senate deposed him and named Galba his successor.

In Corinth one may still see fragments of the paved road that crossed the isthmus in ancient times and along which boats used to be portaged. It was a good source of income for the city. Strolling through the forum we passed stones that were part of the structure from which Saint Paul may have addressed the Corinthians and farther off, in the agora, the public stone privies are still in place. Excavations on a low adjoining hillside are revealing new finds in what was probably the residential district.

It is not far from Corinth to Mycenae and the ruins of the palace of King Agamemnon rising between two hills of the Argos plain and dating back to the thirteenth century B.C. It was from the graves of Mycenae that the German archaeologist, Heinrich Schliemann, took the priceless treasure of gold ornaments and masks and cups that are now in the Archaeological Museum in Athens.

The Lion Gate is in a good state of preservation although the lions' metal heads have long since vanished. They were said to be so fierce that simply to look at them scared the enemy away. Even under the benign skies of Greece the ruins of the palace loom primitive and stark and it is not hard to believe the bloody legend or to recall how Agamemnon offended Artemis by slaying a hind sacred to her and proclaiming himself the better hunter, a challenge the lady did not receive with equanimity.

To punish him she caused the winds to drop, as his fleet lay at Aulis and he was powerless to leave for Troy. It was Calchas, a soothsayer and a nosy parker if ever there was one, who put him up to the terrible idea of calling his daughter, Iphigenia, to Aulis in order to kill her because such a sacrifice, said Calchas, would propitiate Artemis who would then cause the winds to blow and the fleet would be able to sail.

According to some accounts the unnatural father did just that but a more humane version has it that Artemis rescued the girl by substituting a hind in her place.

In view of the hind Agamemnon had killed this might be construed as a touch of irony and indeed irony would appear to have been the goddess' forte, for having rescued Iphigenia from a cruel demise she set her up in a shrine where she had the hospitable little chore of slaughtering every stranger who passed that way.

Time went by, the Trojan War ended and then, as may be remembered by the younger and more recently tutored reader, one fine day who should come to the shrine but Orestes, Iphigenia's brother. Fortunately, ere the knife could strike, the siblings recognized each other and lit out for home, Mycenae, the very spot on which we were standing.

Besides Iphigenia, Orestes had two other sisters: Chrythosemis, who seems to have been a quiet girl and Electra, a real mixed-up kid who was convinced that their mother, Clytemnestra had murdered their father when he had returned from Troy eight years previously.

She and Orestes went to Agamemnon's tomb and plotted how they would dispose of Clytemnestra. Electra was all for tearing out Iphigenia's eyes too—that poor child had her troubles—because she was convinced that her sister had liquidated Orestes to whom she, Electra was devoted—if the word is not too namby-pamby an expression for her emotions.

However, meeting the lad alive, well, and in killing trim she relaxed and concentrated on their parent. Orestes carried out their filial little plot, murdering Clytemnestra and tossing in her lover, Aegisthus, for good measure.

Here again there is a difference of opinion, some saying it was Aegisthus who had done in Agamemnon, others plumping for Clytemnestra, pointing out that she had every reason to be miffed assuming, A, that her daughter Iphigenia was dead at her father's hands and B, taking a dim view of Cassandra, the daughter of Priam, who had accompanied Agamemnon home from Troy. She had, Agamemnon said, fallen to him by pure chance, part of his war booty. He couldn't care less about her but what could he do? It would have been ungracious to send her back.

Clytemnestra's wifely response to this ploy was to kill him in his bath, first throwing a net over him so he couldn't escape. A few more such historic murders—Agamemnon in his tub at Mycenae, Marat in his in Paris—none with a sense of history will venture to be clean.

Legend is fascinating, but it was past one o'clock and our stomachs began sending up little signals. However, since one of the famed beehive tombs was nearby, although we had seen it on a previous visit we complied willingly enough when Mando suggested a quick look before lunch.

"What we are doing," she said, "is to leave the tour and meet them later but by going over to the tomb now we'll see it by ourselves. Much more agreeable, no? Then we will walk to the restaurant, get there ahead of the others and have the best table and service." She looked very pleased at having conceived so shrewd a maneuver.

The part about seeing the tomb alone sounded like a good idea but the restaurant we had passed on the way to the palace seemed a relatively far piece to cover on foot.

"Nonsense," said Mando with a merry trill, "you are mistaken, it's just around the bend in the road."

She was a guide, she was Greek, she ought to know, so drawing the tour guide aside I told her what we were up to. "Don't worry about us," I said, "we'll be at the restaurant before you."

She looked surprised. "You want to walk all that way?"

"It's nothing, just around the bend in the road."

"But . . ."

"No, no, I assure you."

The distance to the tomb was all right. It was short and the party ahead of us was leaving as we arrived so as Mando had foretold, we had it to ourselves. Dug deep into the hillside the hill itself forms an enormous dome lined with blocks of stone that have held through the centuries without cement or adhesive of any kind. The spacious central chamber was used for feasts and funeral ceremonies and the small dark apartment opening off it was the crematorium.

"Come on in," said Mando, stooping as she went through the low doorway, "it's interesting." But we had no flashlight and it was very dark.

"Thank you, dear," we said, "we'll take your word for it. How do you know the ground doesn't drop away or something?"

"No, no, it's perfectly all right. I've been here before."

Moments later she emerged intact. "Now to the restaurant, yes? How envious the others are going to feel when they see us practically through lunch."

"You don't think we'd do better to wait till they get here and drive down in the bus?"

"But the walk is nothing. I assure you." She was so full of vigor Norton and I were ashamed to appear chicken. We set off. We tramped for well over a mile in the blazing sun. We were hot, tired, hungry and our feet hurt. Even our athlete began to grunt a little.

"My God, Mando," I said, "what an idea."

Secretly we were each keeping an ear cocked for the sound of the bus and Norton voiced our thoughts.

"It's going to be pretty damned humiliating if they pass us on the road, all comfortable and relaxed and we smarty pants stumble in after them, our tongues to our knees."

We were spared this ultimate degradation by a gnat's eyelash. Arrived at the restaurant we ran up the steps, across the veranda and flung ourselves down at the nearest table as Mando urged them to hurry with the Ouzo and beer. When the poor sods who had driven down the hot road in comfort arrived, we graciously raised our glasses as they crowded through the doorway. After that, with one exception, if we had so much as to cross the street Mando suggested a cab.

Luncheon finished we went on to Epidaurus. In the bus. On our previous visit in 1959 we had been there for two evening performances. That is the way to see the theatre where the plays of Aeschylus and Euripides were first performed 2500 years ago. But even in the daytime it is a fascinating spot.

A rehearsal was in progress for the festival and dozens of school children were wandering about chattering and exploring, and I thought how simple the classics and classical history must seem when it is all in the family and on home territory. At a word from their teacher down on the stage they came swarming up over the hillside seats, the girls in their bright ultramarine school uniforms, the little boys ragtag and bobtailed. They ran to the very top row where it was fun to hear people speaking in normal voices on the stage far below but for some reason the teacher was annoyed and he came bounding up over the stone benches after them, shouting and brandishing a stick and scattering them like bright birds back down the hillside and out of the arena.

Norton and I thought of his son, Peter, who with his mother had been in Greece when the military junta seized power. They had, in fact, learned of it on this very spot. They were up on the rim when his mother said, "Peter, I've just heard the most extraordinary thing. People down there on the stage are saying something in English about the government and a military coup."

"Nonsense," said Peter, who is theatre-oriented. "They're talking about a play, one of the productions."

"I don't think so," said his mother. "From the few words I could make out it doesn't sound like a play at all."

In a sense perhaps it was a play but not one by Aeschylus, nor his peers. None of that august company was produced at the 1967 festival. The ringing voices of the civilized were silenced by military decree and Greek theatrical producers had to make do with second best. The first string lads had spoken out against tyranny in tones too penetrating for the tender eardrums of dictators.

Among the banned plays were *The Trojan Women* and two other tragedies that had scores by Mikis Theodorakis. They were forbidden because he was a Communist.

Similarly treated were compositions by Rimski-Korsakov and Tchaikovsky. It may be difficult to grasp how notes of music can be political but it should be remembered that during the First World War very little Wagner was played in this country and there were people who threw stones at dachshunds to show their hatred of Germany and their loyalty to the Stars and Stripes.

Our Greek friends cannot help noting that we are quick to support right wing movements no matter how harsh and dictatorial, whereas when such behavior comes from the left we denounce it, and rightly, with loud cries of anguish. Yet the American government is distressingly naive if it fears communism to be the only danger to liberty. Let us not forget such champions of freedom as Hitler and Trujillo and "Papa"

Daladier not to mention our own Joseph McCarthy none of whom could be labeled leftist.

After we had watched the rehearsal for a while we went to the museum adjacent to the theatre where is displayed a collection of statuary fragments and masonry, enough for scholars to have been able to reconstruct the plan of the enclave which is rendered in graphic drawings. Here one sees the rotunda, the labyrinth—nobody knows quite what *that* was for—the stoa and locations where patients went to be treated, for as well as being a theatre Epidaurus was also a shrine to Aesculapius.

We were to spend the night at Nauplia and arrived at the Hotel Amphitryon in the late afternoon. Despite its poetic name the Amphitryon is a Xenia hotel overlooking the harbor and our beloved Bourdzi which we consider to be the most romantic hotel in which we have ever stayed. It is on a tiny island in the harbor and was originally a Venetian fortress, later a prison and, in recent years, a hotel. Travel bureaus are not likely to recommend it for we gathered that the manager who rents it from the government is a prickly individualist none too eager for tourist trade. Also, in honesty, when we were there in 1959 the food was not good but if you are going to be in that part of the world I would still recommend inquiries about Bourdzi. If it is functioning it is a unique spot.

The chief features of Nauplia are its harbor, the piazza, rendered endearing rather by its small size than by any notable architectural feature, and the crumbling walls of the Acropolis crowning the summit of a mountain. A covered tunnel into which were built 999 steps runs down the side of the mountain and for thirty years laborers made the steep ascent lugging the enormous stones used in the construction of the temples.

From Nauplia we went by bus to Tripolis over the high winding roads of the Parnon Mountains in the central Peloponnesus. The drive was superbly beautiful and superbly terrifying. The chauffeur, Paniotis, was expert at wrestling the huge bus around the hairpin bends and while the important consideration was that the wheels clung to the road the rear end of our behemoth hung over empty air much of the time. Norton and I were up front near the driver but even so our places were no haven from the nervous little jokes and quips of the other passengers about how young we all were to die.

Norton said later he thought the driver was having us on a bit, swooping around curves for the sheer hell of it "but" he added "he never took any chances" and certainly the guide who had made the trip often seemed totally relaxed. Speaking for myself the only time I have been as frightened in transit was when we flew in a small plane through the Alps of the south island of New Zealand. In Greece when I dared to open my eyes I could appreciate that the scenery was magnificent and marvelous in color, the high gray flanks of the mountains covered with dark green bushes and shining golden gorse but even so crossing the calm fertile plain of Mainalon was an enormous relief.

On reaching Tripolis we bade farewell to the bus tour and while Norton and I drank coffee Mando negotiated for a private car and chauffeur.

We went south, still climbing, from Sparta to Mystra, passing on the way tiny plots of land, literally only a few yards square, separated by low stone walls that were private farms. The district we were in was Arcadia but it was not the land of pink nymphs and shepherds with contours softly curved. It was stark. This time the mountains we were driving over were the Taygetus Range, also immensely high but in a small easily controlled car less frightening. On a brilliant day the view would have been exhilarating but the overcast that had recently plagued us grew heavier and blue and golden Greece turned to drab and dour Scotland although that is a cliché for in Scotland we have experienced days of rare loveliness.

It does not sound very cultured but we passed through Sparta without stopping. A couple of our Greek friends having shrugged and murmured, "Well, yes, Sparta if you like but it's nothing much, you know. Now Mystra on the other hand . . ."

Mystra, a mountain stronghold, four miles west of Sparta and one of the glories of the Byzantine era, flourished between the thirteenth and fifteenth centuries. There we lunched and very well in a hillside taverna where the meses and stuffed vine leaves were especially good and where I bought three strings of goatbells, two for friends, one for us, the most melodic way imaginable for summoning wandering guests to luncheon in the country.

Classicists and those who thrive on mysticism and arcane Teutonic myths may recall that it was at Mystra that Faust consummated his love for Helen on her return from Troy but for earthy types requiring more meaty information we may say that the original fortress was built by the Frank, William of Villehardouin, a Crusader and able architect in 1249. Through the centuries it was destroyed, remodeled and rebuilt by Greeks, Turks, and Venetians.

The Greeks took over in 1262 when Villehardouin lost a battle with the emperor Michael Palaeologus in the northern part of the country. He was nonetheless a tenacious chap, he wanted his fortress back and he led his troops into the valley of Sparta. When the Spartans heard the Franks were coming they were terrified and decided to get there fustest with the mostest. They headed for the hills, taking refuge in the disputed fortress itself. The maneuver proved so successful that rather than evacuate they stayed on and little by little built up a city of churches and monasteries, palaces and dwellings. Mystra became a metropolis with aqueducts, squares, fountains, walls, and eventually between 40,000 and 50,000 inhabitants and the splendor of her court rivaled those of some of the princes of Renaissance Italy.

Today, with the exception of the compact, finely proportioned Byzantine monastery of Pantanassa, with its fluted tiled mushroom roofs, which is still inhabited, only crumbling arches, broken walls, a few deserted chapels and at the very top the remains of the mighty fortress, drowse on the green hillside overlooking the plain.

The chapels are small and they house some lovely mosaics. There is a moving descent from the cross with Jesus being lowered into his mother's arms while in the upper corner two angels, unable to witness so poignant a moment, cover their eyes with their hands. There is also a curious nativity with Mary swathed inappropriately in black, the baby lying beside her in what appears to be a little coffin. It is probably symbolic but the somewhat macabre conception is mitigated by a benign ox peering over the edge of the coffin-cradle while crouching angels garbed in pink and blue hover overhead.

Unfortunately, we could not get into the cathedral. The nuns who live in the monastery, which one assumes is now changed to a convent, had locked the doors and disappeared.

We went back to the taverna to pick up our driver. Because of his involved and unfathomable reluctance to take the short route to Pylos, our destination, we drove over one hundred kilometers out of our way but I could not grumble unduly for much of the countryside was more beautiful than any we had previously seen in Greece. We wound down from the mountains, through the hills, dropping finally to sea level and the little port of Pylos on the bay of Navarino where we stayed at the Hotel Nestor. The Nestor is not distinguished but it is clean and reasonably comfortable.

We had no balcony and Mando was distressed. To her a balcony was mandatory but we did not feel the need of one since our windows overlooked the bay where a rusty freighter lay at anchor. Also a curious junk-like vessel with a high poop which the doctor found fascinating.

Our dinner was quite good but there was no butter so thinking to emulate the natives I spread my bread with salt and olive oil. The results were disastrous and I am convinced no Anglo-Saxon should ever try it. Sleep was reduced to a minimum but would have been hard to come by in any event for our windows had no shades and a glaring electric light bulb on the quai shone in our eyes all night.

Any belated dozing we may have hoped for was shattered by the clear and brilliant light of a glorious morning and a group of women chattering beneath our window. As they departed a muscular young Greek with a close cap of curly black hair, clad in blue bathing trunks with a white towel slung over his sun-browned shoulder crossed the quai and dove into the bay, a Chirico come to life. Another compensation for a fragmented night and an inadequate breakfast was a gigantic pot of blazing geraniums on the terrace. They proliferate all over Greece, the colors fairly shouting aloud to passersby.

Our goal for the morning was Nestor's palace, about 22 kilometers from Pylos, a highly rewarding ruin since the foundations are so well preserved that with the help of the water color reconstructions painted by Piet de Jong one gets a clear idea of what it must have been like and of the life of the times between 1300 and 1200 B.C.

A guidebook printed by the University of Cincinnati states that it was undoubtedly built by Neleus, a royal prince of Thessaly whose son Nestor ruled for three generations. This was the same Nestor who was featured in the *Iliad*, who knew Odysseus and Menelaeus and who, with his good friend and fellow king, Agamemnon, also sailed against Troy, equipping ninety ships to the one hundred of his pal.

He returned and avoiding the strained family relations of poor Agamemnon, lived in his palace for many years, being succeeded by his son, grandson and in all probability great grandson. It was home to them and they must have felt desolated when the horrible Dorians swept down from the north and wholly destroyed it by fire.

It is a large complex with many rooms, halls, and courtyards. The residential quarters were two stories high and the interior walls, ceilings and floors were of stucco covered with brilliantly painted frescoes; abstract designs and animal scenes. It must have been as gay and varied as the paintings of Matisse. Supporting columns were tapered at the base like those of Knossos.

Adjoining the rooms where visitors waited to be presented to the king was a pantry with wooden shelves and hundreds of wine cups. Apparently his majesty was a humane man wishing no parched throats in his presence.

The ground plan and foundation stones through which people are allowed to walk are now covered by a metal roof protecting them from sun and rain.

We left the palace on the way to Olympia, stopping off for coffee at Kyparisia and an unpleasant little brush with our unpleasant driver who said he was tired and hungry and had no intention of going on until he had had his lunch. This struck us as unreasonable since he had had the same opportunity as we had to breakfast before leaving Pylos. However he also had the key to the car, so although it was we who were paying we cooled our heels while the piper called the tune.

When we started off again he turned on the radio so loud we could not hear ourselves think but we were too angry and too haughty to tell him to stop. In retaliation I opened all the windows. The rush of air obliterated the sound and I noted with malicious pleasure that he found it extremely irritating. He snapped off the radio. I closed the windows, and we proceeded in comfort to Olympia and the Hotel S.P.A.P. where Norton paid off our truculent chum and we watched him depart with relief.

The S.P.A.P. is large, old-fashioned and comfortable, and used to be a railroad hotel. Norton and I felt that in Olympia we were achieving an ambition because we had wanted to go there when we were last in Greece but through a series of miscalculations and misunderstandings it had not worked out. We discovered that our desire had been a sound one for Olympia is one of the glories of the country.

After a brief rest and lunch we decided we would go first to the museum and then into the Altis, the grove on the banks of the River Alfios that was the site of the temples, lodges, and administration buildings in the days of the Olympic Games.

Set along the walls of the museum are the figures remaining from the pediment of the Temple of Zeus. They are impressive, they are noble, one is grateful for the opportunity to see them and that, to my way of thinking, is that.

They are not moving, they are not appealing and they lack the rich humanity of, for example, the terra-cotta figure of Zeus full of gusto and humor carrying off Ganymede. Ganymede, supposedly the most beautiful of mortals, was cupbearer to the gods on Olympus. He was, I am afraid, even more. Yes indeedy. They were a lascivious bunch, those ancient Greeks, and philosophers and slavery weren't the only props their exalted civilization was built on. I divulge no secret in saying that pederasty was a common practice. The corrupt form of Ganymede, the vulgarization of the name in Latin is Catamitus. Today catamite is the flossy or more literary version of our assorted colloquialisms for homosexuals.

However, whether or not we approve Olympian morals there is great enjoyment to be derived from the delightful renderings of the protagonists. In this particular statue Zeus is depicted as being very large because he is a god and Ganymede, held in the crook of his right arm, is child-sized, being but human. He looks pleased as punch at the way things are going and wears a charming little bonnet with a fluted brim.

There is also an adorable head of a girl dating from about 500 B.C. A ribbon binds her tightly crimped hair and through the centuries the glaze has peeled from the tip of her nose giving her the rakish expression of one who is slightly squiffed.

There is a marble bust of Antinotis, the favorite of the Emperor Hadrian for whom he built the superb villa outside Rome and who, despite a nose also flawed by time, was obviously a boy of rare beauty.

The two great *pièces de résistance* are the Hermes of Praxiteles holding the infant Dionysius and the immortal

Nike of Paeonius. Hermes holds Dionysius in his left arm. The right arm is broken off above the elbow but authorities agree that when the statue was sculpted he held in his hand a bunch of grapes. That is what the baby is reaching for and those grapes were the reason the little rascal grew up to be the god of wine.

We know from letters he left that Paeonius had seen Praxiteles' Hermes. He says so, but he makes no comment on it. Professional jealousy perhaps.

In any event, his Nike today though minus her face, most of both arms, her wings and back draperies, still floats from her pedestal, an ethereal and lovely form.

One may buy a postcard of her reconstructed and although I do not quarrel with the authorities and sculptors responsible in contemporary reconstruction she reminds me of the tombstone cutters' art and one appreciates that on occasion time in its passing may enhance rather than diminish that which it touches.

The museum also boasts some exquisite small bronzes and a scale model of the Altis so that one can see exactly what it must have looked like before walking down to the grove of trees in a sunlit meadow where lie fragments of the great Temple of Zeus. A few Ionic columns have been replaced in their original setting and wild flowers and tall rippling grass grow among the foundation stones and toppled pillars. We were fortunate when we were there because there were no other visitors. The grove was quiet, peaceful, and timeless. Even when the heat and splendor of the Olympic Games were at their height the Altis was often tranquil since the games took place only once every four years and in between times few people, other than caretakers, came there.

To the east of the grove lies the stadium and there are still remnants of the tunnel where the athletes waited to make their appearance. The games lasted for five days and as many as 50,000 people thronged to the low slopes surrounding the track. Good Dr. Brown, his lifetime training behind him, shook his head. "The sanitary set-up must have been a pip," he said. The thought is unsettling.

Olympia was not only an athletic capital but also a religious and political center with Sparta usually acting as policeman so that all the Greek city states could meet there in games that may have been hotly contested but were peaceful rather than militant.

Its most brilliant period was in the fourth and fifth centuries B.C. although the catalogue of Olympic victors starts in 776 B.C. and continues until A.D. 393. Two hundred and ninety-three games were held over a period of 1170 years. It was a healthy institution.

Athletes were obliged to train for ten months, rather like American presidential candidates, and in the beginning the contests were largely feats of strength and endurance: foot races, wrestling, javelin and discus throwing. Later came the spectacular and thrilling four-horse chariot races that drew the wealthy of the pan-Hellenic world to vie in speed and splendor as well as writers with their poems and plays. Nor was Nero's the only name of political renown among them.

People who could not compete in the Olympics were "women, foreigners, slaves and dishonored persons." Indeed women were not allowed as spectators.

In about 720 B.C. the loincloth was abolished and athletes began appearing naked. The legend goes that the custom started because a woman, disguised as a man, did gain admittance to the stadium as a member of the audience. Her husband was competing and when he won the contest in her excitement she jumped up shouting. Her abrupt movement disarranged her tunic and a breast appeared giving away her secret. Pandemonium broke out, the judges were furious and their displeasure might have had grave consequences but our lass was stout-hearted. She proclaimed her right to be there as a woman of Rhodes, the grandchild and wife of Olympic victors. The judges simmered down, and the lady escaped without mishap but, oddly enough, in view of the fact that it had not been a competitor who had dissembled, the decree went out that from then on the chaps would appear naked. Possibly the judges thought that if women knew they would see male genitalia exposed they would be shocked and stay away although I can't imagine where they got such an idea.

At last, after more than a thousand years, sunset crept over the great days and Olympia gradually sank into desuetude. The old vigor petered out, buildings were demolished and the stones used to build fortresses. The majestic chryselephantine statue of Zeus by Phidias was carried off to Constantinople where it was destroyed by fire in A.D. 476 and the Altis itself was engulfed by an earthquake during the sixth century. When German archaeologists began excavating in 1875 they were obliged to dig through sixteen feet of silt and clay that in the course of 1500 years had drifted over one of the glories of the world. In case, by the way, there are any other ignoramuses who think, as I used to until recently, that chryselephantine meant that the statue was large, I am now in a position to enlighten them. The word refers to the materials used in the composition; specifically gold for the draperies and hair, ivory for the flesh. Chryso is Greek for gold or yellow and the elephantine part stems, I suppose, from the ivory. Also, as a rule, the statues *were* of heroic proportions.

After an afternoon immersion in history, we returned to the hotel where we sat on our balcony having drinks and listening to the radio from which we gathered that the Arab Israeli war was drawing to a close with the Israelis making a clean triumphant sweep. Peace lay upon the lovely Olympian valley and we were telling Mando about our safari and all the magnificent wildlife we had seen. Greece is marvelous but it is different. Had we been keeping a log, as in Africa, we would have had to jot down wild game seen: one donkey. Heard: one invisible bleating goat.

The next morning we joined another tour traveling by bus through fertile fields rich in vines, cotton, rice, and poplar trees. We were amused to see across the aisle from us a young honeymoon couple. The groom, spent with the delights of love, slept with his head on his bride's shoulder but she seemed in better shape, reading the morning paper with brisk concentration.

At Achaia we stopped at a little restaurant on the water where some of the travelers bathed and where we had coffee and bread and cheese. The restaurant owner put on a bouzouki record and he and the bus tour hostess danced on a small round cleared space on the terrace weaving in and out of the sunshine and flickering shadows of the pine trees.

We looked across the bay at the mountains of Missolonghi rising into the milky haze of a warm summer's day and spoke of Byron, "very slightly lame." He arrived in Greece in 1824 and died shortly thereafter of a kind of stroke and subsequent exposure at the age of 36. His heart lies at Missolonghi but his body was returned to England. Despite poetry and fame he is not buried in Westminster Abbey. Apparently some efforts were made to have this done, but the authorities, not having cut their teeth on the Ptolemies, were horrified by the revelation that he had had an affair with his half-sister and refused him Poets' Corner. Recently they appear to have limbered up a bit and now that he has been safely dead nearly one hundred and fifty years are, I understand, installing a plaque in his honor.

Arriving at Patras on the Ionian Sea, we again bade farewell to the bus and while waiting for the ferry to Kephalonia sat down to one of the best meals we have eaten in Greece or any place else. Run by a Mr. Evangelatos, it is one of those plain clean looks-like-nothing-much Greek restaurants and the food is superb.

The little voyage to the island which takes about three and a half hours is pleasant and the ferry roomy and comfortable. At one point, in the lounge, we became aware of a chattery dry clicking sound. It was made by a couple of men slipping their patience beads through their fingers. I believe it has no religious significance, the beads are not like a rosary, but it is a habit and a pastime. The doodle balls now on the market at home serve the same purpose.

Followed by an escort of seagulls planing in our wake, their white wings glittering against the blue sky, we moved slowly into the harbor of Sami and dropped anchor. The quai is a delight lined with columned houses gaily painted. One was pale blue with pink columns, yellow shutters and a dark green awning. Another was periwinkle with Dubonnet trim, a third oyster white and yellow. It looked like a stage set and we expected the orchestra to strike up at any moment.

Kephalonia, Cephalonia, Kefalinia—take your choice, it's the same place. I plan to use Kephalonia because I like the sound and look of it. It is the largest of the Ionian islands and one of great natural beauty. It is as mountainous as the Parnon area of the mainland but less scary.

Kephalonia was named after the mythological Kephalus who killed his wife Prokris while out hunting. He claimed it was an accident. "I didn't know it was loaded, your Honor," but the authorities were skeptical and he was exiled from Attica to the island. Ulysses, although supposedly born on Corfu, was his descendant and was accompanied to Troy by the "great hearted Kephalonians" in twelve ships.

To get to Argostoli, the capital, lying across the island from Sami, one drives for about three-quarters of an hour through superb scenery. The mountains are crowned with feathery pine trees, their sides and the valleys are a patchwork of wheat, olive groves and vineyards, and battalions of cypress trees troop to the sea.

Argostoli itself is less picturesque. The terrible earthquake of 1953, which damaged several Ionian islands, very nearly destroyed Kephalonia and the little capital was obliterated.

It is unfortunate that having been able to start from scratch, a rare opportunity, they did not take advantage of it. The best architects of Greece might have been persuaded to compete and a beautiful homogeneous small city could have resulted. Instead banal buildings have gone up in haphazard fashion and such charm as there is must be ascribed to the climate although when we were there, the second week in June, it was cold. Mando assured us that was *most* unusual.

One pleasant thing about the island is that while it is comparatively large it is uncrowded, the prewar population of 130,000 having been reduced by the war and earthquake to around 37,000. The means of reduction was tragic but the results are agreeable.

It is quite unspoiled by tourists and if the hotels remain as poor as they are now the condition is likely to continue. The Zenia is rated Class B and that is an exaggeration but our beds were comfortable and we were offered a beguiling distraction; a mother swallow raising a family in a nest up in the corner of the balcony. She sailed swiftly back and forth filling the cavernous mouths of her offspring but she was so timid that when we had our before dinner drinks we sat on the edge of our beds talking in whispers and peering out at her from the shadowy room.

We also discovered an extremely good little restaurant, the Tourist Pavillion of Platis Ghialos (Ghialos Beach). When it had been recommended by the manager of the hotel and he had said that his sister-in-law was the cook and a good one we had feared nepotism but he was an honest man. She gave us, among other things, the best pork chops I have ever eaten— sliced thin, grilled to perfection and served with a light dry *risotto* and dry white wine.

The day after our arrival was Sunday and strolling around town we stopped at a church where a service was being conducted. It was a bright little place, cheap but cheerful with a sky blue ceiling, a clouded crystal chandelier, candles— both wax and electric—and a spanking new altar screen painted scarlet and gold surmounted by a crucifix outlined with small red, green, and yellow bulbs in accordance with the Greek passion for outlining everything in electricity.

An ancient Metropolitan with long hair and a long beard clad in a cream colored silk robe officiated and a chorus of young men and boys chanted continuously.

I saw the collection plate approach with some apprehension since I had not a bean in my pocket so I ran out to corral a few drachmae from Norton who was patiently waiting, seated in the crotch of a tree.

"How long are you going to stay there?" he asked. He was bored but I wasn't. The place was sparky and filled with apparently amiable people. Besides I had an affair going with a young man aged about five months who clutched my finger and gurgled and chortled at me over his mother's shoulder. It was where the action was. I was not prepared, however, to stay the entire course so we went off to join Mando who had routed out the head of the tourist bureau from his Sunday morning gardening to organize a car and chauffeur to drive us around the island.

We started with Saint George, a fortress and the medieval capital of Kephalonia until 1775. Sixteen acres are enclosed by ancient walls on a hill so high it can rank as a junior mountain. The fortress was begun in 1350 by an Orsini of Italy and passed to other Italians some 200 years later when captured by the Venetians.

The old wells are still there, one of them gave water until the time of the earthquake, the dungeons are still very evident and a tunnel, eight kilometers long, leads down inside the mountain from the summit to the plain. The garrison could descend the sloping subterranean passageway unseen by the enemy, either to escape or perhaps to pounce upon them from the rear.

The view from this eyrie is, of course, magnificent but unhappily the blazing blue Ionian Sea of yesterday was now a smoky void.

The place is wonderfully peaceful for the ancient walls confine nothing more belligerent than grass and scarlet poppies and feathery pine trees about twenty-five years old. There was a little discussion between Mando, our driver, and the guardian of the fortress as to whether the Greeks themselves had planted the trees or whether it had been done by Italian prisoners of war. Whoever did it it was a fine idea and the result is delightful.

The Italian always seem to have a very civilizing influence in wars. They usually stop shooting, surrender, and as prisoners behave far more constructively than most soldiers do, building roads, planting trees and cooking well. I have heard that in the American army, in the last war, there was brisk rivalry among the officers who had the duty of inspecting the Italian prisoner of war camps, each man claiming it as his prerogative, since the mess was greatly superior to that of the Americans.

Back at sea level we passed excavations of the Mycean era including a few shaft graves and rudimentary beehive tombs but I cannot say they proved irresistibly fascinating. It was more fun driving through the model village of Kourkoumelata built in its entirety after the earthquake by the wealthy and generous Vergotis family who handed it over lock, stock, and barrel to those whose homes had been destroyed.

The village has everything: a community center, dispensary, commissary, school, private houses, new, clean, roofed in red tile and when we were there all as shuttered as the tomb. Talk about Philadelphia on Sunday! It is a swinging town compared to Kourkoumelata although I think the pervading somnolence had to do with the siesta hour. Nearby is the village of Marco Polo, said by Kephalonians to be the birthplace of the explorer. I have been unable to find any confirmation for the theory, but if to believe it makes the Kephalonians happy it's all right with me and certainly there were Venetians on the island.

The village has another claim to fame which imposes a greater strain on the visitors credulity than the one just mentioned. It is said that every year around the 15th of August, on the anniversary of the Virgin's death, great quantities of harmless white snakes with black crosses on their foreheads make their appearance. The faithful flock around trying to catch them in their hands, cradle them in their bosoms and put their heads in their mouths. I never heard of such a thing! The snakes who escape disappear for a year which is understandable. They must find the experience unnerving.

Having absorbed about all we could of myth we decided on something a little more solid and returned to our dear Platis Ghialos for cheese pie with a strudel crust so delicate tissue paper seemed bulky by comparison. There was also delicious fresh lobster, tomato and zucchini salad, a nice local wine and Turkish coffee. We felt better.

There is a fine beach just below the restaurant, the whole shoreline offers excellent bathing, and Norton swam while Mando and I shivering, cheered him on.

On returning to Argostoli we found the town wakening to life. A crowd of two or three hundred people including masses of children had gathered on a vacant lot just off the main square to applaud a strong man, New Samson, who was about to begin his performance. At the moment of our arrival he was exhorting his public. "You are a noble race, honorable and responsive. I have no theatre but I am an artist, entitled to admission as much in the open air as within closed doors. Pay admission generously, for the unique opportunity to behold feats you will never see equalled."

He then passed around a cup and we were interested to see that very few members of the noble race welched on their obligation to so fine an artist and orator.

The performance started with a boy selected from the audience standing on a table with a sledge hammer with which he whacked in two a heavy stone balanced on the great man's head. Leaping nimbly aside from under the impact New Samson tore a pack of cards in half by way of warm up. We did not doubt that more stupendous feats would follow but I am afraid we wandered away from art to join the social swim, or more precisely, promenade.

It was the hour of the passeo, that evening stroll dear to the hearts of Mediterranean people. From all directions they came, gradually filling the big square, whole families walking leisurely up and down. Parents with nubile daughters, grandparents keeping an eye on scrambling grandchildren, babies in their carriages and adolescents casting discreet glances at one another, giggling and strutting.

We managed to get a table on the cafe terrace and soon they were all taken. A few beers were in evidence but the standard refreshment was ices and iced water. We persuaded Mando to have a bottle of soda but that was as far as she would go. Shamefacedly Norton and I ordered Ouzo. It was crass but we didn't care, we were cold. Besides it was nearly seven o'clock which we considered a reasonable hour for an *apéritif* but we were counting in American time. Seeing everyone else filling up on ices and cake we asked Mando when they would dine, when they would get their appetites back? In a small town on an island they kept Athenian hours. "Probably around ten," she said.

Norton and I were willing to brazen out our drinking habits but we did feel remiss about our clothes. Everyone was in his Sunday best—the men in sack suits and ties, the women in flowered dresses, high heels and pointed toes. Dr. Brown wore his turtleneck sweater and a wool cardigan and I was in a sweater and skirt wishing for a top coat. Our identity was obvious; tourists who didn't know enough to dress up on Sunday afternoon.

A group at the table next to us drew our attention. Mother, father, grandmother, and daughter aged about sixteen or seventeen. The poor child was chaperoned to death and looked bored but Mum was in her element. Her dyed blonde hair was coiffed in the mode of 1830; a large bun on top, puffs and curls at the sides. She was swathed in flowered silk and redolent of scent. She knew everyone and was constantly waving, bobbing up and down, smiling and bowing to acquaintances.

The strong man had finished his performance and came striding across the square on the way to his hotel. New Samson was stitched across the back of his dressing gown like a prize fighter and a throng of juvenile admirers crowded at his heels.

The whole scene had so much the aspect of a ballet that one expected at any moment to hear the director's voice.

"All right, places everybody . . . Afternoon in the Square. Action! Provincial Lady, leave your table, come over stage right, gossip with the young married couple. You, Angry Young Husband, pound the table. Good, good. And you, Disdainful Wife, give him the Look . . . There we go. More animation, Provincial Lady, still more. You're the social leader. You have a maid who comes in twice a week. Besides you want everyone to see your new hairdo and those spike heels. Now then, Strong Man, Samson . . . where the hell? Oh, there you are, get cracking. Hurry up you kids, crowd around him, you want his autograph. Chaperoned Girl, I must see something in the making between you and the Boy with Pink Ice Cream. No, no don't twist your handkerchief, this isn't 1812 . . . flick some invisible dust off your skirt . . . O.K. All right, Provincial Lady, flutter back to your table . . . Now, then, once more from the top. With gusto!" The setup was made to order.

Our interest faded before the pageant did for we were assailed by hunger and despite the hour, only 8:30, the doctor gave the order to march.

Mando had heard of a taverna up the hill. "No more than five minutes' walk," she assured us. It was the one time since Mycenae that she had not suggested a taxi and in view of Mycenae I don't know why we believed her. We did look at her skeptically but she returned our gaze with round candid brown eyes. "No, no, it is so, everyone says so."

We started the upward trudge. Up we went and up. The darkness deepened, the hillside steepened, still we climbed. As the walk lengthened the doctor's temper shortened. He was hungry and he had a gouty toe. We passed several houses that were completely dark but people sat talking by the open window. Although the town is electrified I suppose they wanted to economize or perhaps they preferred it that way. We discerned chinks of light only behind tightly closed shutters or drawn curtains. Sometimes, passing an open doorway, looking through it we would see one feeble bulb dangling from the ceiling, a table, two or three straight chairs against the wall with people sitting upright talking to one another across the room. There appeared to be little cosiness or comfort.

The farther we progressed upward the farther away Excelsior seemed to recede but frequent inquiries from Mando to passers-by elicited the information that we were indeed on the right path to the taverna.

Just as we had given up hope we reached it and a wretched place it was: a big ugly room with distorting mirrors on the wall and an uninspiring kitchen. The menu was stringently limited which wouldn't have mattered at all had the food been good but it was virtually inedible, as the wine was undrinkable. The only really bad meal we had in Greece.

Shortly after we had been served three pitiably thin cats crept in from the garden and I gave them what was on my plate. Norton was angry, the old man who was the owner was put out and Mando was in the middle. She knew the food was awful but the owner was her countryman and she didn't want him to be offended. I *was* wrong to do it when the man was looking but the cats were hungry and I could not eat what was on my plate yet that is the kind of thing that gives Americans a bad name. "She gave food to *cats* when people are hungry!" Still, the moral values must surely depend to some extent on the state of the cats, the food and the people.

Even Norton, when he overcame his disapproval of me, agreed that the reason we were the only people there was probably because the rest of Argostoli had got wind of the quality of the victuals but not at all, it was simply that we were early.

As the evening wore on several groups came in including a wedding party. The bride had removed her veil but wore her short white wedding dress, white slippers and a rhinestone band in her high-piled hair. The matron of honor was in shimmering blue and there were two little flower girls in fluffy white frocks. One of them was restless and whining, exhausted, I should think, and an old party whom we took to be the grandfather didn't look too happy either. He took the child outside and when they returned a few minutes later they both appeared greatly relieved. They rejoined the table where the women were seated on one side, and the men on the other. They all seemed cheerful enough but I was sad that the ugly room and the poor food was what they had to settle for for the wedding supper. They would have fared infinitely better at Platis Ghialos.

Seeing the bridal party reminded Mando that the manager of our hotel had been very curious about Norton and me. Apparently many Greek women wear their wedding rings on their right hands. My right hand was bare, my left he had not seen. He was in the dark.

"Tell me," he had said to her that morning, his voice dropping to a conspiratorial whisper, "that doctor upstairs, are they married?" Norton and I were charmed to think that at our ages we should be suspected of illicitness.

The manager was a romantic. He had been born in Lixouri, a fifteen-minute ferryride across the bay from Argostoli and about sixteen miles by road. He had come to the capital as a young man and in twenty years had never once returned home. "I took an oath," he told Mando. "I hate them in Lixouri." He didn't care for the Argostolians either. "These people," he cried, "they are not people!"

"No?" said Mando in surprise.

"They are monkeys," he snapped and departed to the kitchen, what to do we could only surmise. The Xenia served no meals.

Argostoli, as I have said, is a town without much character but walking about the next morning we came upon an excellent drug store and visited a small museum with the usual pots and jars taken from tombs and one notably touching exhibit: two skeletons lying in dust in each other's arms. They were found that way when excavated. Beside them is a small jar, the kind that used to contain poison and also a knife.

Perhaps it was a suicide pact. Surely they must have been very young.

> Lovers lying two and two
> Ask not whom they sleep beside,
> And the bridegroom all night through
> Never turns him to the bride.

But this time it was not as A. E. Housman wrote it. On the contrary. For more than eighteen hundred years neither lover has turned from the other.

Waiting for Nikko our driver to pick us up we sat in the square having coffee and watched the Strong Man, a little pathetic minus his flamboyant robe and entourage of buggy-eyed youngsters, trying to cajole a couple of kiosk proprietors into hanging up his posters. He met with stony eyes and cold shoulders and we hoped today's performance would be as successful as the Sunday matinee but as all theatrical artists know, if there are going to be any lean nights usually they are Mondays.

We were going to Poros, a beautiful drive over terraced mountains and through fertile valleys, and from a height above the beach one has a quite marvelous view of Ithaca across the bay. While waiting for our luncheon to be prepared at a small roadside restaurant we went for a swim. The beach was stony rather than sandy but the water was limpid and the temperature perfect; cool enough to be invigorating but not cold and the sun blazed in a radiant sky. For lunch the grilled fish, cheese, olives and lettuce and tomato salad was delicious.

Kephalonia is a beautiful island ringed with inviting beaches. Life there is extremely simple and not expensive and the temptation to lift the lid of Pandora's box just a tiny tiny bit is almost irresistible. Were they to build, say two small hotels but really small, and improve the roads—not much, just a little—would it not be an entrancing spot for a holiday? Yes, and travelers going there would tell their friends and the first thing you know syndicates would move in and high rises would destroy the beaches and an endless stream of cars would go screeching around the acute bends of the mountain roads and there would be juke boxes and discothèques and people, people, people. Slam down that lid!

Strolling beside the harbor in the afternoon we discovered that two magnificent yachts had dropped anchor while our backs were turned. One was an English sailing yacht and the other a sleek snowy altogether glorious affair from the United States. On one of the life preservers were the letters D.Y.C. and Norton and I concluded, rightly or wrongly we did not know, that she was from Detroit. If so, we decided that the cream of the automobile industry must be in our midst. As we were walking away Norton said, "If you were thinking of giving me something for Father's Day that yacht would be just about right." I promised to make a note of it.

Even were I rich as a Greek or a scion of American industry I am not yacht oriented but in European waters I could be tempted. There are so many fascinating ports and islands to put in at.

The next morning leaving Argostoli in a distinctly plebeian bus we observed that the beautiful visitors had slipped away in the night. We drove along the tortuous road to Sami and rolled on to our ferry for the return trip to Patras. From there it was 132 miles to Athens, a fairly long haul in our bumbling conveyance but we could not complain about the price. Five dollars per person for the whole trip.

In the seat ahead of us two children, sisters aged about three and five, whiled away the time alternately hitting each other or sleeping in their mother's arms. At that they were good little kids for they had no toys or picture books to distract them throughout the bumpy tiring hours.

We arrived in Athens around six o'clock and later in the evening went to dine with our friends, the journalist Leslie Finer and his Greek actress wife. There was another couple there, Muriel and George Spanopoulos. He was a doctor, handsome in a thin nervous febrile way and he had what

Americans tend to think of as Greek hair; very black, curly, sleeked down and shiny.

He was a strong advocate of the military coup and the junta, confident that at last the corruption which he claimed infected every stratum of Greek life would come to an end.

Since all human beings, especially those in high office, are subject to corruption, I felt he was overly optimistic but then I do not care to see thousands of people imprisoned without trial. Norton felt the same but since we were foreigners we maintained a polite silence. Our host and his wife, living there, felt free to voice their opinions. It was an interesting evening.

The next morning we were flying to Rome and could only hope to find in Italy the marvelous weather which had at last seemed to be permanently settled in Greece. At the airport, and it is true of most European airports, the red tape and inefficient bureaucracy were infuriating, inevitably tarnishing one's last impression of lovely lands.

When everything was paid, including tips and that outrage, the exit tax, I had twelve drachmae left in my purse. Norton had gone off for some final checking and looking around I saw a French paperback copy of Colette's *Chéri*. It was years since I had read it but I considered it an old friend and wanted to renew acquaintance. Unfortunately, the price was fifteen drachmae. There was nobody at the bookstand or at a nearby counter. The few passengers in the vicinity were engrossed in their own affairs and the temptation simply to pick it up and put it in my bag was strong. "Who'll know? How many people are going to want to read *Chéri?*" I said to myself. "Fifty cents, who cares? What's the harm? It's not the money, it's the principle of the thing," said I to myself. "It's merely a question of degree. Petty or grand, it's still theft." I sighed but the training of a lifetime held. With some difficulty I routed out the young lady at the souvenir counter and explained my problem. Price fifteen drachmae. Cash on hand twelve. "Take it," she said. "Put it in your bag. I'll make out the sales slip for twelve. Give the money to the bartender." The bartender! Irritated but docile I handed over my twelve drachmae. He looked at them surprised and tossed them into the cash register. At that point I deeply regretted not having stolen the book. If Colette's estate wasn't going to get so much as a centime from the sale I saw no reason for the airport bar to profit but by that time it was too late.

The flight to Rome was only a little over an hour and a half but the golden light of Greece did not span the time zone. The Roman temperature was 66 as opposed to 80 and the skies were overcast.

Although usually reluctant to eat in hotel restaurants, with the exception of the Connaught in London, we did lunch at the Grand where we were staying and went around patting ourselves on the back (and stomach) the rest of the day. There was prosciutto with fresh figs, grilled prawns, white wine, salad, wild strawberries, and good Italian coffee, a meal I prefer to the one so widely advertised in American magazines and on those great illuminated signs in airports: a club sandwich or a hamburger on a bun topped with a flaccid piece of cheese and a bottle of Coca-Cola.

Our day and a half in Rome was spent largely in arranging our trip to Spain, in shopping, doing a bit of museum work and eating. In retrospect, we seem to have done a good deal of the last, going to restaurants which we had known before and where we thought the food still of high quality.

We dined at Georges where an excellent dinner for two cost between fourteen and fifteen dollars. The Café Greco in the Via Condotti has a little the atmosphere of the Konditorrei Demel in Vienna and although the cakes do not have the melting succulence of the Viennese it is a cosy place for mid-morning coffee or chocolate and afternoon tea. After a foray into the shops of the Via Condotti one needs a restorative for the price strata is rarefied. The tenants number among others such high-flying purveyors of luxury goods as Signora Emma Bellini with her exquisite linens and the Gucci dynasty with all that incomparable leather. These artists are also aware of the tourist season. European merchants are luckier than their American counterparts for they have two Christmases from which to profit handsomely.

Otello, on the Via della Croce, still serves delicious and reasonable meals under its vine-covered pergola and we dined one evening at the Cecilia Metella on the Via Appia Antica. Our companions were dears—Colleen Moore and Prince Edmund Ruspoli, a tall lean white-haired aristocrat who has lived for many years in New York, speaks perfect English and is widely read and traveled. The food, regrettably, did not match the company.

In Triade's, a shop not far from the Grand Hotel on the Via Barberini—the number is 92—I fell in love with some witty and whimsical figurines. They are made of a composition eggshell thin, charming in color, modern in workmanship and romantic in concept. I ordered several.

Shortly after we got home we discovered a shop in East 53rd Street in New York that sells the same thing. They cost a great deal more than those in Rome but on the other hand you do not risk the almost inevitable damage in transit and the difficult and delicate job of reconstruction with toothpicks, tweezers and Elmer's glue that the doctor had to embark upon due to their fragility.

It is a pity to go to Rome and not to visit the Villa Giulia, one of the most delightful museums in Europe, entered through a curving arcade with a gaily painted vaulted ceiling and housing a matchless collection of Etruscan art, the exhibits dating from the sixth century B.C. The two gems, to my way of thinking, being the sarcophagus of the man and wife and the bust of Apollo. What enchanting people they must have been, with their elegant dress, full almond eyes, long delicate noses, pointed chins and smiling mouths.

That part of our Roman sojourn we enjoyed. When he came to pay our hotel bill the doctor was shaken. Rooms at the Grand vary with the location and the season but they are in the neighborhood of $30 a day. That does not include meals. It does include the 18 percent service charge but you are of course expected to give more than that. "The 18 percent," the management explains, "is mostly for the staff you do not see; the kitchen help, the night cleaning men and so forth."

The population you do see—chambermaids, waiters, bell boys, the *portieris*—is extensive but the cowed traveler reaches once more into his pocket, the prudent one thanking his stars that his passage home is paid for.

Norton, however, was still smarting as he replaced his depleted wallet. "Why are we racketing around the capitals of Europe, traveling in dribs and drabs this way? It's costing a damned fortune!"

"Because of that bloody awful war, that's why. We should have gone to the Middle East first. We should never have . . ." and in unison, "listened to John Owen." Then we burst out laughing. In reality we are very fond of John, our whipping boy. The fatal phrase "migration of the herds" was the root of all our troubles.

The flight from Rome to Madrid took two and a half hours and after a festive Alitalia luncheon I plunged into my almost stolen Colette.

The characters and the world of *Chéri* have vanished but they were at one time very real, perhaps reaching their apotheosis in French society at the turn of the century.

There is Léa, the aging mistress whose past lovers kept her in luxury and whose own prudence and shrewd investments kept her rich. Also the young callous gigolo whom she saw through and loved and who needed her. He loved Léa in spite of himself and inevitably left her for an advantageous marriage to a rich young girl. In the end of course he comes genuinely to love his wife and Léa is left alone, a ravaged figure, returning finally to her circle of aging demi-mondaines.

The story is dated, the skill and compassion of the story teller survive. Those who would like to refresh themselves with wisdom, talent and a passionate love of life can do no better than to get hold of Robert Phelps' admirably organized and edited book of Colette's work *Earthly Paradise*. Seven translators are involved in the achievement and their ability is outstanding.

At Madrid we were obliged to change planes for Valencia—to our relief the flight, filled when we left Rome, had produced some vacancies and we were able to get aboard. After we arrived, we rented a car and feeling like pioneers set out for Benisa and eventually the Parsons. One could not say it was precisely raining but the clouds were leaking and there was a heavy, somewhat ominous feeling in the air. When we heard a terrific explosion and saw a shower of earth and rocks fall into the road ahead of us, with one voice Norton and I cried, "Shifta!" We were wrong. They were Spaniards and the explosion was deliberate for the road we were traveling was being widened with the aid of modern technology gleefully employed.

By dint of poring over the map, frequently asking our way and borrowing the native intelligence of those we met, we at last arrived at Casa Cristina and our old friend Drue.

The Costa Brava has gotten the publicity. The Costa Blanca of which Alicante is the central city is less exploited and has a very special quality. That part of Spain was familiar to the Phoenicians and the Greeks, the Romans and the Moors but no one seems to know who conceived the terracing of the mountainsides. The slopes flow into one another in wide undulations, every terrace planted with almond trees, the wealth of the district. When wide enough, they also support the pale stone houses of the few Parisians and Americans who, in the last few years, have come quietly seeping in.

Don Rasmussen, an American artist, was one of the first foreigners to settle there. He remodeled an old farmhouse, invited a few friends who told others and the hegira from the north was on. It is a discreet one, however, largely because the properties, while not of many acres—three to four or five would seem to be the largest holdings—are going up financially in leaps and bounds, people buying for investment and protection and the ones who are already there not wanting to be crowded by neighbors.

We visited some of the other houses but we felt, and I do
not believe it was prejudice, that the Parsons' was by far the
handsomest and most comfortable although they all had the
quality of being part of the landscape, solid, unobtrusive, and
appealing if not quite as picturesque as a feature in the
French edition of *House & Garden* had led us to believe. I
have great respect for professional journalists but they would
appear to be euphoric by nature, certainly in the glossy magazines. It is advisable to temper their enthusiasms with a grain
of salt.

The great promontory of Ifach stands guard over the Bay
of Calpe, included in the magnificent sweeping view which
is largely what the landowners pay for, but the beach itself
is about seven kilometers away from the terraced holdings
and one must follow a steep and winding road to get there.
Hence bathing is not practical. Marketing is. One day we
went down and bought tiny fresh clams and a bucket of
great succulent prawns which we ate grilled for dinner.
To Drue they were a revelation because although she was mad
about them she had once contracted hepatitis from eating
shellfish and feared she could never have it again. Dr. Brown
was able to release her from this fallacy and explained that she
was now immune. The only way she could ever get hepatitis
again was from a dirty needle.

Norton and I had been in Ifach on our first trip to Spain
in 1951 and we thought the beach more attractive at that
time. The *parador* or inn had been run down and was still
bedraggled from wartime neglect but the place itself was
simple and unspoiled. Now the port has been enlarged and
every hillside is spiked with hideous high rise apartments,
half of them no more than concrete and steel skeletons. The
contractors, full of ambition and dreams of profit, take off
half cocked and run out of money when only part way up to
the sky and the buildings disintegrate before completion.

The Parsons are not dependent on the beach for they have
built an Olympic-sized swimming pool on their terrace. It
is a handsome hole but Norton and I looked at it sullenly

for we could not enjoy it. We stayed at the Casa Cristina for four days and for four days it rained. The morning of the fifth we awoke to splendor and that was the day we left.

Still, the weather gave us time to catch up on our news and to enjoy the house. It isn't that there are so many rooms, eight or nine I think, but the living-dining room is about forty-nine feet long and half as wide and the bedrooms are proportionate. A lovely loggia with wide archways gives onto the terrace, the pool and the View. They heat with almond shells, of which they have several, and the kitchen is an eye-popper; coal, electricity and gas, a professional butcher's block and marble counters for working. Señora Parsons has never been one to skimp in the culinary department.

America is a great country but there are certain compensations in living in poverty-ridden Spain where one may floor and wall the kitchen with beautiful old tiles and where the bathroom washbasins are of marble since it is so much cheaper than porcelain or steel.

The retaining walls of local stone, masterpieces of engineering and architectural beauty were put up by Tomás, their gardener. Even in Spain they cost money but I prefer not to think what the price would be at home. Tomás, small, dark and lean with an intensely intelligent face, is the gem caretaker and general handyman of dreams. He is also a good veterinarian caring for Apollo when the Parsons are away. Apollo, today, a splendid if indeterminate dog with shining black fur, tan legs and markings and a plume of a tail was picked up on Saint Apollo's Day when he was a poor beat-up puppy with no nails, pads torn and bleeding and bones sawing through his skin. He was worse off than most derelict pups for it was obvious even then that if he survived he would be large and thus costly to feed. Drue and Geoff rescued him and today he runs the establishment.

The master and mistress do not spend a great deal of time there now but they are looking forward to the day when Geoff will no longer be working so hard for his airplane company and when they will sell the Paris apartment and retire.

"The thing to do," they said, "is for you and Norton to retire here too." Norton does not feel it so strongly but for me the Mediterranean has always held great fascination and we were not averse to a little idle sightseeing while in that part of the world, with vague background notions of *maybe* . . . someday . . . We did look at several properties but as I have said the prices have already gone up. Yet there is no question that in a few years from now the upped prices of today will seem bargains.

We stayed with our friends until it was time to resume our schedule in the islands.

We bade them an affectionate goodbye and drove into Valencia arriving at the old Hotel Astoria Palace around six in the evening to find it overrun with five tours; American, French, and German, and the staff nearly crazy.

I decided to have my hair done and joined Norton back at the hotel shortly after nine. The lounge in front of the dining room was packed with starving Americans clamoring at the doors but they had to wait until 9:30 before they would open.

We ourselves went off to dine at Las Graelles, an extremely good restaurant in the Avenida Conde de Serrallo. Although ten would have been the more distinguished hour we had to be up at 6:30 the next morning to catch our plane. Besides we too were hungry. Also, Norton insisted on Paella. It had to be made from scratch and by the time it was ready we were the most In couple in Spain, dining at the traditional hour of eleven.

The next morning flying north to Barcelona, where we were to have a five-hour wait before our plane to Rome, I marveled at the symmetry of the orange groves seen from the air. One has come to accept the meticulous plowing and planting of the fields but trees! How is it possible to place each one so precisely? They were accurate to the millimeter, not a leaf out of place. And the product was delicious. We knew, because we had had toothsome orange marmalade and orange juice at breakfast.

Although our stopover was brief we were pleased to be back in Barcelona, a big prosperous frisky city with broad tree-shaded boulevards and narrow streets, no more than slits between old buildings. There are good restaurants, cafes and two big department stores. In summer the traffic policemen wear white jackets and white solar topis and are helpful.

We had intended going to the Church de la Sagrada Familia (Holy Family), with its four extraordinary towers, but we got sidetracked and ended up instead at the Gothic Cathedral of Santa Eulalia, a vast edifice rising into high umbrageous canopies and filigree spires and lighted by thousands of votive candles. Masses were being held in countless chapels and one could confess in many languages. Signs on the confessionals are in Italian, French, German, English. If one has sinned gravely and cannot wait to get home to pour it out to his own confessor he may take advantage of this international cleaning establishment and depart shriven.

Our own departure struck me as being not entirely in a state of grace. The Rome plane was half an hour late taking off and in the Eternal City itself the pace quickened to a wild stampede. We tore through customs and flung ourselves into a taxi for the brief ride from the International to the Domestic terminal and the flight to Cágliari.

There we were herded into the bus that drives across the field to the plane. Among the passengers was a little old lady in heavy widows weeds walking with a cane and wearing a white patch over one eye held in place by dark glasses.

Everybody, including the little old lady piles out expecting to mount the plane steps and depart immediately. We do not. We wait. The bus doors reopen, we are herded back in again and return to the departure building where the little old lady is warmly greeted by the crowd of relatives who have just bade her farewell. The loudspeaker announces there will be a delay of twenty minutes since the machinery is not working.

My Italian is minimal but I understand quite a bit. It was not reassuring to understand this last phrase. Actually the announcer was mistaken. In two minutes the plane was ready. With loud sobs the relatives embraced the matriarch.

Again we are herded into the bus, drive out and again make an abrupt return. The little old lady is swept into the literal bosom of her family. At the next call to battle the farewells mount to a crescendo with louder sobs, a great flailing of arms and passionate embraces. One son detaches himself from the coagulated group and accompanies his mother in the bus and out to the flight of steps leading up to the plane where he hands her over to the stewardess, turns and walks smartly away. The little old lady is helped up the stairs and carefully deposited in her seat. Her tears immediately stop, she adjusts her clothing and announces briskly that she will have a glass of juice.

In one hour we touch down at Cágliari, pronounced Calyary. It is the capital of Sardinia and I did not know it until we started planning our trip.

Sardinia's history is as ancient as the rest of the Mediterranean world but compared to her recent emergence in travel agencies and the public conscience she has been lying fallow, a sleeping island brought to life by the kiss of the young Prince Karim, the Aga Khan. The love affair began in 1962 or '63, when a syndicate of European investors of which he was the leader gradually bought up about two hundred square miles along the island's northeast coast now known as the Costa Smeralda—the Emerald Coast—and began turning it into an enormous resort area.

We went there later on and stayed at the Cala di Volpe, one of the most widely publicized of the hotels. Much of it we thought colorful and amusing and as giving promise of more to come but our first stop at a Sardinia beach resort was at the pretty, unpretentious and less well known Hotel Is Morus. It is at Pula on the southeastern end of the island, about forty-two kilometers from the capital. Until one is nearly there the countryside is not noteworthy; indeed just outside Cágliari itself there is a sort of Jersey City flats atmos-

phere, that smelly desolation the traveler must traverse en
route to the Newark airport outside New York City. Nearing
Is Morus, however, matters greatly improve and the hotel
and its surroundings are attractive in a flat sand-and-pine-
grove way, although it is backed by the spine of arid mountains that bisect the island.

The evening of our arrival we were shown to our room
which while comfortable and reasonably attractive was on
the ground floor. We had a small terrace balcony but our
view was limited by oleander bushes and pine trees. Since
the sea lay just beyond the high hedge it would have been
nice to be able to glimpse it.

I asked the young man from the concierge's desk who had
shown us to the room if we couldn't have one on the second
floor. "No," he said abruptly, "if you don't like this, see the
manager." We returned to the front lobby, Norton reluctantly. He hates rows about rooms. I think all men do. The
manager, also young, appeared. "I am wondering," I said,
"would it not be possible to get an upstairs room with a
better view?" The query which seemed to me innocent enough
produced outrage. "No," he snapped. "We consider the room
you saw one of our best. If you don't like it you can go back
to Cágliari. I'll call you a cab right now."

He had us. We were tired, the little we had seen of Cágliari we had not warmed to and we obviously had no intention of going back there. I observed grandly that insolence
was unnecessary but angry as I was I couldn't help a giggle.
There was a kind of swishy irritation about the young man
that made him sound like a peevish mistress. "All right, if
that's the way you feel, go *back* to your wife. See how you
like it."

We unpacked and went to dinner. The dining room is a
long broad veranda overlooking the water and in the course
of the evening an enormous orange moon climbed the sky.
The hotel seemed pleasantly populated and the food very
good. We had no complaints about our table but we suspected the manager had had a change of heart when the
headwaiter came over to us and assured us that the next day

we would be given a situation more in keeping with what he
apparently considered our exalted status. There was, however, a fringe benefit at the table we had for it was close
to that of a French family; father, mother and an entrancing
little son, one of those geniuses who at a tender age can
speak the language. When we picked up the thread of his
discourse he was obviously asserting his independence.

"Now that I am eight years old . . ." he said.

"You are four," said his mother. The conversation
languished.

After dinner we meandered into the cardroom and observed with sadness the sleek small heads of antelopes
mounted on the wall. A friendly member of the hotel personnel, obviously trying to make up for the unfortunate contretemps earlier in the evening, murmured sympathetically
about the idiocy of wanton slaughter while nevertheless
hastening to assure us, just in *case* he had miscalculated and
we had itchy trigger fingers, that gazelle abounded in the
central part of the island.

The next morning . . . hearts and flowers. The sky was
radiant, the garden shimmered in color and fragrance and we
made up with the manager. He apologized, we assured him
it was nothing, not to mention it, and we all three embarked
upon what, in that climate, was a cosy honey sun. Norton
and I had already concluded that he had perhaps been un-
nerved by a tiff with his loved one and my inquiry about
another room had been the last straw.

The profusion of bloom in the garden was delirious—nasturtiums, lemon verbena, white, blue and purple larkspur,
geraniums, zinnias, lilies, lantana, bougainvillea, mimosa,
cactus, pines, and cypress trees. It was puzzling though. If
the earth supported such marvelous flowers would it not
also support vegetables? But the fields adjacent to the hotel
lay untilled and the mountainsides uncultivated. We missed
the lovely productive terraces we had seen in Spain.

The hotel is set on a fine sandy beach furnished with
chaise longues, mats and sheltering umbrellas of dried

eucalyptus branches. Two catamarans are provided for the guests' amusement but one pays extra to use them; 500 lires (80 cents) the ride and there is no time limit except that imposed by good manners, and consideration of others. The cabanas for changing clothes are convenient but one's own room is so near that there is no particular need for them.

On an upper terrace they have built a salt water swimming pool, there is a tennis court and a fragrant pine grove through which to stroll and where I came upon a curious arrangement of little cement bridges and runways which turned out to be a miniature golf course.

I roamed alone through the pines, for Norton had already started work on his mahogany Buddha appearance. I too am a child of the sun but as sometimes happens in human relationships I can take my parent only in small doses and sun or not I found it too cold to bathe. An English couple we met said they had been traveling around Sardinia for two weeks and that today and the day before were the first times they had seen real sun and this was the latter part of June.

There were other English among the clientele as well as French, quite a few Germans and even a sprinkling of Italians enjoying their own island, mostly well-to-do industrialists from Milan, a good many of whom owned property around the hotel. The accent was on youth with children, adolescents, and young couples predominating.

We were amused to watch our little French boy who had become enamored of a lean, very blond German youngster of about ten or eleven. He was a handsome child, proud possessor of impressive beach equipment; a snorkel, flippers and a belt with a sheathed knife which he wore clasped around his non-existent waist. He also had a kite which I found fascinating. It was not beautiful like a Japanese kite but I considered it an engineering triumph and it was one of the few plastic objects I have ever coveted. Shaped like an airplane with blue wings and a yellow body, it was attached to a reel the boy wore strapped to his wrist. With a spinning sound he would release the wire and flashing and glinting in the sunlight the plane shot upward titillating the sky. The little French boy followed this godlike creature around with the eager air of a puppy but the god, as befitted a mature Olympian, ignored him. I suspect there would have been more rapport had it not been for the language barrier.

Since Sardinia is famous for its ceramics we drove into Cágliari one afternoon to try to ferret some out and to see the town. There are about 200,000 inhabitants and industry is composed largely of salt and oil refineries and of iron mining. Agriculture, despite the aridity, is also a large part of the island economy. A few of the old streets are picturesque but most of the ancient walls have been pulled down to make way for new buildings and Progress.

We did not think so much of the vaunted sacristy of St. Michael's Cathedral but its baroque façade is unusual with graceful female figures carved in bas relief, their arms upraised, their flounced skirts narrowing down to tassels.

The Archaeological Museum contains some fascinating small bronze figures of humans and animals dating from the same period as the Etruscans and like theirs lean and curiously modern in feeling. There were also stone steles carved with Egyptian motifs. This seemed to us rather surprising but Egypt is not so far away, after all.

Not far from the museum is Rinascente, a large department store where I bought an amusing ceramic figure, a peasant woman on a horse. The doctor observed with pained disapproval, as he watched it being carefully wrapped, that toting it about all the rest of the trip was going to be a damned nuisance. He was right but the red tape involved in having it sent was worse.

We continued on down the Via Roma, a long arcaded street like the Rue de Rivoli in Paris, till we came to a small shop with the imposing name of Instituto Sardo Organizzazione Lavoro Artigiano—I.S.O.L.A. for short—where they sold handsome handwoven fabrics and imaginatively designed ceramics. They were not so colorful as a couple we already had at home but we were assured that they were the modern vogue and highly regarded. We bought two or three of the most attractive and this time there was no nonsense about lugging them.

"We will wait," said the doctor firmly, "three months if necessary. What does it matter?" He was right, it didn't, but inevitably it is later than we think and it is nice to enjoy the goodies while there is still time.

With vague thoughts of a possible purchase of land still nibbling at the back of our minds, we spent a little time walking and driving around the point on which Is Morus is situated. Our companion and informant was Antonio Cappellari, one of the young managers of the syndicate which controls the property. Farther down the road they own another hotel which is at present distinctly second rate but they are planning to improve and embellish it so that it will become Class A. The beach there is magnificent, superior I should say to even the very attractive one we were on. They are also going to put in a golf course for the two hotels.

The plots we saw around Is Morus were zoned to one acre each, the growth was pine and while some of them had views there was little private beach frontage. The beach was there but one had to descend a steep little palisade to get to it. The price per plot was $20,000 which we considered high, but island life is not cheap anyplace. The few houses that had already been built were not overly attractive although obviously given taste and money that drawback could be remedied. The true lure is the climate, the bathing and the flowers. Summer seemed really to have settled in and day after day there was hot sun, dry air, a little breeze and a light blanket welcome at night.

Since, if one is in that part of the world, Is Morus is such an attractive place to stay I append the rates. From 15th April to June 30th, approximately $11.50 and $13.00 per person. From 1st July to 30th September double rooms 10,600 to 11,600 lires per person or roughly $18 and $19. Meals, service, and taxes are included as are all the beach facilities with the exception of the catamarans already men-

tioned. Transportation is provided between the hotel and airport to Cágliari and the charge for one to four persons each
way is $13.

Compared to the rates in many other parts of the world
all this is reasonable but little extras accrue that one should
be aware of. We got quite a start, when on paying the bill,
Norton discovered that for four mornings a dozen breakfast
eggs, two for him and one for me, came to $9.60. We could
understand the Continental preference for coffee and rolls.

Mr. Cappellari had kindly taken the trouble to discuss
our route to Cale di Volpe with Orlando who was to drive
us there, insuring that we should pass through the most interesting part of the country. That immediately adjacent to
Cágliari was flat, dry, dusty and hot but before too long
the hills and outcroppings started and history began.

The iron mines of Sardinia were known to the Carthaginians and the Romans and during the Bronze Age the island
was fairly heavily settled. Between about 1500 and 400
B.C. we come to the Nuraghe and although that was not my
favorite civilization—I am more of an Akhetaten woman
myself—one must say for them that they were a sturdy and
durable race. Their round squat towers of enormous stones,
serving the same purposes as the fortresses and strongholds
of the Middle Ages, dotted the countryside and in the part
we were driving through many ruins still remain. After passing
Barúmini where we came to an undulating plain from which
rose a particularly large tower, we stopped the car and got out
to reconnoiter. The tower was doubtless the abode of the
boss while surrounding it were low walls and circular chambers which we surmised must have housed troops and re-
tainers or, when numerous enough, the villagers themselves.
It was in these settlements that they found the bronzes we
had seen in the Archaeological Museum in Cágliari. Like
so many ancient edifices the towers of the Nuraghe were constructed of stones held together by nothing but sweat and
know-how although sometimes a kind of clay appears to have
been spread over the interiors, but probably more for dé-

cor and warmth than for any adhesive quality. As usual the
view of the surrounding country was unimpeded.

We lunched a few miles farther on at Láconi where the
small albergo was spotless and the food very good and then,
through country growing more mountainous and beautiful,
drove on to Désulo.

The road winding through groves of cork trees was well
made and Orlando commented on it approvingly and as we
quickly learned with a professional tongue. During the
war he had been a prisoner of the British and for six long
years had built roads for them in Kenya. We were curious
about the village of Désulo because Antonio Cappallari had
told us that on Sundays many of the villagers dressed in their
local costumes and that it was picturesque and pretty. This
we found to be the case with the women. The men for the
most part were old sobersides but the women and
children wore white frilled bodices, vests and the long skirts
of the traditional peasant dress. We asked Orlando to ask
them if they would mind if we took their pictures. Mind!
After snapping two or three with his Nikon, Norton brought
out the Polaroid and the village exploded. Everyone, every
man, woman and child wanted his picture taken and of
course wanted the print which Norton gave them. During
the minute he held it above his head to dry they jumped and
grabbed and yelled with excitement. The camera itself was
a miracle but even watching me spread the gelatin fixitive was
the treat of the month. It was touching. With the exception
of first communions and weddings and possibly the new baby
I imagine there is little photography in their lives. Finally
Norton was at the end of the pack. Through Orlando, he
explained, "This is the last one. Now everyone get close together and then you can pin it up in the mayor's office or the
barbershop and it will belong to all of you." Solemnly
they grouped themselves. Some smiled, others were cooperat-
ing so intensely they didn't dare risk even that small a
movement. Norton aimed and snapped but alas for pos-
terity and communal ownership they snatched it from his

hand, it was torn to pieces and the fragments fought over in the dust of the road. We broke away with difficulty for they clustered around the car perhaps unable to believe that anything from America ever came to an end.

In the course of the afternoon we passed through the much larger but less colorful town of Nuoro and after heading sharp north to Olbia began our descent from the mountains to sea level, Porto Rotondo and the small bay of Cala di Volpe, the Bay of Foxes.

I don't quite know why we had anticipated that the hotel would be white. Somewhat Moorish in architecture and white. Well you might say it is Moorish in a way but white it is not. It is strawberry sundae pink, buff and dark red and with so many managers, bellhops, and *portieris* in attendance that you know at once, even before being presented with the bill, that it is Class A de Luxe.

The third assistant manager and a bevy of porters escorted us to our room. We reached it by crossing a bridge over the narrow inlet that separates the reception area from the rest of the building. We had to pass through the dining room which struck us as informal in the midst of so much grandeur and proceeding along an outside cloister or arcade eventually reached our door.

Our room and others we saw later was not only luxurious and comfortable, it was witty with amusing *trompe l'oeil* pictures painted directly on the plaster walls and a cupboard bedecked with colorful antique Bavarian make-up: hearts and floral designs and the date 1860 in curlicues. It was charming and was built, I would suspect, in 1966. There were wrought-iron bedsteads, the beds were comfortable and the linen pink and pretty. Much of the furniture was, in the decorator's phrase, "distressed" to the point of crying aloud but the rooms were certainly among the most attractive and spritely hotel rooms I have ever been in. Under such conditions it seems churlish to find any fault at all but I couldn't escape the impression that everything was just a bit *overly* contrived, as if a clutch of delirious decorators had been given their heads and a blank check. Whee! Also, in the midst of the splendor, I thought I detected an imperceptible aroma of drains. Norton said I was plebeian and that it was my imagination but we were on the ground floor on an inlet. There isn't much tide around there.

A long curving pier juts out into the bay and I suppose one could dunk off the end of it although it is actually more of a landing stage for power boats. A huge D-shaped salt water pool is tempting but for the best swimming you have to take the hotel putput for the five or six minute run to a small cove and sandy beach.

The atmosphere is romantic, however, and the bay is surrounded by low hills. Eventually there will probably be an excess of villas but at present there are only a few and the stars still outshine the house lights piercing the dark water.

The syndicate is putting in a golf course designed, I believe, by Robert Trent Jones. Eventually the Cala di Volpe will have a lounge which, when we were there, it did not have and which seemed a rather curious oversight. Guests sat in their rooms or on sofas along one side of a narrow passageway leading to a tiny bar. The manager explained that the large dining room would become the lounge and a new dining room would be added. I like to think a new chef will be added too. The food was edible but lacked flavor.

Since the next morning was chilly we devoted it to research. The Costa Smeralda, the brainchild of the young Aga Khan and his associates is designed as a unit and we wanted to see it all.

Our first stop was the Hotel Romazzino which as a matter of fact was put up by the Rank organization, the British film producers, but it is definitely part of the large complex that includes a ceramics factory, a landing field, and many apartments, hotels, and villas.

While perhaps not Luxury the Romazzino is first class and extremely attractive. Spacious, comfortable, gaily furnished, it was built in 1965 and is on several levels following the contours of the sloping land that borders the bay. There are one hundred rooms all with balconies and all overlooking the water. Here, unlike the Cala di Volpe, one may walk directly onto the beach but like the other places the water is shallow. There is a barbecue bar for picnic luncheons and the management, which is Swiss, told us proudly they were putting in their own lobster pots. The Romazzino struck us as ideal for families and indeed there is an official baby sitter in residence.

The Luci di la Muntagna is I should say definitely Class B with small rooms garishly decorated in poison green and insistent orchid. In this one the management is Pakistani and although they have a tiny beach they too will take you elsewhere to bathe. They were planning on a swimming pool for the following year. The rooms have balconies but little privacy for the partitions between them are cut so low that willy-nilly guests are all members of a big happy family.

The Pitrizza is more like a club than a hotel with twenty-eight rooms divided between six bungalows. A family or a small group of friends could rent a whole bungalow. In the height of the season they are shared by three or four couples. Built of stone the main house and cottages have flat roofs with heavy stones on top and the overall effect is squat and dwarfish. "Troglodyte," said the doctor and he was right. Despite the architecture however we thought the swimming facilities the best we had seen. There was a nice little beach, the water looked deeper than at the other hotels and their pool was extraordinary. Above sea level and big, the salt water was pumped up into it and flowed back down, fresh and constantly changing.

The gem of the collection, to my way of thinking, was the Hotel Cervo right on the port. The rooms were prettily furnished, had big closets, the baths were gaily tiled and it was built around a little patio. I love patios. The harbor, full of small boats, is diverting and rooms overlooking it are the most popular but indisputably they are noisy. There are sixty-two rooms, they all have balconies and those on the back are quieter.

The hotel is lively because it surmounts an arcade of shops and markets and although you have to go to the nearby bathing beach in a motorboat it is the one hotel of the group where it is not necessary to have a car to get around. You are in the heart of the picturesque baby metropolis.

Herewith the maximum daily rates for two people in the height of the season (approx. July 1–Sept. 30) including at all hotels, meals, service, taxes, and beach facilities.

Cala di Volpe: $64.00   (Inflated in our opinion)
Romazzino: 40.00
Luci di la Muntagna: 27.00
Pitrizza: 64.00
Cervo: 42.00

We ended our day's research with dinner at a pizzeria on the quai at Porto Cervo. It was run by a small group of the fraternity in their uniform: black short sleeved sweaters or shirts open to the navel, cuffs unbuttoned, gold chain around neck, tight pants. The food and wine were good, it was not expensive and looking out over the little harbor with the lights gleaming and twinkling on the boats was a relaxed and contented way to spend the evening.

Travel brochures make irresistible reading but like Chambers of Commerce handouts they should be scanned with a fishy eye. Always in the brochures the sun shines, always in the Chambers of Commerce hymnals the air is balmy and Aegean and Mediterranean summers are undiluted bliss. They are, eh? In the middle of June it had been cold in Greece, it had teemed in Spain and at the end of the month in Sardinia it was so chilly the morning we first went to the Cala di Volpe's bathing beach that when the motorboat came over to pick up a Swedish couple who had preceded us we asked if we might accompany them back to the hotel. Swimming was more an exercise in fortitude than any voluptuous delight.

Deciding that other areas might make more rewarding exploring than the beaches, we drove with Orlando about thirty miles to Palau where we took a ferry for the fifteen-minute crossing to Isola Maddalena. Once on *that* island we went by causeway to another smaller one, Isola Caprera. The reason for going there is because it was the home of Garibaldi.

He bought the island in 1854 with money he had accumulated in New York working as a chandler and later on as a trading skipper. A big pine tree, the lower part of its trunk horizontal with the ground is an attractive feature of the property and the guide told us that Garibaldi planted it in 1867 to celebrate the birth of his daughter.

Which daughter he did not say nor is it surprising for the great man's marital life appears to have been confused. His first wife, or at any rate loyal companion—let us not split hairs—was a South American named Anita by whom he had a daughter and two sons. She died in 1849. In 1859 or '60 he remarried but like Sam Houston, another indomitable character in all save his relationship with women, he and his bride ricocheted off each other on surprisingly short notice. The eighteen-year-old Mrs. Houston departed her husband's bed and board approximately eleven weeks after their marriage. Garibaldi seems to have left his bride on their wedding night or almost immediately thereafter.

He subsequently had two children, a son and daughter, by his mistress—perhaps it was *that* little girl who inspired the tree—and later, having obtained an annulment, he married their mother.

For a man of Garibaldi's incomparable courage and wildly venturesome temperament the house seems singularly tame and middle class. Perhaps it made a welcome change from the death sentence imposed upon him in his youth in Italy, and from the torture he had undergone in Brazil which left him with some deformity. In any event, with the exception of an uncharacteristic interlude spent writing novels, he could not have passed much time there. His days both prior to and following the purchase were passed in battles, marches, triumphs, and defeats vis-à-vis the French army and assorted Italian states.

In 1882 at the age of seventy-five he decided to call it quits. One may say he did not rust out. The bed in which he died is still in the house under a large glass case and he and his family lie in sarcophagi on a slope in the garden.

Returning to La Maddalena to wait for the ferry we bought a few bright souvenirs in the local shops and sat in the neat new-looking little square drinking delicious cappuchino coffee. I do not know how the canard originated that we have good coffee in the United States. Ninety percent of the time it is nothing but black acid.

That evening we had drinks and dinner at the hotel with the Swedish couple who had rescued us in the morning from the chilly beach. They were attractive and she looked remarkably young to have two children in their twenties but she said she had and they probably existed since very few couples other than George and Martha in *Who's Afraid of Virginia Woolf?* invent offspring.

We left them and went to finish our packing and the next morning at seven we took off for Santa Teresa Gallura and the ferry for Bonifacio and Corsica. Napoleon, we are here!

The approach to Bonifacio, only an hour north of Sardinia is unusual. One sees no town, only a blank wall of cliffs. Then, as the ship noses nearer, one becomes aware that there are small headlands pitted with large grottos. The ship makes a sharp turn to the right entering the narrow channel between them and the island proper and comes to anchor in a pretty little Mediterranean port with gaily colored buildings rising straight from the narrow quai.

Norton had to wrestle our luggage as there were no porters and, although one had been ordered, no car. "What of it?" I said. "We'll take a taxi to Ajaccio. It's only about five or six miles." Considering the money one's dear parents lay out for one's education it is depressing to realize that one grows to maturity still an ignoramus. Ajaccio lies ninety miles from the southern port and takes a good three hours to reach.

Corsica, topographically, is richer, more intricate than Sardinia. There is rolling cultivated country and the mountains are heavily wooded with oak and chestnut, bay and beech. Plane trees line the roads and ancient stone villages cluster on hilltops and in hollows. A low dark shrub growth, the Corsican maqui covers huge patches of land and the fragrance of thyme permeates the air. Corsica smells delicious. This, we decided at once, would be the place to buy property.

Ajaccio too has skyscrapers, reduced in scale to be sure but definitely high rising. We drove through the city to the Hotel Cala di Sole four or five kilometers farther on. Its location, right on the water, is first class, the hotel itself is second. Indifferent motel architecture, cheap furniture, not very comfortable beds and the male guests dine in their shirt sleeves. The food they eat in this informal attire is very good. The waiters pet phrase is O.K. but so are the meals and so is the bathing. Room and full board for two 140 francs or $28. Half board, 120 francs or $24.

Through the afternoon in still air and hot sunshine we toasted and bathed, and around six took a cab and drove into Ajaccio. The cabs we were to discover were not cheap, the fare between the hotel and town came to $2.50 but about Ajaccio itself we had no complaints. Smaller even than such small capitals as Lisbon or Copenhagen or Dublin it has, nevertheless, their capital quality as well as the verve and muscularity of a little Barcelona. The low cost apartments, though probably cramped within, from without are very pretty, the balconies foaming with deep purple morning glories, geraniums, and nasturtiums.

We were amused and a bit bewildered by the number of learner-drivers. Every other building seemed to house a driving school and in the comparatively small area comprised by the city there were more cars with the cautionary sign than I have seen in all the towns of England put together. Perhaps Corsica was in the middle of an economic boom and everyone was splurging on his first car.

We strolled about making a few necessary purchases and pounced happily on a good bookstore. We bought a couple of paperbacks and sat at a cafe over beers reading the European edition of the *Herald Tribune* and learned with no pleasure that President Johnson had blown his top again, lambasting his critics and shouting that "Everybody should think about how great America is, not complain and criticize."

According to the paper the speech was greeted with wild cheers yet the deliberate cultivation of complacency would seem a remarkably short-sighted policy since few attitudes make a nation more vulnerable to her foes.

We returned to the hotel, dining around nine and afterward had coffee on the terrace. The view was lovely, the stars shining on the quiet water, the sharp dark hills silhouetted against the sky. We thought they were hills on the mainland but they are in reality a string of small islands called Les Iles Sanguinaires, no one seemed to know quite why. Possibly because they glow red in the setting sun or perhaps they were the scene of ancient bloody battles. Whatever the reason they punctuate the seascape in decorative and satisfying fashion.

As I have said, the food at the Cala di Sole was very acceptable and although we did not sample them ourselves we were told that there were two good restaurants near the hotel: La Petite Auberge and the Santa Lina. Until we drove past it and saw the name on a sign I had assumed that it was called Saint Helena. Since we were in Napoleon's birthplace it seemed logical although on second thought I expect that would have been a tactless name for a restaurant.

The next morning as we had arranged to see his birthplace proper and ordered a car for nine-fifteen, we had ourselves routed out at eight. Still terribly sleepy, we breakfasted in our room, dressed and went up to the lobby at nine to discover it was a bright and shining eight. I don't know how the knowledge had evaded us the day before but Corsica is an hour behind Sardinia.

Our first stop in Ajaccio was at Corse Tourisme, one of the nicer travel bureaus, presided over by a lean dark intelligent young Moroccan with quite beautiful hands, named Mr. Abdes. There had been some difficulty the day before about our hotel and car vouchers but all had been adjusted and Mr. Abdes had provided us with a guide, an attractive Algerian French girl named Michele. She had a good English vocabulary but her pronunciation was chancy. Speaking of a certain highly regarded Corsican cheese she said it was made of aivi milk. Norton and I furrowed and cudgeled. Aivi. What beast was that? Not cow surely, not goat. Finally, after what I can only regard as inspired detective work, we deciphered ewe's milk. Who shall blame Michele? Who is born knowing that in the so logical English language ewe, yew and you are pronounced yoo?

Guided by our pretty guide we arrived at the house where Letizia Ramolino, married at age fourteen to Carlo Maria da Bonaparte, on August 15, 1769, gave birth to one of the thundering names of history. Joseph was born a year earlier and six assorted siblings who owe their survival value to their older brother quickly followed. Napoleon and John Fitzgerald Kennedy would have understood each other very well.

Unlike the birthplace of many great men the Bonaparte house was reasonably luxurious. Carlo Maria was of a crusty, ambitious, and complex character, but in spite of the difficulties he created, while his children were small, his law practice and his scheming seem to have paid off in practical comfort. The house is four stories high with charmingly painted ceilings. They have been restored but in essence they are the originals as are all the mirrors which are still in place. I never look into an old mirror without thinking how enthralling it would be could it give back all the actions and people that have been reflected on its surface.

We were shown the bed in which Napoleon was born. It is narrow with a high head and footboard and Dr. Brown observed that it must have been difficult for the midwife. For Letizia too I should image.

I regret we have no picures of the house but the street in

which it is located is so narrow that no perspective is possible.

Napoleon, despite his Italian background, was in his turn devoured by that peculiarly French appetite for La Gloire. I myself do not warm to it since it must inevitably involve astronomical extravagance and the death of thousands, usually in extremely unpleasant circumstances but there are many, including General de Gaulle, who consider it great stuff.

We went to visit the Imperial Chapel in the Rue Fesch where the members of the Bonaparte family, excepting of course the most illustrious, are buried. We returned by way of an irresistible small market. The fruits and vegetables were so fresh the dew still clung to them and the peaches were ambrosial. When I exclaimed over them Michele was amused. "Americans always love markets," she said. But it depends on the market. The supermarket near our apartment in New York is a frightful place; dank in winter, glacially cold in summer, selling hard pale vegetables and fruit and frozen meat wrapped tightly in cellophane, devoid of fragrance and flavor, bearing no relation whatever to the bounty of the earth.

As we sat over coffee Michele talked about Algeria which was her home. She and her family had loved it but had been obliged to leave when the French were ousted. Here in Ajaccio she felt confined. "We are a little, little island," she said and there was anguish in her young voice. To us it was picturesque, to her, poor child, it was prison. And indeed how was she to find a job with any potential? Where would she find a husband? She was a pretty girl too and winning, one who would surely attract young men could she only meet them.

She told us that the best restaurant in Ajaccio was the Pardi in the Rue Fesch near the Imperial Chapel, one flight up. She told us true. The whole family cooks and they do not care to have customers going away hungry. We were served fish soup, lobster, French fried potatoes (real ones), pink roast lamb with salad on the same plate to absorb the good juices along with the dressing, cheese, and fruit. Wine included, coffee extra. Price 18 francs, approximately $4. We blanched to think what food of equal caliber would have cost at home.

Still, Corsica is an island and segments of island economy come high. We received the shock treatment when we went to look at property. *If* we saw something that appealed to us, perhaps with an old farmhouse and an olive grove and water front and *if* we could afford it, well then, possibly . . . we are not the first couple to dream the dream.

Mr. Abdes had introduced us to a Mr. Benedetti, a real estate man whom we had liked on sight and his is not an ilk Norton and I automatically warm to but Mr. Benedetti had an earthy quality, rough gray hair and he looked you in the eye. It had been agreed that he would pick us up at the Corse Tourisme office after lunch. He duly appeared in a car driven by a young man. We assumed the car was his and the young man his son or an assistant in his office. The assumption was erroneous. The young man was not his but the car was the young man's and it broke down. Not, however, until we had seen our first acreage which had a good deal to recommend it; rolling land, beautiful old trees, the ruins of a stone farmhouse, and a small purling river although one would not own both banks. Mr. Benedetti thought it comprised approximately twenty acres. He quoted prices in old francs and they run into the millions but reduced to current currency—which though introduced in 1960 most of the French still ignore—the price came to about $55,000. Under the circumstances—no livable house, no road and remote from the source of utilities, we thought it a little inflated.

Disaster quickly followed. The car's hydraulic system, designed to soften bumps, gave way and we jounced and banged, our spines cracking at every turn of the wheel, to the nearest garage where the car owner telephoned to Ajaccio for, so we thought, another car. After a twenty-minute wait we discovered he had spoken to a mechanic friend who would come when he could. Embittered I called my beau Mr.

Abdes and within minutes a taxi arrived and we resumed our quest.

If $55,000 for twenty acres had seemed high the next asking price appeared euphoric: $44,000 for four acres of hillside covered with maquis and nothing else. No house, no trees, no electricity, no water, no water frontage. There was a superb view of the sea and a delightful if public beach nearby. Roads were in and Mr. Benedetti assured us water was being laid on and we believed him for here obviously was a development in the making. We wanted no part of it for living but it was a possible investment could one be assured that other people would be bemused enough to up the original ante. One must suppose that they will be. In recent years the Mediterranean islands adjacent to Italy and France have been quietly invaded by Continental real estate interests who have cannily gobbled up the desirable sites at relatively minor cost and who nightly drift to sleep soothed by the classic lullaby, Buy Low, Sell High. They can't be blamed. One can only blame oneself for having been so lack-witted as to get a good idea too late.

The car that had come to rescue us was in prime working order but the chauffeur proved a menace. He was a real estate agent in embryo urging us to look at another place Mr. Benedetti had casually mentioned and we could see him slithering in on the commission. But it would have taken two hours to get there and back and we were tired. Instead we returned to the hotel and went swimming in the pretty cove with the clean sandy bottom.

Sitting on the terrace having a cocktail before dinner, looking at the sea spread like silk at our feet and the sun sinking behind the islands we felt that one must live on the water or perish. When gazing on rolling fertile farmland, silvery groves of olives and almonds or the lush orchards of more northerly latitudes we feel that only there lies true contentment. Perhaps it is just as well that desirable property comes high.

There is no question, however, that Corsica exerts a pull

for it is breathtakingly beautiful. We traversed a fairish sec-
tion of it and the variety of so small a morsel of real estate is
quite incredible. In looking at the map it takes no great effort
of imagination to see Corsica as either a rabbit's or an American Indian's head seen in profile. In either case the forest
of Tartagine is the eye, the forests of D'Aitone and Valdo
Niello the mouth. If it's an Indian you can also find a beard
but the salient feature, ear for rabbit, feather for Indian, is
Cap Corse, the long peninsula jutting north at the base of
which is the port of Bastia, our destination prior to sailing to
Elba. There is a reasonably direct inland route from Ajaccio
or a longer one around the coast which is a scenic wonder and
that is the one we took.

Golfe de Lava is a gem. From the Golfe de Sagone one
has a supreme view of mountains and sea as well as a great
beautiful beach, at the time blessedly deserted. We continued
on to the village of Carges where we became involved in a
wild goose chase. We were seeking a man Mr. Benedetti
had told us about. Mr. Benedetti was uncertain of his name
but we would have no difficulty finding him since he was
the father-in-law of the gendarme Paoli who owned four
hectares adjoining the property of Monsieur Lefevre. The
four hectares might be just the thing we had in mind. They
might have been but we never saw them, stumbling instead
upon Sebastien, a competitor of Mr. Benedetti who up until
now had played no part in the saga but who took us to see
property our man had not mentioned.

There seemed to be two pieces: one of four acres, the
other of twenty with two little coves, one rocky, one choked
with thick white seaweed which, said Sebastien, was most
unusual. It would be nothing at all to rake it away revealing
a delightful sandy beach. The property was on a hillside but
did not take in the crest. That belonged to Sebastien's sister
but she might be induced to sell. There was a cistern and
springs, a few old olive trees and a small broken-down farmhouse. The place had definite possibilities but it was the en-
visaged improvements Sebastien mentioned so eagerly that

were unsettling. Light and water were not far and were coming nearer. The small dirt road was to be improved and
lengthened. Their first thought had been to bring it along
the shore, what did we think? We thought it a repulsive idea.
"What? Destroy the waterfront? That's the reason people
buy property in a place like this. To have a private beach."
Well, yes, he understood that, others had said the same thing
so now they were thinking of running the road along the
crest of the hill and only three or four families, the property
owners, would have the right to use it. However, a long point
of some hundred-odd hectares, thrusting into the sea, ad-
joined the main plot. It could easily be divided into tiny lots
and undoubtedly the owners could legally establish a right
of way. Sebastien assured us that was impossible. No water
out there. But water can be brought in. Had he not just
said that water could be brought to us?

He glided over this, eager to get to the next piece of news,
the plum that would really fetch us. "Very shortly, within
a few days, in fact . . . guess what?" His eyes were dancing
with pleasure. "What?" They were starting work on an airport, in that field, just over there.

"An airport!"

"*Oh, tout petit, tout petit, Madame.*" Something stirred in
my memory. Where had I heard? . . . I had it! The old quip:
"Just the least little bit pregnant."

This little small thing was to be for private planes so
tourists could fly in to swim and hunt. Norton and I were
shaken but we steeled ourselves. All right, how much? For
the small parcel, $70,000, for the larger, $100,000. I turned to
my husband. "These people are unhinged." Not understanding the words, Sebastien understood the attitude. He
shrugged. He and his family were in this together and he felt
they had a good thing. If they did not sell to an individual
they could doubtless make a deal with a syndicate.

"Look," said Norton, "they're small operators. If we're
really serious we'll make a sane offer and I bet you we get it."

"Let's think about it," I said.

P.S. We did not buy the property and I do not know whether or not it is still available.

On to Golfe de Porto with its tiny enchanting village on the left bank sloping to the water and then into Les Calanches, an extraordinary area on a vastly different scale. Here mile after mile of rocks rise straight from the water, corroded into fantastic formations: towers, battlements, spires, even human beings. Jacques, our driver, pointed with amused pride to one in the shape of an enormous seated bishop complete with mitre and staff and to another one, a great head with a Lincolnesque nose and chin whiskers.

From Les Calanches the road winds down to the village of Porto, with its two or three hotels and few houses. They are right on the water but because of the enormous towering peaks surrounding them there is a disturbing air of confinement even on a bright day. However we had a good luncheon at the Hotel Riviera and then leaving the coast took the road inland to Evisa and started the climb through twenty-five kilometers of pine forests. The stand is magnificent and though lacking the awe-inspiring majesty of the redwoods has an asset denied those noble trees. It is protected from commercial interests and cannot be destroyed through greed and gross stupidity. One hopes that the officials in charge will continue to have more perspicacity than California's governor Mr. Reagan who is purported to have remarked of that state's incomparable heritage that "If you've seen one redwood you've seen them all."

One emerges from the forests of D'Aitone onto the Col de Vergio, an isolated peak of approximately 13,000 feet. Spread out below lies Corsica and in the clear thin air we could hear the melodic tinkling of bells. Ah, we thought, a flock of sheep. What appeared in a few moments was a flock of putty colored hogs peacefully grazing.

From there the road runs through another forest, Valdo Niello, before penetrating the great gorge of Santa Regina. The Golo River runs through it and when we passed that way a hydroelectric plant was in the process of construction.

It is good for the economy I know but you can't warm to a hydroelectric plant, especially when it scars so much natural beauty. After a bit the road straightened and we made much better time but our interest in our surroundings petered out proportionately.

We reached Bastia around a quarter to six. The atmosphere was far more commercial than that of Ajaccio, the streets were crowded and the noise was deafening. Our first stop was the travel agency where we picked up our tickets for the next night's boat trip to Elba and then on to the Hotel Bonaparte, a dreary if clean hostelry and a small room right on the street reverberating with scooters and motorcycles.

Our hearts sank for it became evident that the American Express Company had goofed in sending us there. There is no conceivable reason to spend a night and a day in Bastia. The only reason for going there at all is to get out of it. If you are sighting Elba from Ajaccio it is a must and the drive is an exhilarating experience but do not arrive, as we did, a whole twenty-four hours too soon. Allow yourself only a few hours, preferably minutes, in advance of sailing time. That way you not only cut down expenses, you save yourself one of those tedious bouts of unnecessary packing and unpacking.

The hotel did not serve meals so we dined Chez Matieu which was, the woman at the desk assured us, "Supérieur." I would not echo her opinion but it wasn't bad and once more it was brought home to us that even a mediocre wine is a life saver when food and surroundings are prosaic.

We had coffee outdoors in a large kind of park-plaza where unaccountably it seemed to be autumn—dry brown leaves rustled on the bare earth. Norton and I made a list of our most unfavorite cities: Macao, although so near beloved Hong Kong, we consider pretty bad. Then there is Suva in Fiji, Addis Ababa in Ethiopia, Mombasa, our recent debacle, and Bastia. If you pronounce it bearing down hard on the B and S it sounds like a swear word. This we did several times. It released our adrenalin and we felt better.

As we strolled back to the hotel we noticed across the way

a large building. It had a rather commercial atmosphere and most of the windows were shuttered but in one of them two women leaned on their elbows gazing down into the street. A sign over the front door read BAINS, DOUCHES. Seeing the women I said, "The building seems to be closed, I wonder what they're doing there." Norton looked sly, sophisticated. "What do you think? Look at that sign." I gave him a little lesson in the use of the word *douche* in French and in English.

The next morning we woke to find bad Bastia enveloped in beautiful weather and drove through more lovely country to a sweet little village, Patrimonio, where they make good wine and on to the Hotel La Roya. La Roya was a provincial version of the Bonaparte with a scruffy little lawn but the bathing was good and the luncheon unexpectedly excellent. Delicious hors d'oeuvres, rouget, grilled veal, frites, wine, cheese, and coffee.

Returning to the hotel we were delighted to find that quite a stack of mail had been delivered to us. Unprepossessing Bastia had been on the itinerary left with friends at home and we could only conclude that the dear creatures, psychically foreseeing our depression, had sent letters winging our way. We took them out to read in the Grande Place on a bench overlooking the water. I was amused by one from Bob Merriman who had been our stage manager in *Barefoot in the Park* during the ten months I had been in the play in New York. I had left the cast early in April and we had flown to Rome on the 29th.

"Well honey," wrote Bob, "you may not have been smart about timing your trip to the Middle East but you sure as hell knew when to leave the Biltmore Theatre." The play was well into its fourth year and business inevitably was declining. In a companion letter from Jeanne Johnston, our wardrobe mistress, I learned they would be closing July 25. No matter how much it may have been anticipated no play ends its run without the company feeling a pang of regret yet those two could certainly use a rest and change.

Norton and I decided that a little change wouldn't hurt

us either. A noisy family had moved onto the bench behind us and seemed engaged in an all-out family row. Shrieking children and screaming parents. This is not usual in Europe, but from the little we had seen we did not think the Corsicans were very affectionate with their children. The only terms of endearment we had heard were Cow Head and Imbecile.

Dining again Chez Matieu, by this time we were habitués, we found everybody there engaged in the real estate business; the bartender, the waiter and a couple of passers-by who, overhearing the conversation, had hurried in from the street. Maps were brought out and we were urged to go the next day to see the opportunity of a lifetime. Nothing, we assured them, would give us greater pleasure and we would return in the near future but for the present we could not cooperate, we must indeed leave that very minute to catch the ship, the *Citta di Tripoli.* We had ample time but the thought of escaping Bastia was so heady that we were down on the pier before the ship opened for business.

A large percentage of the passengers were beatniks of various nationalities and watching them we thought how square they were. There is no more dedicated conformist than your youthful rebel and these children all had to be exactly alike, unkempt, unshaven, dirty, and quite smelly. In my own youth we all wanted to be alike too but we didn't smell and the idea was to look as prepossessing as possible.

As we were sitting in the bar waiting for the ship to sail one of the boys came up and asked us how many francs and lires there were to the dollar. All at once he seemed young and defenseless and human and his ignorance was understandable. Sardinia and Elba are, of course, Italian and there, right in the middle, is French Corsica. Confusing.

Some hours later we emerged from our hot cramped cabin to find ourselves steaming slowly into Portoferraio just as the sun rose over the saddle of two rounded hills. As in most Mediterranean ports the quai side houses were sturdy and well-proportioned, the colors appealing; terra-cotta and dusty rose with green shutters tight closed against the malign night air. Struck by the sun's rays the few unshuttered panes blazed with light, in brief conflagration saluting the new day. I should imagine the outer port has changed but little since Napoleon first saw it. The inner harbor is another matter. Here is high rise ubiquitous cheap motel construction. Reservations had been made for us at the Hotel Massimo and a taxi voucher for getting there duly issued. It turned out to be unnecessary. The boat docks, one disembarks, and walks twenty yards across the quai to the front door.

After a very poor breakfast we returned to our room. Once again I had mounted my charger and cantered up to the *portieri*, lance at the ready, in a brave effort to improve our situation, one on the top floor with a balcony, maybe?—and once again I had gone down to defeat. *Tutti Occupado*. We resigned ourselves and tried for a catnap but by that time the town was awake and swinging and sleep out of the question.

It was a beautiful day so we hired a cab and drove out to Biodola, a beach with fine sand and no flies or seaweed. Since it was Sunday a good many people were about but it was not unpleasantly crowded. The only flaw was the transistor radios. It seems to me that the British handle this problem simply and well. Barbarism is not tolerated in public. In Richmond Park, for example, radios are forbidden. I myself would forbid them in all public places including the streets and if that seems too austere then I feel that there should be a ruling, stringently adhered to, that those who can find happiness only in bedlam may tote their transistors about with them *provided* they use earphones so that less maniacal citizens may pursue their tranquil ways.

There was a beach-side cafe that looked attractive and where we would have liked to lunch but the juke box drove us away so we wandered down the beach to the Hermitage. It seemed a nice hotel with a shaded dining terrace overlooking the water and a swimming pool and decorative straw parasols set about but we were disillusioned by the overly familiar waiters and conventional hotel food. I do not want to go to Europe for a shrimp cocktail and well done lamb with mint sauce. The location, however, cannot be faulted and the rooms during the height of the season run from about $14.25 to $17 per person including, as we found to be customary everywhere, full board, service, taxes and, when on the beach, a beach umbrella.

Back in our room in the late afternoon we were amused by the drama being played out on the quai below us. The mainland is only ten miles away and on summer Sundays crowds come over on the ferries to swim and picnic. The ferries have enormous maws which they open and into which they are capable of engulfing an incredible number of cars. We at first thought they were trying to show no favoritism, between the three or four lines that converge upon them. However, one fellow in a deluxe green Mercedes got up to the ramp three times and three times was turned back while more humble vehicles were allowed to board. We decided this was gross discrimination against the rich and when he finally made it we cheered.

The trip to Peombino is short and the supposition that thousands of years ago Elba was part of the mainland is strengthened by the fossil remains of bears, hippos, and rhinoceros that have been found on the island.

There is another small harbor beyond the main one we overlooked in which yachts from all over the world lie at anchor. It is a colorful spot and reminded us of the harbor of Papeete.

Like so many Mediterranean towns the streets of Porto-ferraio are frequently broad shallow steps, a few forming unexpectedly steep staircases. We saw two or three attractive-looking restaurants and finally settled for Zi Rosa, near the hotel, a happy choice. The food was good and Signor Rosa had an English friend in the real estate business whom he telephoned and who agreed to pick us up the following afternoon.

The morning we had decided to devote to history. Elba has a good deal of it, Portoferraio having been founded by Cosimo de Medici in 1548. It has quite a literary aura too for Victor Hugo lived there as a child and the tiny island of Monte Cristo, which owes so much to Dumas père, is not far away. However, I think it will not be disputed that its greatest fame stems from the exalted exile it briefly harbored.

Napoleon arrived early in May of 1814 and settled first in the Villa dei Mulini in the heart of town. It is a commodious house overlooking a garden and the sea lapping against the wall. Today the garden has rather run to seed and although there are palm trees, only two remain of the long row of cypresses that stood in Napoleon's time. His bed with gold rococo ornamentation and, so they tell you, the original blue silk curtains, is still there as are many handsomely bound books from his library. I doubt that he would have had much time to read before 1814 but possibly in exile he was a bookworm. Yet I often wonder how much people really read beautifully bound books.

While appreciating the invaluable service rendered by paperbacks on the whole I am a hard-cover devotee. Exquisite bindings make me suspicious. They are marvelously decorative and usually turn out to be the *Lives of the Queens of England* by Agnes Strickland.

As there were in Napoleon's boyhood home in Corsica there are in the Villa dei Mulini charming frescoes on ceilings and walls. In a large case is the island's first flag. Napoleon had it made on board the *Indomitable*, the British ship that took him to Elba. It used to be white with a diagonal crimson stripe and three gold bees, symbolizing the industry of the three maritime provinces of Elba, but time has dimmed the brightness that fluttered over the ceremonies welcoming the Emperor to his new domain. The ground is now oyster, the proud crimson strip is brown, the golden bees have tarnished and are barely discernible. It is sad when a flag dies.

I remember once seeing in a New York courtroom Old Glory propped in a corner. Had I been called upon to acknowledge it I could only have saluted with such patriotism as I could muster the brown, gray and purple, long may it wave.

On disembarking at Portoferraio, Napoleon was received by the mayor, Signor Pierro Traditi, whom he tactfully appointed court chamberlain. There were other civil and ecclesiastical authorities besides, we may be sure, a throng of curious Elbans. On his side, Napoleon, from whom all the glory had not yet flaked off, could present Marshal Henri Bertrand with his wife and family, Generals Antoine Drouot and Pierre Cambronne, a veritable gaggle of officers, French, Italian, Corsican, and Polish, as well as four hundred troops. The record recounts a rather endearing contretemps in the arrival ceremonies and also indicates quick thinking and ingenuity on the part of an unsung hero.

What was a welcome to so illustrious a newcomer without the keys to the city? The only hitch was that if they in fact existed they could not be found. Quick as a flash our lad scrambled through bureau drawers and cupboards and came up with the keys to the mayor's wine cellar, plunged them in a pot of gilt paint and the day was saved. Considering what his state of mind must have been Napoleon might well have preferred them to keys that just unlocked some old gate.

Yet even if low in his mind he was barely settled in before embarking on emperor-like activities such as road building. Although it now seems peaceable enough, in Napoleon's day the neighborhood in which the Municipal Palace was situated had gone to pot and was surrounded by malodorous inns and shops and dubious haunts frequented by the local ragtag and bobtail political element. It was noisy and non-classical so he decided to move to the country and withdrew to the villa of a well-to-do peasant, two or three miles from town.

As we followed the long avenue of yews leading up to the house we decided that the peasant must have been a wizard at extracting the riches of the earth, for with its long one-story façade of yellow granite with transverse wings at either end the building looks like an art gallery. Somewhat embarrassed by our ignorance, we discovered it was. It was commissioned in 1852 by the Russian Prince Anatoli Demidov who had married a niece of Napoleon's and who thought it would be a good place for exhibiting memorabilia of his distinguished late connection. The memorabilia did not materialize and today the gallery houses an undistinguished art collection, although it is fun to see Antonio Canova's *Galatea*. This is the well-known statue of a crouching nymph for which Pauline Bonaparte, Napoleon's sister, a girl who shed her clothes at the drop of a chisel, obligingly posed starkies.

The farmer's house where the emperor lived is behind the museum and is comfortable and attractive without being pretentious even though the reception salon does have a marble floor with a small sunken fountain in the middle and walls delicately painted with scenes of Egypt. I really don't know why Napoleon wanted to be reminded of it.

His bedroom was not large but again the walls are painted with draperies, the floors are tiled and the single bed is solid Empire. We had a nice English girl from Manchester as our guide. She worked there in a bookshop but she studied Italian in night school. "It sounds different when you first hear it spoken in Italy." She loved Elba. This was her third trip and she was still full of enthusiasm. When I said I wondered if the pink silk window curtains were by any chance the originals she said respectfully, "Oh they *must* be, you couldn't *make* them today." I suspect a reasonably adroit seamstress could.

Leaving these monuments to how the mighty have fallen we drove to Marina di Campo, a pleasant small beach where we swam and ate luncheon.

Any thoughts of a siesta back at the hotel were rudely shattered for the waterfront of Portoferraio is not the place to get one. What with honking horns, motor scooters, and horses hoofs clopping on the cobblestones the town sounds far larger than it is.

We finally gave up and went down to meet the real estate chum of Signor Rosa, Signor Smith, a cheery charmer in his early fifties born of a Florentine mother and an English or Scottish father, he wasn't sure which. He had an American wife, a Swedish mother-in-law, a four-year-old daughter and another baby on the way.

He himself could not have been more ingratiating. His only shortcoming from our point of view was that he represented a British investment company with large real estate holdings in Elba so he could show us only company property.

The views were almost all spectacular, the drawback was the ground itself: plots measured in meters instead of acres at high prices with few trees, soil covered with the famous Mediterranean scrub growth, the maqui, no place for a garden and no beach frontage. One plot $40,000. I yield to none in my appreciation of the great classic views of the world but I also require something beneath my feet. The mountains and the sea, rich farmland, orchards and blossoming almonds and the plains of Africa where the animals are . . . all that is incomparable to look at but where are you going to cook and eat and sleep and read and work?

Not too long before I had gazed upon what might be called a comparable urban spectacle from a brand new apartment house that pierces heaven itself. All New York lies deployed before one's eyes. Our island, embraced by its two great watery arms, shimmered in the daylight haze and at night companion towers blazed against the sky. The spectacle was marvelous and for the privilege of looking at it one is requested to pay between $600 and $1000 a month for living space in which a small cat would feel confined. Inside bathrooms, wretched closets, a microscopic kitchen, small bedrooms and a living-dining room that is no more than a long hall; the view on one side and no possible space in which to group furniture for companionable purposes. Of course no wood-burning fireplace. I myself would not live there if they paid me the money instead of demanding it, but it is very nearly completely rented, which goes to show I suppose that people get what they will put up with in architecture politics, domestic service, art or anything else.

Leaving the Development plots to those who might come after us, we drove to Porto Azzuro, another delightful little bay on the island's east coast and sat at a cafe watching the world go by. An elegant gray Bentley slipped past and Mr. Smith told us it belonged to a lady from New Zealand who had left her native land and adopted Elba as home. "She lives alone, spending her days working in her garden and she loves it," he said. Whether she had arrived at this happy condition independently or as a disciple of Voltaire's he did not say.

That night we dined again at Signor Rosa's ordering lobster, the expensive dish. We felt it was the least we could do to thank him for putting us in touch with the charming if, in a sense, sterile Mr. Smith who had, in any event, supplied us with a pleasant outing. Elba is a place we would like to go back to but not to the Hotel Massimo.

The Aliscafi, the hydrofoil in which we left Portoferraio for the mainland, was fun. It was our first trip in one and they are fine vehicles; roomy, comfortable, speedy, and cheap. Our only complaint was the windows, so salt encrusted it was hard to see anything.

From Piombino, a small local train runs to Campigilia Marittima, the junction where one connects with the Genoa-Rome express but the thought of hoisting our luggage in and out of one more conveyance soured the doctor. "The hell with it," he said, "we'll rent a car." The distance is only about six or seven miles and the fare as I recall was $5. It was worth it.

Discovering we would have a two-hour wait for the Rome train we went to breakfast at a small cafe down the road from the station. There was delicious homemade bread, good coffee, poor tea. The secret of bringing water to the boil before pouring it over the tea leaves has not quite penetrated the Mediterranean conscience. As we were Americans they courteously agreed to eggs. Boiled for *quatro minuti*, we explained, would do them to a turn. When half an hour had slipped by we made known our curiosity as to their whereabouts. Presently they were brought; hell hot, rock-hard and fresh from the oven. With salt and pepper they weren't bad at all.

Returning to the station we found the train was twenty-five minutes late. When pressed to say something nice about Mussolini people used to observe that he made the trains run on time and drained the Pontine marshes but he has been a long time dead and the trains have reverted to normal. As far as I know the marshes are in good shape.

Once aboard the express however we went rocketing at a great rate through the flat fertile countryside. One crop of wheat had already been harvested and they were plowing the earth for a second planting.

Norton and I were alone in our carriage until we stopped at a station where a roly-poly Italian got in. He buried himself in his newspaper until I drew his attention to us in an unfortunate manner. Pulling out my needlepoint I found the bag full of sand. I leaned from the window to empty it and, as would have required no great wit to foretell, the wind blew the sand right back into the compartment and into the eyes of my dear husband and our companion. I made abject apologies, our Italian assured me a little coldly in excellent English that it didn't matter and the two gentlemen cried quietly and kept wiping their eyes all the way to Rome.

It was the Fourth of July and the weather was hospitably celebrating American independence. It was clear and hot and fine and we ate two festive meals separated by a little shopping.

Giggi Fazi, we discovered, had moved from its old location but the new place is atmospheric without being self-conscious. There was lots of good food and lots of Italians enjoying it including a woman with dark red hair, flashing brown eyes and a creamy bosom swelling from a deep decolletage festooned with opulent pearls. That was at lunch. Eying this toothsome morsel the doctor smacked his lips. "I can't wait until dinner," said he.

Unfortunately she did not show up at the Tratoria Romulo so we never learned to what further lengths or depths matters might have gone. The Romulo used to be considered something of a hideaway and very Italian. Indeed as we were driving there in a cab I silently rehearsed a few phrases about how we had been introduced to it by Italian friends just in case the management was averse to foreigners or didn't understand English. There are many things one may legitimately worry about in this world but that was not one of them.

We walked through the restaurant out into the garden to discover three enormously long tables crowded with American youth; girls and boys in their late teens and early twenties. Refreshingly enough they were not hippies but polite, well-dressed and quiet. The loudest sounds they made were plaintive little cries for Coca-Cola.

At a table near us a group of half a dozen youngsters appeared to be shepherded by an older Italian man. We overheard one of the young sophisticates say loftily, "They're here because this place was mentioned in *Europe on 5 Dollars a Day*. They're the tour we've been trying to avoid." Like parents, like child, despite the generation gap. What Americans do not yearn to be the only Americans in foreign and exotic parts? Occasionally they get their heart's desire, as in our sojourn in Bastia, but the reason for that is that all the other Americans have better sense than to go there.

Vini culture note: our bottle of Chianti Antinou Della Fattoria, we thought very good. The few Italians who were allowed into the restaurant that night apparently thought so too for we saw several bottles. The locals were crowded against the wall at small tables and received poor service thanks to the American inundation. It meant money of course but the lovely stream went to the restaurant not into their pockets. If they felt resentful it would not be surprising.

Our compatriots were imbibing culture as well as nourishment as we discovered the next day when we joined the throng at the Sistine Chapel. The crowd was tremendous so that at 500 lira a head the Vatican does very well.

One of the delightful aspects of the visit has nothing to do with the chapel—the mosaics taken from Hadrian's villa are enchanting, especially those of birds in branches. The enormous library with its vaulted ceiling and walls covered with religious paintings in clear and vivid colors is another joyous bonus.

Thronging the narrow passageway leading to the chapel were people of all nations including, we were happy to see, women from Vietnam in their flowing tunics and rippling trousers. We were grateful that the entire race was not being obliterated in the name of . . . many Americans are hard put to it to say what.

I shall not hold forth on the Sistine Chapel itself. My betters have done that at length, in detail and with varying degrees of eloquence but I should like to restate briefly one or two statistics that I think are interesting. Michelangelo began work on the vault, the *Creation,* in September 1509 when he was thirty-four and finished it in 1512. He expressed his exhaustion due to prolonged labor on a scaffold in a sonnet. I quote a rough translation by Giraldi:

"In this toil I have already grown a goiter similiar to the one that the cats in Lombardy or some other town have, because of the water I drank; my stomach rose up so strongly that I felt it almost joined to my throat. My beard was turned up to the sky, my head turned back over my spine, my chest curved like a harpy: and my brush, letting drops fall on my face, made me look like a richly decorated floor. My loins have entered into my belly, and my buttocks are flattened because of counterbalancing the weight of my body, which is completely reversed. I do not see where I put my feet. My skin in front is getting longer, but behind it is shortening, so that I hold myself like a bow of Soria. In this position even the mind can only give strange and fallacious judgments, which hit the target like a badly aimed dart. So, Giovanni

[perhaps the humorist poet Giovanni da Pistoia], if my painting is that of a dead man, defend it and defend my honor; because I am not in a suitable place to work well and all the
more so because I am not a painter."

We are told that the sonnet is accompanied by a carica-
ture of a self-portrait which shows a nude man standing, in
the act of painting a figure on the Vault.

The poem is humorous but it is poignant and one's own
body aches in reading it.

In the spring of 1536, he was then sixty-one, Michelangelo
returned to his task and worked for another five years on the
Last Judgment, on the end wall of the chapel. As mighty
an oak physically as artistically and despite the woes and
pains of his youth he died at the age of eighty-nine.

Leaving the Sistine Chapel we decided to go to St. Peter's
and a long walk it is in hot sunshine around the high old
Roman wall. On reaching the piazza we were discouraged
to find we could go only part way in the shade because of
scaffolding obstructing the colonnade. When we finally got
inside it was to be brought up short by barricades erected
to hold back the tremendous crowds. Movement was very
nearly impossible but we did manage to work our way to a
carabinieri and asked him where the Pieta was. He pointed to
the other side of the cathedral.

"Over there behind those curtains, but you can't see it."

"Why not?"

A shrug. I have seen the Pieta several times but the pro-
hibition only increased my determination to see it again. With
considerable difficulty we shouldered our way through further
masses of humanity at last stopping in front of another carabinieri who stood guard before the curtain.

"May we have a look?" Pantomime indicative of peeping.
The law shook its head.

"Oh please. We've come all the way from New York."
We might have added, "And Sicily, Kenya, Greece, Spain,
Sardinia, Corsica, and Elba," but we didn't think he'd care.
Our pleading got a little action however for our man glanced

around. The crowd was so great and so self-contained we were as good as alone. Gingerly he pulled aside the curtain, gingerly we peered within. There she was, the exquisite tragic figure, her ex-sanguinated son dead across her knees. We thanked the carabinieri and turned away relieved to see the masterpiece safely back from Flushing Meadow and Mr. Moses' folly.

I would warn readers that getting away from St. Peter's is no simple transaction. Taxi drivers know about it but they prefer to ignore it the way New York cabbies ignore the Pennsylvania and Grand Central stations. At first we thought to take a carriage, the idea seemed picturesque and full of old world charm but the price was new world astronomical so we settled instead for a private car whose driver agreed to take us to the Via Condotti. The doctor did not look happy.

"You're sure that's where you want to go?"

"Dear, of course. It's where the shops are."

"That's what I mean."

We did go into Gucci, that den of gorgeous and costly temptation where dwell the wild and beautiful leathers, but Gucci is so grand and prosperous that they refuse to accept American Express credit cards. It is not for me to tell them how to run their business but had I been able to charge anything their day's take would have been just a little better than it was. Yet perhaps after a while prestige is all and mere pelf ceases to count.

A more crass establishment is Garbo, 42 Piazza d'Espagna. They were *happy* to accept the cards. This is a nice men's shop selling good-looking ties, men themselves think so, and they averaged around $2.88 and were quite as handsome as those one pays $6 and $7 for at home.

The luncheon we shared with friends, Marguerite and John Fornacca, in their apartment, revived us after the morning's activities. It was Italian and good. Gnocchi and veal and white and red wine. Indeed, gnocchi by itself accompanied by a salad makes an excellent lunch and is a pleasant change from meat.

The Fornacca apartment is large but they are trying to buy another room from one that adjoins them. "That way," said Marguerite, "when the grandchildren come I won't be inconvenienced. I love them but at my age why should I be inconvenienced?"

She reminded me of a dear American friend who sold her large country house and built a much smaller one. When some one observed that it would not be able to accommodate her grandchildren she smiled charmingly. "Precisely," she said.

That evening we went to have cocktails with the Irving R. Levines. Nancy, who had gone back to New York to see her father who had been ill, had returned that morning. The two little boys were as beguiling as ever and we were pleased to learn that the tadpoles had thrived and turned, appropriately enough, into frogs. Thus metamorphosed they had been flushed down the toilet by the maid. The foolish woman did not realize that she had completely jeopardized her chances of ever meeting a prince.

Other friends of the Levines came to join us including a family named Stein. They were from the South—the father was a professor at Vanderbilt University—and rarely have we met a more delightful family. Besides the parents there was an older boy, a youngster, and a daughter of eighteen, one of the prettiest girls in one of the prettiest pink dresses I have ever seen. The whole family was incandescent with intelligence and charm. I have southern friends who are dear to me but sometimes I am able to control my enthusiasm for denizens of Dixie. The Steins, however, seemed universal rather than regional and we got to talking real estate for they loved Italy and were considering buying a farm in Tuscany.

At last, in a murmured aside but not without difficulty, I persuaded the doctor that we had not been asked for dinner and that even in Europe ten-thirty was a chic hour to leave a cocktail party and go to dine.

I plumped for the Piazza Navona but Norton wanted another hotel meal so we returned to the Grand. It was as I suspected, a mistake. Not the food, that was excellent, but the Grand caters largely to Americans and as it was then nearing eleven o'clock our compatriots had dined and retired. We were the only people in the dining room and I felt hemmed in. On our last night in Rome I wanted a fling.

"All right," said the doctor as he signed the bill, "we'll fling, God damn it. Where do you want to go?"

"The Piazza Navona."

We hailed a cab and drove off, the idea being to have coffee at the Tre Scalini but once arrived we found the Piazza so jammed with people that after making a slow laborious tour of my dream precinct we returned to the hotel without having got out of the cab. It was not our very best last night in a foreign country.

The next morning, having completed a final bit of shopping, I stopped in at Santa Maria della Vittoria. It is a nice church, sensuous and rococo, dark and gleaming. I watched with interest a woman gazing at a statue of the Virgin Mary in rapt ecstasy. The worship of statues has always seemed to me curious. I remember when I was a child in a convent I used to watch the nuns lighting candles and genuflecting before plaster of Paris statues of the Virgin draped in Virgin blue and wearing a gold cross and of Jesus with curly beard pointing to a red heart on his chest. Religion is one thing and I understand about symbolism, but art is something else and no one should be taught to reverence poor work.

Coming out of the church, as I went down the street back to the hotel, I all but bumped into a representative of a rival sect; King Hussein of Jordan. He was staying at the Grand and was just getting into his car to drive to the Vatican for an audience with the Pope. Dressed in European clothes he appeared small and nondescript despite his large black Cadillac and motorcycle escort.

I had been entertained by an interview with His Majesty that had appeared in the morning paper. When asked what he could discuss with His Holiness he had replied, "Of course we will talk about the Arab case, the Jordanian situation,

Jerusalem and the holy places of Jordan of which we have always been the proud custodians."

When it was pointed out to him that under Jordanian rule the holy places could not be visited by Jews the King said, "This problem would never have existed if the problem of Palestine had never arisen. There never would have been a state of war and tragedy in that area."

It had a kind of wild *Alice in Wonderland* philosophy that I found piquant—innocent of logic, realism, and common sense.

Our moment finally came. We drove past the Arch of Constantine and past the Colosseum on out to the airport and the nine-hour flight home where, although it was a beautiful day, we circled the field for forty minutes due to the traffic jam before we could land. I do not enjoy this in clear weather. In foul weather I am apprehensive and nothing can persuade me that the crew is having a good time either.

I always remember a pilot who, when a new crew boarded the plane on which we were traveling across America, came back from the cockpit and sat down beside me. We fell to chatting and he asked me if I traveled much and I said yes, I imagined I did for a normal civilian and I added, "It probably seems silly to you but after all the miles I've flown when we come down I still say to myself, 'That's nice. We made it.'" He smiled. "Miss Chase, I will tell you something. The chances are I *have* flown more miles than you have but every time we come down I say to myself, 'That's nice. We made it.'"

As we turned into our driveway in the country, Norton and I looked eagerly around. Due to the rainy spring the foliage was luxuriant and glowing. In the evening light the lawn sloped to the pale sand and the Sound glimmering through the trees.

Our friends Sally and Tony came running to meet us and Thor, the Weimaraner, gave us an exuberant reception although we were later spurned when he remembered we had deserted him for two months.

Puss Cat was more indulgent and tail erect walked with us among the roses when we went into the garden to see how things were progressing. Norton and I looked at each other and smiled. "Do you think," I said, "we could persuade the people who own this place to sell it to us?"

TRAVELERS TIPS

1 Keep your passport and vaccinations up to date. Who knows when opportunity may knock?

2 Register cameras and typewriter in your passport.

3 Cold statistic to remember. Like building a house, travel always costs more than you anticipate. Unexpected contingencies arise. Be prepared.

In alloting your budget include cost of film and developing of same. It's a big item. Also make some allowance for postage which can balloon unexpectedly.

Relevant to cameras: The native residents of many countries are shy birds, reluctant to pose. If you can manage a Polaroid and make them the dazzling present of a picture of themselves they will more willingly let you get a permanent record with a conventional camera.

Even if a color fiend have some black and white film for late day shots.

A camel's hair or sable air brush to blow dust from the lens is an invaluable aid.

If you are going to be in places where you can have color film developed take along a hand viewer. Admiring your masterpieces is fun and a grand way to pass the time on long flights.

4 Keep a little American money in small bills in your wallet. Use it sparingly as you are probably paying more in dollars than you would in native currency but it is always negotiable in an emergency.

5 Find out from your travel agent who is his correspondent

in foreign parts. Should any hitch occur it is good to know where to turn.

6   When coping with letters of introduction make a double list. On one side the people to whom you are sending the letter with a covering one of your own, on the other the name of the person who gave it to you. This is especially important in Asia and Africa where names bear little relationship to the sounds you are accustomed to and where telephonic communication is often faulty. The name of your mutual friend gives you a clue as to who they are.

7   If you have difficulty sleeping on soft or sagging beds consider a light weight folding board that fits in the bottom of your suit case. It may be a nuisance, it can also be a life saver.

8   Make a list of people to call before leaving home. Man to take down, clean and store curtains. Also rugs. Man to repair furniture. Head off milkman. Stop papers. Car in dead storage. Suspend insurance, etc.

9   Make a packing list starting at the top of your head, descending to the soles of your feet; supplies for the care of the person. A systematic checkup at the start saves time and frustrations later on.

10   Take a small stiff nail brush. Invaluable for scrubbing collars and cuffs on drip dry shirts.

11   Carry cream and lotions in small containers rather than in one large one. Thus, as they get used up, they can be discarded.

12   Take a couple of small bottles or flasks. Plastic are the lightest but they can affect the taste of liquor yet you will need something when the residue from a large bottle is too much to leave behind but not enough to make toting the parent bottle worthwhile.

13   There are bound to be slack moments, sometimes depressing ones. Have a few paperbacks handy including a hair-raising murder or two; they will tide you over the bad spots.

If you are game people cards and traveling chess and checker sets may be welcome in the evenings, especially when the light is inadequate for reading. Needle point addicts will want a small piece of work in hand.

14   Pack a Do Not Disturb sign. Some hotels have them, some do not, but English is spoken over a large portion of the globe and the message will get through.

15   Take matches. They are available but they are never where you are and you have to buy them. In Africa they are more precious than pearls.

16   Take a flashlight. One you can set on a table for reading or writing is a good idea.

17   Take hangers either inflatable or the folding kind. No hotel or lodge ever has enough.

18   Pack Scotch tape, labels and a few manila envelopes. Invaluable for sending home scarves, handkerchiefs, post cards, catalogues, small guide books, and the like.

19   Equip each member of the family of writing age with his own pen for filling out the countless forms dispensed by officials.

20   Even if flying around the world make sure that an airline, foreign to a country through which you may be traveling, has the right to transport you if you intend deplaning within that country. Theoretically on an around the world ticket they are allowed to do so but it doesn't always work out that way.

21   Despite tags on the outside lay a paper or card with your name and next address on top of your clothes inside your suitcases. That way, should the tags get ripped off you still have a chance of getting your luggage.

22   Pack a hobby when you go. Seeing the world is marvelous but one's enjoyment is greatly enhanced if it is focused. If besides what may be termed the automatic sights . . . museums, châteaux, churches, and the countryside itself one has a special interest. Schools, old carriages, boat yards, markets, musical instruments . . . it doesn't matter what. A hobby is fun.

23   Try to hold on to a sense of values. New impressions will be flooding in on you and strangers will be giving you information you cannot always check. Common sense is as valuable on a journey as it is at home.

24   When traveling abroad, if you see something you yearn for and can afford it at all, buy it. If you don't you'll regret it all your life.

25   When you get home you'll be tired and excited at being back. Try to keep twenty-four hours for readjustment. Forty-eight are better.

2 —

9205

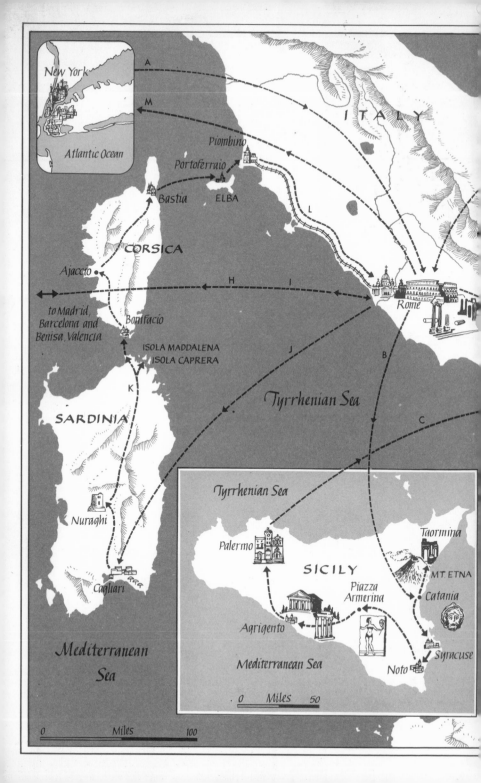